Germania:
The Ancient Germans in Greek and Roman Sources

Also by Raoul McLaughlin

Rome and the Distant East: Trade Routes to the Ancient Lands of Arabia, India and China

The Roman Empire and the Indian Ocean: the Ancient World Economy & the Kingdoms of Africa, Arabia & India

The Roman Empire and the Silk Routes: The Ancient World Economy and the Empires of Parthia, Central Asia and Han China

Rome and China: Points of Contact (co-authored with Professors Hyun Jin Kim and Samuel N.C. Lieu)

Germania:
The Ancient Germans in Greek and Roman Sources

Geography, Society, Warfare, Religion and Customs

Raoul McLaughlin

Pen & Sword
MILITARY

First published in Great Britain in 2025 by
Pen & Sword Military
An imprint of Pen & Sword Books Limited
Yorkshire – Philadelphia

Copyright © Raoul McLaughlin 2025

ISBN 978 1 03613 281 1

The right of Raoul McLaughlin to be identified as
Author of this Work has been asserted by him in accordance
with the Copyright, Designs and Patents Act 1988.

A CIP catalogue record for this book is
available from the British Library.

All rights reserved. No part of this book may be reproduced, transmitted, downloaded, decompiled or reverse engineered in any form or by any means, electronic or mechanical including photocopying, recording or by any information storage and retrieval system, without permission from the Publisher in writing. NO AI TRAINING: Without in any way limiting the Author's and Publisher's exclusive rights under copyright, any use of this publication to "train" generative artificial intelligence (AI) technologies to generate text is expressly prohibited. The Author and Publisher reserve all rights to license uses of this work for generative AI training and development of machine learning language models.

Typeset by Mac Style
Printed in the UK by CPI Group (UK) Ltd, Croydon, CR0 4YY.

The Publisher's authorised representative in the EU for product safety is Authorised Rep Compliance Ltd., Ground Floor, 71 Lower Baggot Street, Dublin D02 P593, Ireland.
www.arccompliance.com

For a complete list of Pen & Sword titles please contact

PEN & SWORD BOOKS LIMITED
47 Church Street, Barnsley, South Yorkshire, S70 2AS, England
E-mail: enquiries@pen-and-sword.co.uk
Website: www.pen-and-sword.co.uk
or
PEN AND SWORD BOOKS
1950 Lawrence Road, Havertown, PA 19083, USA
E-mail: uspen-and-sword@casematepublishers.com
Website: www.penandswordbooks.com

For my family and my colleagues.

Contents

Maps and Illustrations		ix
Acknowledgements		xi
Introduction		
The Ancient Germans		xv
Roman Appraisal of the Germans		xvii
Chapter 1	Northern Europe in Early Greek Myth	1
Chapter 2	Roman Sources and Attitude to Enquiry	6
Chapter 3	Overview Description of Germany	11
Chapter 4	Germany: Position in the Ancient World	19
Chapter 5	German Habitats and Wildlife	32
Chapter 6	German Resources	36
Chapter 7	Perceptions of German Origins and Character	55
Chapter 8	German Appearance and Reputation	69
Chapter 9	Germanic Society	73
Chapter 10	Germanic Women and Families	82
Chapter 11	Germanic Religion	91
Chapter 12	Germanic Politics and Law	119
Chapter 13	Germanic Chiefs, Warlords and Kings	123
Chapter 14	Germanic Warfare and Military Threat	144
Chapter 15	Service in the Roman Army	172
Chapter 16	German Bodyguards of the Roman Emperors: Germani Corporis Custodes	177

Chapter 17	The Baltic Coasts and Scandinavia	203
Chapter 18	Baltic Amber	214

Epilogue	226
Chronological Index of Ancient Authors	229
Chronology	234
Appendix A: Germanic Bodyguard of the Roman Emperors: Inscriptions from Rome	237
Appendix B: Details of Germania: Claudius Ptolemy's Map Data	245
Appendix C: German Tribes in Tacitus and Ptolemy	252

Maps and Illustrations

Maps

Map 1. Roman world view: reconstruction of Agrippa's map (12 BC–AD 14).
Map 2. Claudius Ptolemy's reconstruction of western Europe (AD 150).
Map 3. Claudius Ptolemy's map of Germania (reconstructed from ancient data).
Map 4. Peoples of Ancient Germania.

Illustrations

1. Scene of warriors fighting bulls on the Gundestrup Cauldron, found in northern Denmark. The silver panels display Celtic-style artwork and may date to about 100 BC.
2. A warrior youth fights a bull. Inner base of the Gundestrup Cauldron.
3. Roman relief depicting a northern European fighting a legionary, second century AD (found in the Forum of Trajan, currently in the Louvre, Paris).
4. Germans depicted on the Portonaccio Sarcophagus, AD 180 (Museo Nazionale Romano).
5. Head of a Suebic German depicted on the Mušov Cauldron – a Roman bronze cauldron found in the grave of a Germanic chief, from the second century AD.
6. Bronze figurine of a Germanic warrior (National History Museum of Romania).
7. German spear carved with the sacred image of a fylfot and triskele, first century AD.
8. Gravestone of a Roman cavalryman named Titus Flavius Bassus (Cologne).
9. Roman gate pillar depicting Germanic captives (Landesmuseum, Mainz).
10. Roman Triumphal Arch of Orange, depicting captured northern European war gear including shields and animal standards, 27 BC–AD 14.
11. Silver denarius of the Emperor Augustus: Germanic Surrender, 12 BC.
12. Silver Roman cavalry helmet found in Batavian territory at Waal, near Nijmegen (Valkhof Museum).
13. Roman silver drinking cup depicting King Priam of Troy appealing to Achilles for the return of his son Hector's body. Found in a Germanic

chieftain's grave at Hoby, Denmark, from the first century BC. The Greek champion Achilles is depicted as Augustus and the cup was possibly a diplomatic gift.
14. Germanic chiefs depicted on Trajan's Column, AD 113.
15. Germanic warriors depicted on Trajan's Column.
16. A Roman attack including Germanic warriors, depicted on Trajan's Column.
17. Roman auxiliary cavalry, perhaps Batavians, depicted on Trajan's Column.
18. Germanic bodyguard on Trajan's Column.

Acknowledgements

I was educated at Lagan College in Belfast, the first integrated cross-community school to be established in Northern Ireland, founded for young people of all cultural and economic backgrounds. I am grateful for an education free from the divisions of race, religion, or social class.

My undergraduate degree was in Archaeology and Ancient History at Queen's University Belfast and I am indebted to the Northern Ireland Department of Education and Learning for financing the early stage of my doctoral research.

In the absence of further funding, I used my spare time and limited earnings to continue my research. In 2010, I completed my monograph, *Rome and the Distant East*. This was followed by the publication of *The Roman Empire and the Indian Ocean* in 2014 and *The Roman Empire and the Silk Routes* in 2016, presenting a new model for the ancient world economy.

For eight years I taught tutorial groups in Ancient History at Queen's University Belfast. From 2016, I worked in a clinical care home that provides nursing care for patients with complex medical needs, including palliative care for elderly people with dementia. During the Covid-19 pandemic, a specialised Covid care unit for the elderly and infirm was opened at the facility. I left health care in April 2024 to resume my research.

I would like to thank Dr John Curran for his steadfast support throughout my academic career, and my all colleagues at the Classical Association in Northern Ireland who strive to preserve the relevance of Classics and ancient history. I especially mention Dr Peter Crawford and Dr Helen McVeigh. I am grateful for their friendship.

Publishing this work in a series of books without an academic position has created personal hardship. This book is therefore dedicated to my immediate family: my parents, my brother Leon and my sister Thayna. Thank you for all your support.

Dr Raoul McLaughlin
Bangor, Northern Ireland
June 2025

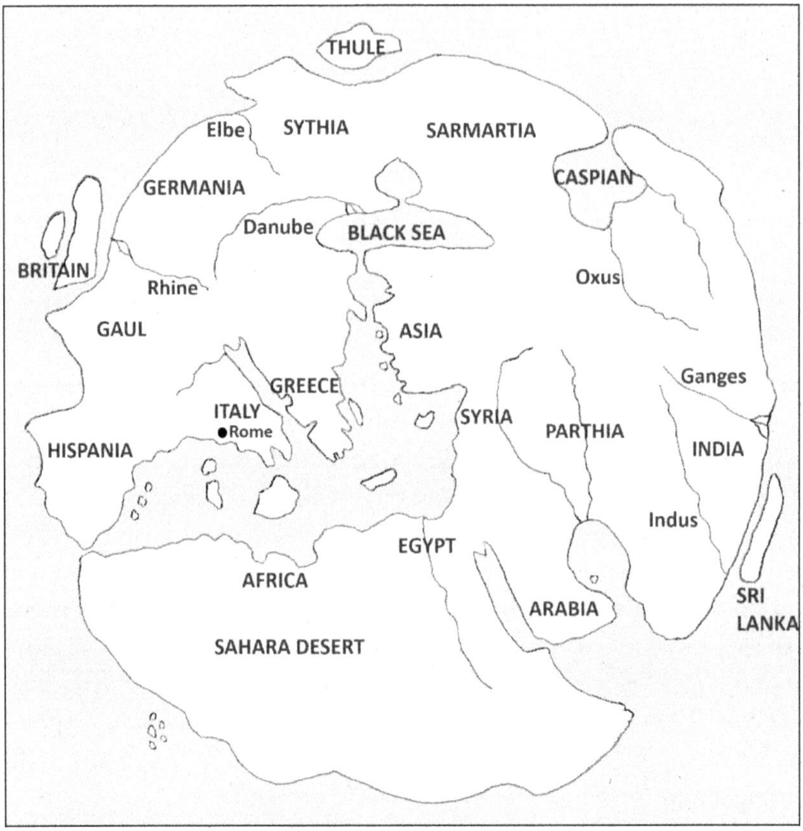

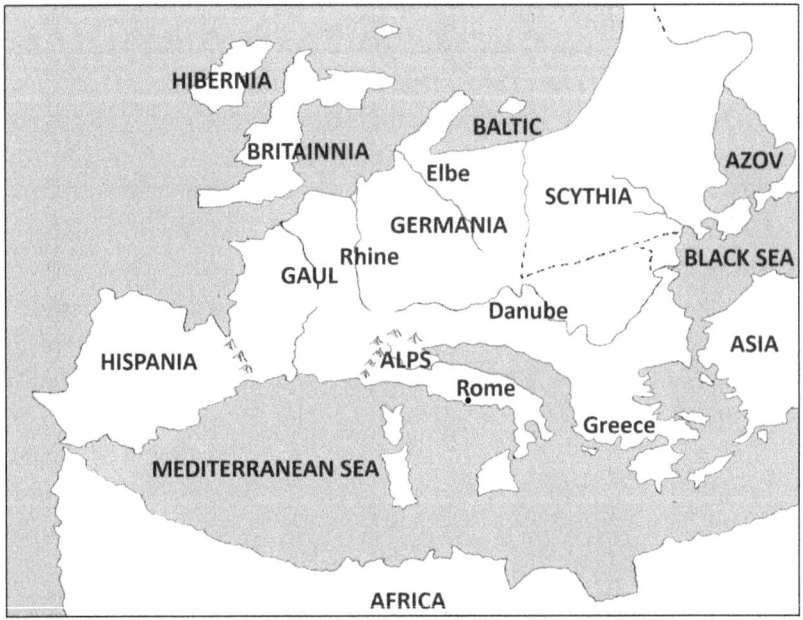

Map 1. Roman world view: reconstruction of Agrippa's map (12 BC–AD 14).

Map 2. Claudius Ptolemy's reconstruction of western Europe (AD 150).

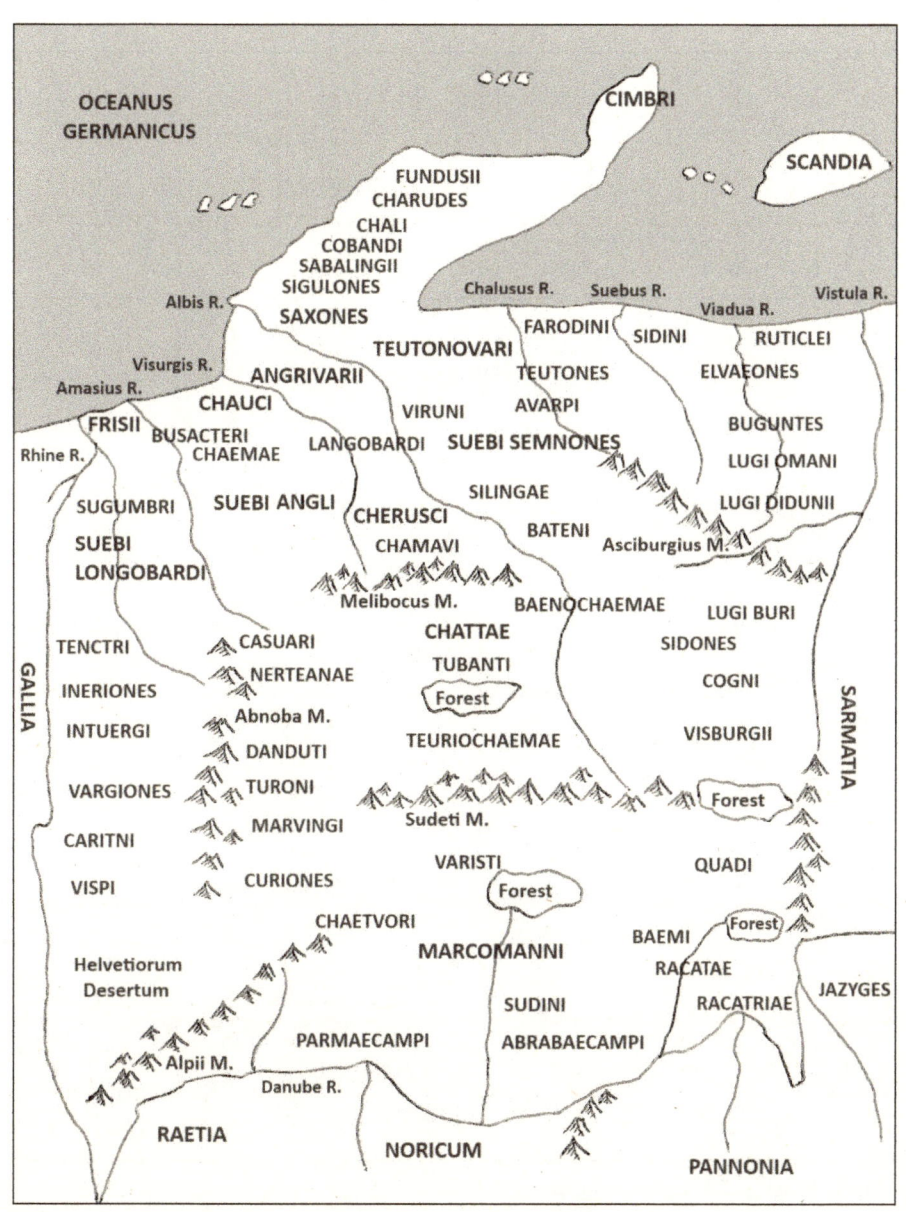

Map 3. Claudius Ptolemy's map of Germania (reconstructed from ancient data).

Map 4. Peoples of Ancient Germania.

Introduction

The Ancient Germans

This sourcebook contains new translations of the principal Greek and Roman texts concerning the ancient Germans and their kindred peoples. It is designed to allow archaeologists to contextualise their work, and for classicists and ancient historians to develop a more authentic understanding of this ancient population and their culture. This book is designed to be accessible to a wide readership, including individuals with no prior knowledge of ancient Classical civilisations. It is the sourcebook for a university course entitled 'Beyond the Empire: Ancient North Europeans'.

There are at present no wide-ranging academic books written about the ancient Germans from the perspective of Roman history. Likewise, despite the abundance of textual evidence, no accessible sourcebooks have been produced providing ancient Classical accounts of the Germans. The subject has been either left to archaeologists examining material cultures or considered piecemeal by historians in various journals. Any books that do exist on this subject generally focus on individual Germanic groups that migrated into the Roman Empire during Late Antiquity, including the Goths, Visigoths, Vandals, Lombards, Franks and Anglo-Saxons. The topic of Germanic relations with the early Empire is considered significant, but it has not been addressed by a single author in a comprehensive study. This is an important subject that deserves greater academic attention.

This sourcebook considers the period between the end of the Roman Republic in the first century BC and the collapse of the Western Roman Empire in AD 476. It therefore presents approximately five centuries of ancient testimony from the earliest Classical knowledge of the Germans to the final fragmentation of Roman Europe after various Germanic invasions. Readers who are familiar with later Nordic accounts will recognise the antecedents of many of the beliefs and practices attested in the medieval era.

In ancient times there were two main population groups in northern Europe. The Celts dominated the Atlantic-facing territories of the continent, while the Germans emerged in the Nordic North and spread across central Europe. Roman expansion into northern Europe was achieved by the conquest and annexation of Celtic territories, usually after prolonged campaigns and devastating conflicts.

By contrast, the Roman Empire tried, and failed, to subdue the homelands of the ancient Germans. The militarised northern frontiers of the Empire therefore became a 'German phenomenon' extending along both the Rhine and Danube river systems. Some Germans were accepted and incorporated into the Roman regime, but throughout much of ancient history, the Germans were an external and foreign population. This changed in the fourth and fifth centuries AD, when Germanic populations broke through the frontiers and dismembered the Western Roman Empire.

Throughout history, due to their population movements, Germanic peoples had a significant impact on global events. The ancestral English were part of a Germanic population that migrated into Roman Britain during the fifth century AD. This included Franks, Angles, Saxons and Jutes who overcame the Celtic Britons and underwent an ethnogenesis to become '*Angelcynn*' (Germanic-Celts, the Ancestral English). The Scandinavians (North Germans) developed into the medieval Vikings who spread as seafarers and settled across the Atlantic territories. In northern France, their descendants became the Normans, and in Scotland and Ireland, the Vikings progenitured the Norse-Gaels ('*Lochlanns*'). The Germans of central Europe also formed a dominant group within the northern European population that settled and established the early United States of America. This sourcebook is intended to be an account of their ancestors, collected from the ancient Greek and Roman sources.

Roman Appraisal of the Germans

The Roman historian Tacitus explains the German threat to the Empire. Writing in about AD 98, he reviews almost two centuries of engagement and conflict.

001 Tacitus, *Germania,* **37**
Rome was in her 640th year when we first heard of the Cimbrian invader (108 BC). This was during the consulship of Caecilius Metellus and Papirius Carbo, about 210 years before the second consulship of the Emperor Trajan (the time of writing). This is how long we have been involved in conquering the Germans.

In this period many losses have been sustained on both sides of the conflict and no people have given us as many frequent alarms and dangers. Not even the Samnite peoples (of Italy), nor the Carthaginians, the Spanish, Gauls, or even the Parthians (the rival empire of ancient Iran). German independence truly is fiercer and more challenging than the despotism of an Arsaces (the Iranian dynasty). The east can taunt us with the slaughter of Crassus (commander of a Roman army annihilated by Parthian cavalry in 53 BC). But they lost their own prince Pacorus when they were defeated by Roman forces led by Ventidius (in 38 BC). But the Germans have deprived the Roman people of five consular armies. They have routed or captured the Roman armies led by Carbo, Cassius, Scaurus Aurelius, Servilius Caepio and Marcus Manlius. They also deprived the Emperor Caesar Augustus of his commander Varus, along with three legions (in AD 9).

Even when the Romans are victorious, the Germans have inflicted significant losses on them. This occurred when Marius defeated the Cimbri in Italy and when the great Julius Caesar gained his victories over the Germans in Gaul. Later, the Roman commanders Drusus, Nero and Germanicus all took substantial losses to gain their victories in Germany. Soon after these events, the Germans treated the grandiose threats and menaces of Caligula with contempt and ridicule (AD 41). Then there was a lull in the conflict until the unrest caused by the Roman civil war (of AD 68).

The Germans stormed the winter camp of our legions and even prepared for the conquest of Gaul. But once more, they were driven back by our forces. Even in recent times, we have celebrated triumphs over German armies, but we have never claimed their homelands through conquest.

Chapter One

Northern Europe in Early Greek Myth

In the third century BC the Greek writer Apollonius recorded legends concerning Jason and the Argonauts. Apollonius suggested that Greek ships in the Black Sea could enter the Danube and by sailing west, reach the Baltic or the Adriatic coasts of Italy. This route crossed territories that were Celtic or proto-Germanic.

002 Apollonius of Rhodes, *Argonautica,* **4.300–330**
There is a river on the furthest extension of this sea (the west coast of the Black Sea). It is broad and extremely deep, and merchant ships can enter its waters. This river is called the Ister (the Danube) and its outflow is visible from a long way off because it forms a separate stream (the freshwater does not easily intermix with the sea). The source of the Danube lies far beyond the blast of the north wind (Hyperborea) and the distant Rhipean Mountains. It springs forth with a roar (to cross these territories) and flows through the boundaries of the Thracians and Scythians (next to the Black Sea). When it enters these regions it divides into two streams. One course fills the Ionian Sea (via the Black Sea) and the other flows south to enter a deep gulf beyond the Trinacrian Sea (the Adriatic north of Sicily).

Voyage of the Argonauts

Apollonius offers a confused account of western geography. In his retelling of Greek myth, the Argonauts sail from the Black Sea upstream along the Danube to the Isle of Electra (the goddess of sea storms) in the Sea of Cronos (the Far North). From there they enter the 'Eridanus', the 'Ocean Stream' encircling the earth. This could be the amber-producing coasts of northern Europe, which had a trade link to the Celtic regions of northern Italy via the river Po.

003 Apollonius of Rhodes, *Argonautica,* **4.570–580**
The Argonauts quickly boarded their ship and toiled ceaselessly at their oars on their way to the sacred isle of Electra ('Amber'). Electra was the most distant island near the flowing Eridanus (the 'Ocean Stream').

When the Colchians learnt that their prince had been slain, they were eager to pursue the *Argo* and the Minyans (Greeks) to the Cronian Sea. But Hera (the Greek matron goddess) prevented them by casting terrifying bolts of lightning from the sky.

004 Apollonius of Rhodes, *Argonautica,* **4.600–610**
The heroes (the Argonauts) sailed onwards and moored in the land of the Hylleans (people descended from a son of Hercules – Germans?). There were numerous islands in the river (the Upper Danube?) that made the sailing dangerous for those who passed by. But the Hylleans did not do any harm to the Argonauts and even voluntarily assisted their passage. As a reward they were given a mighty tripod of Apollo (a stand on which sacrificial offerings were made, or a seat from which divine oracles were delivered). Phoebus ('Bright Apollo') had given Aeson's son (Jason) two tripods to carry on his voyage. This gift was received when Jason visited sacred Pytho (Delphi) to enquire about his voyage (from the oracle). It was foretold that whatever land the tripods were placed in, the territory would never suffer from the ravages of an enemy. One of the tripods is still hidden in the pleasant land near the city of Hyllus, but it is preserved deep beneath the earth where it can never be seen by mortal men.

The Argonauts Reach the Land of Amber (the Baltic)

005 Apollonius of Rhodes, *Argonautica,* **4.660–730**
Hera considered the warnings and the anger of (her husband) Zeus. She therefore devised an ending for the voyage of the *Argo*. She stirred up storm winds in front of the ship that drove the *Argo* back to the rocky isle of Electra ('Amber'). But suddenly a human voice came from the Dodonian oak beam that Athena (goddess of wisdom) had placed at the stern of the ship (perhaps a carved figure like a masthead). The crew were filled with great terror when this voice told them about the wrath of Zeus. It proclaimed that they could not escape the anger of the god, not even on an endless sea, or the midst of the greatest tempests. Only Circe (the sorceress) could purge their guilt for the ruthless murder of Apsyrtus (the Colchian prince). The voice then told Polydeuces and Castor (the demigod brothers) to pray to the immortal gods. They must pray for a safe passage through the Ausonian Seas (surrounding Italy), so that they could reach Circe, the daughter of Helios and Perse (the solar god and a water nymph).

As the crew of the *Argo* cried out through the darkness, the sons of Tyndareus (the Spartan king) stood up. They lifted their hands up to the immortal gods and prayed for safe delivery. But the rest of the Minyan (Greek) heroes were overcome with despair and despondency. Meanwhile, the *Argo* sped forwards under the power of its sails and entered the deep flowing passage of Eridanus (the 'World Stream' – the outer ocean in the Far North). It was here that Phaethon (son of Helios) was struck on the chest by a blazing lightning bolt (cast by Zeus). Half-consumed by fire, he fell from the (sun) chariot into the opening of that deep gulf (the Baltic Sea?). Even now, the waters belch heavy steam clouds from that smouldering wound (the impact site of a burning god). No bird can spread its fine wings and cross that water. Mid-course (it will be caught by the heat) and plunge fluttering and burning into the flames.

All around the site stand the maiden-daughters of Helios, enclosed in tall poplar trees (thin evergreens). They wretchedly wail a piteous lament and from their eyes they shed bright drops of amber. These amber drops are dried out by the sun upon the sand. Then, with a blast of the howling winds, the waters of the dark expanse rise over the wide beaches (ocean tides). The waves roll and drag the amber drops back into the swelling mass of the Eridanus.

But the Celts tell another story about these amber pieces. They say that these are the tears of Leto's son, the god Apollo, that have been taken and carried away by the eddies of the ocean (perhaps material shed by the setting sun). (The Greek princess) Coronis (lover of Apollo) gave birth in bright Lacereia (in Thessaly) at the outlet of the Amyrus (the Greek myth). But the youth sought to leave the 'shining god-realm' of his father Apollo. Apollo reproached him and became wrathful (on discovering his absence). But, when he travelled to the sacred race of the Hyperboreans (the Far North), the god shed countless tears (when he saw the site of his son's death). This is the story told among the Celts.

The crew of the *Argo* despaired (as they entered the 'World Stream') and for a long time, they had no desire for food or drink. Every day they felt weak and despondent due to the repulsive stench which was difficult to endure. This was the smell coming from Phaethon who was still burning (producing volcanic-like fumes). And at night, they heard the piercing lament of the daughters of Helios, wailing with their shrill voices. As the daughters lamented, their tears fell and rolled across the water like drops of oil. Finally, the *Argo* entered the deep stream of the Rhodanus (perhaps the Rhine rather than the Rhône) which flows into Eridanus. There was a great roar as the waters mingled (joining the river to the sea).

This river rises at the edges of the earth where there are dark portals and vast estates of night (an indistinguishable Celtic territory where the great rivers are interconnected). One part of this river bursts out into the Ocean (the Rhine entering the Atlantic), while another pours into the 'Sea of the Greeks' (the Rhône flowing into the Mediterranean). A third part flows through seven outlets into a great gulf beyond the Sardinian Sea (the river Po).

Moving up the river (Rhine/Rhône), the *Argo* entered vast stormy lakes which spread across the immense Celtic landscape (the Swiss Lakes including Lake Geneva). Here they almost met with catastrophe, because one branch of this river leads back into a vast gulf of the Ocean (perhaps an imagined passage through the Loire). In their ignorance and confusion, the Argonauts were about to enter this stream, from which they would never have returned safely. But suddenly Hera (the matron goddess) leapt forth from heaven and uttered a great cry of warning from the Hercynian Rock (the Caspian). The crew were all shaken with fear for the terrible noise crashed through the mighty firmament. But the warning from the goddess succeeded and they turned back from the wrong course. The *Argo* instead entered the ordained outlet and followed the correct passage devised by Hera (down the Rhône). The goddess poured a dreadful mist along the river, so the *Argo* passed unseen and unharmed through countless tribes of Celts and Ligyans. Finally, after a long time, the *Argo* came to a beach beside the surging sea. Sailing through the middle outlet of the river they safely reached the Stoechades Islands (off southern Gaul in the Western Mediterranean).

Baltic Amber

Amber found within Roman territories provides evidence for trade contact with the Baltic coast of northern Germany. Diodorus Siculus, writing in the first century BC, provides an early description of this trade network and the myths that it engendered.

006 Diodorus Siculus, *Historical Library*, 5.23
I will now describe the material which is known as 'electron' (amber). Beyond Gaul the continent extends as far as Scythia (the Ukrainian Steppe). To the north of these territories there is an island in the exposed ocean which is called Basileia (Heligoland in the North Sea). The waves striking this island cast up great quantities of the material known as amber. No other place in the known world produces this great quantity. Many ancient writers have devised incredible stories about this territory, but all have been disproven by later events.

Many poets and historians tell a story concerning Phaethon, the son of (the Solar God) Helius. It is said that Phaethon persuaded his father to allow him to drive the four-horse Sun Chariot across the sky for the passage of a single day. Helius agreed, but due to his youth and inexperience, Phaethon could not keep control of the reins. The Sun Chariot careered away from its sky course and set the heavens ablaze. This is the origin of the Milky Way (the band of stars that is our Galaxy, as seen obliquely across the northern sky). As the vehicle hurtled out of control the scorching rays of the sun burnt parts of the earth. The God Zeus was horrified by the sight and launched a thunderbolt to halt the rampaging chariot. Phaethon was dislodged from the vehicle and tumbled down to the earth near a northern river. The earliest Greek accounts called this river the Eridanus, claiming that it was near the Padus (the Po River in northern Italy). The sisters of Phaethon gathered near this northern river to mourn their brother. They vied with each other to bewail his death until their excessive grief caused them to metamorph into thin trees. At the same season every year, these sister-trees drip sap-like tears from their bark. It is this substance that hardens into amber.

This account of the sisters is fiction and has been disproved by later discoveries. It is now known that amber is gathered on the island of Basileia (Heligoland). The natives collect it on their shore and bring it across to the seaboard opposite their island. From there amber is conveyed into regions that are better known to us.

Amber exceeds all other saps in its brilliance and endurance, but it is still commonly used in connection with mourning and bereavement, especially involving the young.

Chapter Two

Roman Sources and Attitude to Enquiry

This source is an example of Roman approaches to writing history including ancient studies concerning the Germans. Pliny the Elder wrote an account of Rome's German Wars during the mid-first century AD. The work has not survived into modern times, but it was a sourcebook for Tacitus' *Germania*. Pliny's nephew provides further details.

007 Pliny the Younger, *Letters***, 3.5** From Pliny the Younger to Baebius Macer. I was delighted to learn that you are a zealous reader of my uncle's books (Pliny the Elder). As you would like to possess copies of all his works, you have asked me to give you a complete list. I can give you this information and include the order the works were completed, because students like to know these details. The works are:

> *Throwing the Javelin from Horseback*. He researched and composed this ingenious study while on active service as a cavalry officer (on the Rhineland frontier).

> *The Life of Pomponius Secundus*, in two volumes (the governor of Germania Superior during the AD 50s). Pomponius was very fond of my uncle who composed this book to thank him for his assistance and honour his memory.

> *The German Wars*, in twenty volumes. This study is an account of all the wars we have waged against the German peoples. He began this work while he was on active military service in Germany. The task was inspired by a dream where the spirit of Drusus Nero appeared to my uncle. Drusus had won sweeping victories in Germany and had died in that country (in 9 BC). But his achievements were in danger of being forgotten. He urged my uncle to rescue his name from ill-deserved oblivion and entrusted him with the task to restore his fame.

> *The Student*, a work in three volumes, which was afterwards split up into six volumes because of its length. This study discussed the proper training and equipment for an orator, starting in youth.

Ambiguity in Language, in eight volumes (a study of linguistics). He wrote this work in the final years of Nero's reign when tyranny had made it dangerous to write any book on any subject.

A Continuation of the History of Aufidius Bassus, in thirty-one books (a famous Roman historian who died during the reign of Tiberius leaving his historical study incomplete. Bassus also wrote a *Bellum Germanicum* – *The Germanic Wars*).

The Natural History, in thirty-seven volumes. This learned and comprehensive work considers the study of Nature.

Perhaps it surprises you that a busy man had time to finish so many volumes filled with detailed discussions. It is even more remarkable, because for many years he also presented cases in the law courts. My uncle died aged 57. His studies were hindered by the many duties he performed in the important offices he held (during the AD 70s governorships in Gallia Narbonensis, North Africa, Hispania Tarraconensis and Gallia Belgica). There were also duties arising from his position as 'friend' (senior advisor) to the emperors (Vespasian and Titus).

But my uncle had a keen intellect and a marvellous capacity for work. His powers of application were enormous (concentrated effort and focus). He used to begin to study at night, like the Festival of Vulcan (a Roman Fire Festival that began with the pre-dawn lighting of candles). He would study long before sunrise. Even in winter he would often commence work during the sixth hour (after nightfall) and still be studying at the eighth hour. He could sleep immediately and without difficulty whenever he felt the need. Sometimes he would pause in the middle of his work for this purpose (a short period of restorative sleep).

Before daybreak he would meet Vespasian to perform his official duties (in an advisory council) because the emperor was also a night worker. On his return home he would devote any further free time to study.

Often in summer he would eat his usual simple and light meal which was always prepared in traditional ways. Then he would recline in the sunshine and order a book to be read aloud (by a slave or attendant). He would take notes and copy extracts from the reading. My uncle never read or listened without taking notes and extracting details. He used to say a book has never existed that did not have some interesting passage or good information. After resting in the sunshine, he usually bathed in cold water. Then he would eat a light snack and have a brief nap. This had the restorative power of a night's sleep and he would return to his studies until the afternoon meal. After eating he would ask for another book to be read aloud and he would take further brief notes on the subject.

I remember an occasion when the reader incorrectly pronounced a single word. One of my uncle's friends corrected him and made the reader repeat the entire paragraph with the accurate pronunciation. My uncle interposed to ask, 'Did you not understand the meaning of the paragraph?' When his friend said he did, my uncle responded, 'Then why did you make him repeat all that information? We have lost more than ten lines of new content because of your interruption.' That is how much my uncle resented the waste of every useful moment.

In summer he used to finish his evening meal while it was still light. In winter he always finished eating before the first hour of darkness had passed. This was a fixed rule in his routine as though the process was dictated by law. This is how my uncle conducted himself when he was extremely busy amid the heightened activity of Rome. When he was in the countryside (at his summer villa) the only break my uncle took from his work was when he bathed. He would listen to a reader or dictate notes to a scribe, even when he was being scraped with the strigil or rubbed down (Roman cleansing routine using oils and scraping tools to remove dirt and perspiration).

When he was travelling my uncle devoted himself entirely to study. He travelled accompanied by a shorthand writer who carried book scrolls and wooden tablets (erasable wax tablets for temporary notetaking). My uncle wore mittens on his hands in winter, so that numbness would not deprive him of the opportunity to rapidly write down his thoughts. In Rome he was always carried through the streets in a litter so that he could continue his work. I remember that once he rebuked me for walking to my destination. He said, 'If you were a real student of knowledge, you would not waste any time in that manner.' For he thought that all time not devoted to study, was time wasted.

This application to study and work allowed my uncle to complete all the many volumes I have listed. In total he left me 160 book-sized documents. Each document has text written on both sides of the scroll in very small handwriting. Consequently, the number of volumes contained in this collection is far greater than the total of scrolls.

The Roman Mind

Pliny the Elder devotes his *Natural History* to the Emperor Vespasian.

008 Pliny, *Natural History*, 1.5
I believe that those who seek difficulties to overcome through service (to state or society) are the best guides to learning. They are more valuable than people who write simply for recognition and pleasure. This has been my purpose. (…)

As (the Senator) Domitus Piso said, 'We do not need single books, but entire storehouses of knowledge.' I have read about 2,000 volumes, including many complex and obscure studies that are rarely seen by students. I have gathered these details into these 36 volumes containing 20,000 noteworthy facts, obtained from about a hundred authors (equivalent to about 10 modern books). These volumes explore many subjects, with a great number of facts that have been ignored by our predecessors or confirmed by subsequent experience (such as the origins of amber).

I expect that many facts will have escaped my notice (by omission), but I am only human and I have many other duties to perform (state official, administrator, legal advocate, advisor to the emperor and commander of the imperial fleet at Misenum). We can only pursue our writing interests in our limited spare time. For me, that is during the night hours when I would otherwise be idle (when custom did not allow visitors or formal meetings).

I devote my days to you (the Flavian Dynasty) and I take the sleep I need to sustain my health. As Marcus Varro says, less sleep adds a little extra time to life. For being alive surely means being awake and conscious? (productive work in preference to excess sleep). And this manuscript is my reward (work achieved in the added hours).

For these reasons and difficulties, the work may have flaws. But you know my capabilities (in imperial service). This guarantees my work and it rates its value. Receive it as a votive offering and acknowledge its value in this regard.

Roman Experience

The Roman writer Vellius served as a cavalry officer in the army of Tiberius, the future emperor who served in Germania. He therefore had direct experience in the region (AD 4–12).

009 Velleius Paterculus, *History of Rome*, 2.104–5

In this period, after I had previously filled the duties of the Tribunate, I became a soldier in the camp of Tiberius Caesar. Immediately after (Augustus) adopted Tiberius, I was sent with the commander to Germany as Prefect of the Cavalry. I was succeeding my father in that position, and for nine continuous years I served as Prefect of Cavalry, or as commander of a legion. I was therefore a direct witness to the remarkable achievements of Tiberius and in some minor way, with my modest abilities assisted him. I do not think that any mortal man will ever again see the sights that I witnessed (on our outbound journey).

Chapter Three

Overview Description of Germany

In AD 234, the Emperor Severus Alexander planned a military campaign to counter a threat from the Germanic tribes living beyond the Danube Frontier.

010 Herodian, *Roman History*, 4.7
Alexander and his advisers also feared for the safety of Italy itself. (…) The provinces of Illyricum are a narrow expanse. There is very little territory between Italy and the Germans under Roman control (between the Alps and the Danube). This means the Germans are in close proximity to the Italians and the two peoples (Germans and Romans) share common borders (along the southern Rhine and Danube).

Account by Tacitus

Tacitus provides an extensive account of Germany including details of the terrain and the main Germanic tribes. He begins his account by considering territories east of the Rhine and then proceeds north. The Chatti occupied the Hercynian Forest, which covered a large part of southern and central Germany.

The Chatti

Hercynian Forest

011 Tacitus, *Germania*, 29
Beyond the frontier zone, around the outskirts of the Hercynian Forest (Bavaria), are the settlements of the Chatti. Like many of these districts in Germany their territory is exposed and marshy. The landscape becomes less hilly towards the east, but the forest extends across the entire southern boundary of the Chatti lands. These Germans have strong physiques, muscular limbs and show fierce expressions. The Chatti have more intelligence and insight than other Germans and the tribe is renowned for its vigorous courage. They promote their best men to power and strictly obey those who they elevate to command. They rely more on the ability

of their war leaders than simply the strength of their army. They maintain their ranks on the battlefield and watch for opportunities, checking any sudden impulses in combat. It is unusual how much they devote themselves to methodical discipline. They divide the day into portions (time periods to allocate military tasks) and entrench themselves at night (fortified camps). The Chatti think that bravery is an unfailing resource and regard luck as a doubtful occurrence.

The Chatti depend on their infantry for their entire military strength. These forces are laden with weapons, tools, and provisions. Other German tribes may go into battle, but the Chatti go on campaigns. They seldom engage in simple raids or casual conflicts. It is the character of a cavalry force to quickly overcome an enemy, but they can suddenly suffer a reversal or defeat. The swift can suddenly faulter, but the deliberate and steadfast confidence of infantry is a better model for courage (this is what the Chatti possess).

Usipii and Tencteri

Scale of Germanic Warfare

Tacitus suggests the scale of Germanic warfare in his account of conflict east of the Rhine.

012 Tacitus, *Germania*, 32–33
The Rhine becomes a substantial river as it reaches the territory of the Chatti. It therefore serves as a boundary between the Chatti and the adjoining Usipii and Tencteri tribes. The Tencteri possess the usual military characteristics of the Germans, but they also excel in cavalry. They are renown as much for their cavalry as the Chatti are famous for their infantry. The prosperity of their forefathers has been maintained (the capacity to raise horses). These mounts provide their children with playful sport, their youths with competitive rivalry, and the Tencteri will ride even in old age. They bequeath these horses through the usual rights of inheritance and the animals are passed between generations, along with slaves and dwellings. Properties are inherited by the eldest, but the horses will be given to the most warlike and courageous son.

The Bructeri tribe used to occupy territories beyond the Tencteri, but current accounts suggest that the Chamavi and Angrivarii have seized and occupied their settlements. They took the territory after joining with neighbouring tribes to expel the Bructeri from their homelands. This conflict eliminated the tribe. These tribes possibly warred against the Bructeri because they were becoming overbearing, or maybe the attackers only sought plunder. Whatever the reason, this conflict demonstrates how the gods favour Rome. The Romans were granted permission to observe this war in which more than 60,000 Germans were killed. They did not die from the efforts of Roman armies, or the effects of our weapons. They were killed by their own countrymen in the pleased view of Roman observers. My best prayer is not that the German tribes will always love Rome. I pray that they will always keep a hatred and a rivalry for one another. The future destiny of our empire will be successful if there is discord among our enemies.

North Coast of Germany

Roman Maritime Explorations, the Chauci and the Cimbri

013 Tacitus, *Germania*, 33
Beyond the Angrivarii and Chamavi are the Dulgubini and Chasuarii tribes. The lands are also occupied by several other tribes who are not so well known (northern Germany). The Frisii occupy territories approaching the Rhine (the Netherlands) and their tribe is divided into the Greater and Lesser Frisii based on population size. Their territory extends to the ocean and is flanked by the Rhine. This coast has vast lakes and sea inlets which have been navigated by Roman fleets. Roman ships have even ventured into the sea beyond this coast to reach another 'Pillars of Hercules' (the Skagerrak Straits between Jutland and Norway). It is commonly claimed that Hercules once visited this country, but we ascribe every great work of wonder to this ancient demigod. The Roman commander Drusus Germanicus was a daring explorer, but the ocean blocked his further progress and he could not find evidence of Hercules or explore the seas beyond (the Baltic Sea). Since that era no one else has made the attempt and it is considered more pious and reverential to believe the actions of the gods, than to seek proof of them.

This description of Germany has included its western regions (bordering the Rhine), but the country also has a vast northward expanse. East of the Frisian settlements is the homeland of the Chauci. The Chauci occupy part of the coast and their territory stretches south to flank all the tribes previously mentioned (the Angrivarii and Chasuarii). In the south it reaches an extended territory of the Chatti tribe. The lands of the Chauci are densely populated. They are the noblest of the German people who maintain their greatness with honourable dealings. The Chauci live a peaceful and secluded existence without ambition for conquest or lawless violence. They do not provoke wars or injure other peoples with plundering raids. The fact that they can maintain their superiority without harming other tribes is evidence of their military valour and strength. Nonetheless, they always have their weapons ready if required and their army can be rapidly assembled with a multitude of men and horses. Even at peace they preserve the renown and readiness for military valour.

The Cimbri dwell in this same remote region of Germany bordering the ocean (Jutland). They once had great renown, but now they are an insignificant tribe. There are widespread traces of their ancient glory on both sides of the Rhine. The remains of vast encampments indicate the warlike strength of the tribe and confirm that a vast emigration occurred from their homeland.

Inner Germany

The Suebi

Julius Caesar wrote accounts of Germany from direct experience.

014 Julius Caesar, *Gallic War*, 4.1
The Suebi nation is by far the largest and the most warlike Germanic nation. They are said to possess 100 districts and each year every one of these territories sends a thousand men with weapons to participate in their wars (potentially 100,000 warriors). The kinsmen who remain at home can maintain their own households and provide (sustenance) for their absent comrades on expeditions. The following year they themselves will take up arms to fight while their returning comrades remain at home (managing communal resources and producing food). Consequently, their herds are not neglected, and their skill and practice in war are continually maintained.

015 Tacitus, *Germania*, 39
The Suebi occupy the greater part of Germany, but they are not a single people like the Chatti or the Tencteri. Until recently the Suebi were divided into separate tribes that each had their own names, but they accepted the general designation of 'Suebi'. (…) The Semnones say they are the most ancient and renowned branch of the Suebi and their great antiquity is attested by their religion.

Eastern Germany

The Langobardi

The Romans never conquered German territory east of the Elbe River. The Langobardi occupied lands near this boundary.

016 Tacitus, *Germania*, 40
The Langobardi regard their small numbers as an honour and a distinction. They are surrounded by a host of the most powerful tribes, but they have preserved themselves. They have done so, not by submitting to stronger adversaries, but engaging them in the hazards of war. Beyond this land are the territories of the Reudigni, Aviones, Anglii, Varini, and Eudoses (the Jutland Peninsula). Then there are the Suardones and Nuithones (Baltic territories east of the Elbe River). (…)

This branch of the Suebi nation stretches into the remoter regions of Germany.

Southern Germany: Across the Danube Frontier

Marcomanni and Quadi

017 Tacitus, *Germania*, 42
The Narisci occupy territories on the frontiers of the Hermunduri. Beyond them are the Marcomanni and Quadi (southern Germany). The Marcomanni are foremost in military strength and renown. Their territory was previously settled by the Boii, but they expelled them from the region and claimed the land by their own strength. The Narisci and Quadi are not inferior to the Marcomanni. Together these tribes form the entire southern boundary of Germany facing the Danube (Roman frontier).

Intermixed Tribes

018 Tacitus, *Germania*, 43
There are other tribes beyond the Marcomanni and the Quadi. These are the Marsigni, Gotini, Osi, and Buri. The Marsigni and Buri resemble the Suebi in both their language and their lifestyles. But the Gotini and Osi are distinct because of their languages. The Gotini speak a Gallic (Celtic) dialect and the Osi preserve a Pannonian language, which confirms their

non-German origins. They are also distinct because they make tribute payments to foreign powers including the Quadi and Sarmatians (steppe nomads). The Gotini are so lacking in self-autonomy that they will work in iron mines for foreign states. These tribes occupy very little land that is fertile and dwell mostly in the forests and mountains.

Suebia is divided in two by a continuous mountain range and there are many German tribes beyond the mountains (east of the Elbe and the Oder rivers). The largest is the Ligii nation, which spreads across a wide extent and includes several states. The most powerful states are the Harii, Helveconae, Manimi, Helisii and the Nahanarvali.

The Far North

Baltic Coast Leading to Scythia

019 Tacitus, *Germania*, 43
Beyond the Ligii are the Gothones (Baltic coast near the Vistula River). The Gothones (Goths) are ruled by kings who have greater authority than other Germanic kings. However, these kings do not restrict the freedom of the people. The Rugii and Lemovii occupy lands adjoining the Gothones, but they live further inland from the coast (between the Oder and Vistula rivers). These tribes are distinctive because they carry round shields, short swords, and demonstrate a servile submission to their king.

020 Tacitus, *Germania*, 45
The tribes of the Aestii occupy the eastern shore of the Suebic Sea (Baltic coast beyond the Oder River). Their behaviour, customs and clothing styles resemble the Suebi, but their language is closer to British (Celtic Brythonic). They worship the 'Mother of the Gods' and wear the image of a wild boar as a religious symbol. The Aestii believe that this symbol can ward off many dangers. Those who wear the emblem believe that the goddess can protect them in battle amid their enemies. The Aestii wield clubs and rarely use iron weapons. Other Germans seem unconcerned with agriculture, but the Aestii are more patient in cultivating grain and other produce. The Aestii also search the seas and are the only people who gather amber on these coasts.

Scandinavia

Specialised Ships and Authoritarian Chiefs

021 Tacitus, *Germania*, 44–45
The Suiones occupy the land on the ocean (Scandinavia). Although they possess men and weapons, they are also powerful due to their ships. These vessels are unusual because they have a prow at both the front and rear of the boat. This can be used to run either end of the boat onto the shore. Their boats are not manoeuvred by sails, or fixed rows of oars attached to the sides of the ship. Instead, the rowing apparatus is unfixed, as on some river craft. This allows the oars to be shifted as circumstances require.

The Suiones respect wealth and a single ruler holds power in their territory. There are no restrictions to his power, and he commands complete obedience. The Suiones do not carry weapons as is the custom with other Germans, and weapons are not at the general disposal of the population. This is possible because the surrounding ocean prevents the sudden incursion of any external enemies. It is desirable because a sizable number of armed men can easily become insubordinate (challenging the chief). For this reason, the ruler of the Suiones is reluctant to place anyone in sole charge of an armed force, neither a nobleman, a freeborn citizen, or even a freedman. All armaments are retained and safeguarded by a keeper who has the status of a slave.

There is another sea beyond the Suiones which is sluggish and almost motionless (the Arctic). It is certain that this ocean surrounds the entire world. The last radiance of the setting sun lingers on this oceanic expanse until sunrise. Throughout the night it remains visible with a brightness sufficient to dim the light of the stars. In this region, the sound of the sun rising can be heard and the forms of gods can be glimpsed in the glorious light (the Aurora Borealis). The rumours seem truthful and this must be the limits of the world.

East Sweden

A Female Chief

022 Tacitus, *Germania*, 45
The tribes of the Sitones closely border the Suiones (eastern Sweden). The Sitones resemble the Suiones in all aspects except they are currently ruled by a woman. They have in this way given up their freedom and fallen below the dignity of even a slave. This is the final territory in Suebia.

East Edge of Germania

Sarmatian-Germanic Tribes, the Fenni (Finns?)

023 Tacitus, *Germania,* **46**

I am not certain whether to call some of the furthest tribes Germans or Sarmatians (mounted nomads on the edge of the Pontic Steppe). This includes the Peucini, Veneti, and the Fenni. Some authorities claim that the Peucini tribe are Bastarnae, but their language, mode of life and settlements appear German. They live in squalor and general inactivity (no towns or state-managed building projects). The Peucini are beginning to resemble the Sarmatians because their chiefs are intermarrying into that population.

The Veneti claim the forested and mountainous region that exists between the Peucini and Fenni. From this region they launch plundering raids into adjoining territories. These Veneti have adopted the characteristics of the Sarmatians, who are nomads, dwelling in wagons and conducting their lives on horseback. But they are better described as Germans because they have fixed habitations, carry shields, and depend on the speed and strength of their infantry. These practices are in complete contrast to the Sarmatians.

The Fenni are more beastlike people and even more impoverished (the Finns?). They forage for food, wear animal skins and hunt with bows. They lack iron so their arrows are armed with pointed and sharpened bone. When the men hunt, the women are present, and they take a share of the prey. Their infants take refuge in shelters made from interlaced branches. This is their only protection from storms and wild animals and both young and old must find rest in these simple structures. The Fenni are more content in this hardship than they would be labouring in a field or toiling in the construction of buildings. They would rather live an existence suspended between hope and fear. They reject the concerns of other men and the example of the gods, for they have obtained the hardest goal because they do not desire more than they need. All accounts of nations beyond this tribe are too incredible to be accepted. It is said the Hellusii and Oxiones have the faces and feelings of men, but the bodies of wild beasts. But all this is unauthenticated and cannot be confirmed.

Chapter Four

Germany: Position in the Ancient World

Roman accounts reveal the significance of ancient Germany and the importance of the Rhine and Danube river systems.

The Size of Europe

024 Pliny, *Natural History,* **4.23**
For those interested in this information, the dimensions of Europe, are as follows: the length of the continent from the Don to Cadiz (the Ukraine to southern Spain) is estimated by Artemidorus and Isidorus to be 7,714 miles. Polybius previously stated the breadth of Europe from Italy to the ocean (south to north) to be 1,150 miles, its exact measurement had not yet been ascertained (during the Roman Republic).

The length of Italy as far as the Alps is 1,020 miles. Polybius took a measurement from the Alps through Lyons to the harbour of the Morini, which is the main port for the crossing to Britain (northern Gaul). He gives the figure of 1,169 miles for this distance. However, a more accurate measurement would start from the Alps and extend north-west through the camp of the legions on the German frontier to reach the outflow of the Rhine. This measurement is 1,243 miles.

Crossings through the Alps

The Alps were a major barrier protecting Italy from invasion. But the Romans were aware that the Germanic territories were close to this frontier.

025 Pliny, *Natural History,* **3.19**
Cornelius Nepos records that in some areas the Alps are only 100 miles across, but Livy gives the figure as 375 miles for a crossing through the mountains. This is because they take their measurements at different points in the mountain range (and its surrounding districts). The Alps are over 100 miles across in the place where they divide Germany from Italy, but in other parts the passes are very narrow and barely exceed 70 miles.

Limits of Germany

Scandinavia, the Rhine and Danube Rivers

026 Tacitus, *Germania*, 1

The rivers Rhine and Danube separate Germany from the Gauls, the Rhaeti, and the Pannoneans (France, the Balkans and Switzerland). Mountain ranges, or perhaps mutual fear, divide the Germans from the Sarmatians and Daci (Hungary and Romania). Elsewhere, the country is encircled by the ocean which surrounds broad peninsulas and islands of unexplored extent (Scandinavia). This ocean contains tribes and kingdoms that have only recently been revealed to us by the actions of war.

The Rhine emerges from the precipitous and inaccessible heights of the Rhaetian Alps (Switzerland). It curves slightly westwards on its course down to the northern ocean. The Danube pours down from the gradual and gently descending slopes of the Abnoba (the Odenwald Mountains). It passes through the land of many nations before it empties into the Black Sea through six channels. The seventh channel is concealed in marshes.

027 Seneca, *Natural Questions*, 6.7

The Danube and the Rhine rivers divide the peaceful from the hostile. The Danube deters attacks from the Sarmatians (the eastern steppe nations) and keeps Asia out of Europe. The Rhine holds back the Germans and keeps this warlike nation separate from us.

028 Solinus, *Polyhistor*, 20.1

Germania begins at Mount Saevo (Scandinavia), which is a mountain range similar in size to the Riphean Hills (perhaps the Volga). This territory is occupied by the Inguaeones. The country of Germania lies next to the Scythians (the Pontic Steppe). Germania is rich in resources and inhabited by numerous savage peoples. It extends from the Hercynian Forest to the cliffs of the Sarmatians (near the Black Sea). On one side it is defined by the river Danuvius (the Danube), on the other with the river Rhenus (the Rhine). Very wide rivers, including the Alba, Guthalus and Vistla, flow from its interior north into Oceanus (the World Ocean).

029 Cassius Dio, *Roman History*, 39.49

The Rhine River emerges from the Celtic Alps a little beyond Rhaetia (Switzerland). It flows westwards (and north) to form the frontier of Gaul. All the inhabitants of Gaul live to the west of this river and the Germans inhabit the country to the east. After flowing (northwards) the Rhine finally empties into the ocean (Atlantic North Sea). This river has always been considered a boundary between territories, even down to our own time (the third century AD). The tribes in these regions have acquired different names, but from very ancient times we (the Classical Greeks) have referred to populations on both sides of the river as 'Celts' (populations the Romans divide into 'Gauls' and 'Germans').

Origins of the Rhine

From Switzerland to the Coast facing Britain

030 Strabo, *Geography*, **4.3.3**
The people who live closest to the source of the Rhine are the Helvetii tribe. Mount Adula is in this territory and the river emerges from this region (the Swiss Plateau). Mount Adula is a part of the Alps and another river called the Adda flows from this region southwards into Cisalpine Celtica (Italy). The Adda fills Lake Larius near where the city of Comum was founded. Flowing from the lake, the river joins the Padus (Po River). The Rhine also spreads into a great wetland and lake as it flows northwards from the mountains. This lake reaches the territory of both the Rhaeti and the Vindelici, who live in the Alps and occupy certain lands beyond the mountains.

Asinius records that the Rhine is 6,000 stadia long (600 miles), but this is incorrect. If the river had a straight course, it might be only half this length (300 miles). A further thousand stadia (100 miles) can be added for its winding course (total length about 400 miles).

Asinus writes that the Rhine has a swift current and is difficult to bridge. But he also claims that after descending from the mountains, the river flows on an even slope through low-lying plains. It would be strange for a river to maintain the force of a swift and violent stream down gradual slopes and along numerous windings. Asinus also reports that the Rhine flows into the ocean through two river mouths and disagrees with other authorities who give different figures.

Both the Rhine and the Seine encircle large territories with their winding courses, but they are not nearly as long as some authorities record. Both rivers flow from the southern parts of Gaul towards the north and both discharge into the sea opposite Britain. The Rhine flows into the sea near the headland of Cantium (Kent), which forms the eastern coast of the island. This headland is close enough to be visible from the Gallic coast, but it is quite some distance from the Seine. The Deified Julius Caesar established a navy yard on this coast when he sailed to Britain (Portus Itius near Boulogne).

031 Strabo, *Geography*, 4.3.3

Caesar spared about 8,000 Helvetii so that their territory would not be destitute of inhabitants (Swiss Alps). This was a consideration because their homelands border German lands (and the Germans might settle there if the land was vacant).

Beyond Helvetii territory the Rhine flows into the lands of the Sequani and the Mediomatrici. Their homelands border the territory of the Tribocchi, who are a Germanic tribe. The Tribocchi crossed the river from their original homeland in Germany and settled in this part of Gaul. The boundary between the Helvetii and the Sequani is Mount Jura, which is occupied by the Sequani.

The Rhine in the Augustan Era

032 Strabo, *Geography*, 4.3.4

The (Celtic) Mediomatrici and the (Germanic) Triboci occupy eastern Gaul facing the Rhine. Their lands adjoin the (Germanic) Treveri who also inhabit territories on the Gallic side of the river. Roman officers have recently built a bridge across this stretch of the Rhine for their ongoing war against the Germans (possibly Drusus Germanicus or Varus). The Ubii used to inhabit the part of Germany that lies opposite this region, but they agreed to be transferred across the river. The Roman commander Agrippa allowed them to settle in Gallic territory. North of the Treveri are the Nervii people who are another Germanic tribe settled on the Gallic side of the Rhine.

The final population living along the course of the Rhine are the Menapii. They occupy both sides of the river where it empties into the northern ocean. This region is covered by wetlands and woods that have short, dense and thorny trees. The territory of the Menapii faces the Sugambri who are a Germanic people. But most of the Germanic river-lands east of the Rhine are occupied by the Suebi. The Suebi are far greater in strength and population than any other Germanic tribe. In our era, Germanic tribes driven out of their homelands by the Suebi have been fleeing across the Rhine and taking refuge in Gaul. These fugitive tribes have become dominant in certain Gallic regions and have initiated further wars. When they begin these hostilities, they are always suppressed by the Romans.

West of the (Germanic) Treveri and the Nervii dwell the (Celtic) Senones and the Remi (in the Seine River Basin).

Course of the Rhine

033 Pomponius Mela, *Geography*, 3.24
When the Rhenus (Rhine) cascades down from the Alps it forms two lakes known as Lake Venetus and Lake Acronus (Upper and Lower Lake Constance). Afterwards the river remains as a single stream for a long time and is contained by solid banks. But close to the sea it divides in two separate courses. On the left the Rhine remains a narrow river until it reaches its outlet. But on the right, the bank of the river recedes and the waters extend across a vast expanse. At the point where the Rhine floods the flatlands, the river becomes a huge lake known as Lake Flevo. The water flows around an island called Flevo (Vlieland) before it narrows into another outlet pouring into the sea.

North Rhine Territories

034 Julius Caesar, *Gallic War*, 4.10
The Meuse River rises from the Vosges Mountain, which is in the territories of the Lingones (a Celtic Tribe). It joins with a branch of the Rhine called the Waal and flows past a riverine island occupied by the Batavi (a German tribe). Less than 80 miles from Batavian territory the river empties into the ocean (North Sea).

The Rhine has its source in the territory of the Lepontii (a Celtic tribe) who inhabit the Alps. The river flows north with a rapid current for a long distance through the territories of the Sarunates, Helvetii, Sequani, Mediomatrici, Tribuci, and Treviri (Celtic tribes in Gaul). When the Rhine approaches the ocean, it divides into several branches. These branches form extensive island-like territories which are inhabited by savage and barbarous tribes. Some of these coastal populations subsist partly on fish and the eggs of seabirds found in several streams where the river empties into the ocean.

Outflow to Sea

Batavian Territory

035 Pliny, *Natural History*, **4.15**
In the Rhine region, the most significant territory is that of the Batavi and Canninefates. They occupy an island-like stretch of land flanked on both sides by the river (Rhine Estuary, the Netherlands). Their territory is almost 100 miles long. Other tribes with territories in this region are the Frisii, Chauci, Frisiavones, Sturii and Marsacii. They occupy lands between Briel and Vlieland (Frisia) and give their names to channels where the Rhine divides (the estuary). The Rhine discharges into lakes before reaching the sea. To the west is the river Meuse, which joins with the Rhine. A single small stream in the middle of the channels retains the name 'Rhine' as it flows into the sea.

The Danube River

The Danube flows eastwards to the Black Sea and functioned as a major frontier of the Roman Empire.

036 Strabo, *Geography*, **7.1.1**
I have described Iberia and the Celtic and Italian populations. I have also written about the islands that exist near these territories. I shall now describe the remaining parts of Europe, dividing the landmass into two further regions. One region extends from the river Rhine as far as the Tanais (the Don River) and the entrance to Lake Maeotis (the Azov expanse to the north of the Black Sea). Another region lies south of the Ister River (the Danube) and extends from the Adriatic coast to the Pontic seaboard (the Black Sea). This region extends south as far as Greece and the Propontis (the Sea of Marmora between the Black Sea and the Mediterranean). The Danube therefore divides the eastern part of Europe into two separate sections.

The Danube is the largest of all the European rivers. It rises in the western limits of Germany, about a thousand stadia from the Adriatic coast (100 miles). Near its source, it flows towards the south and then it turns eastwards. By bending northwards, it then flows into the Black Sea close to the estuaries of the Tyras and Borysthenes (the Dniester and Dnieper rivers)

Germany: Position in the Ancient World

The territories north of the Danube are positioned beyond the Rhine and Celtica (Gaul). These lands are occupied by Gallic and Germanic tribes. The territory extends as far as the Bastarnians and the Tyregetans, who occupy lands near the Dnieper River (the Ukrainian Steppe). The tribes between the Dnieper and Don rivers extend from the Azov Sea to the edge of the Black Sea (areas occupied by mounted Scythian nations). Their populations extend northwards as far as the outer sea (the world-encircling ocean).

South of the Danube, the Celtic tribes have mingled with the native Illyrian and Thracian tribes as far as Greece. Consequently, it is much easier to describe the territories and populations on the other side of this dividing feature.

Danube as a Major Waterway

037 Pliny, *Natural History,* **4.12**
The Danube rises in Germany in the range of Mount Abnoua near the Gallic town of Rauricum. It flows from the Alps (Austria) through the territories of numerous tribes. During this course, its volume of water increases enormously and when it enters Illyria it is called the Ister.

The Danube receives sixty tributary rivers and nearly half these watercourses are navigable. The river then discharges into the Black Sea by six vast channels. (…) The outflow from the river is so great that for 40 miles the sea is overpowered, and the water tastes fresh.

Outflow of the Danube into the Black Sea

038 Solinus, *Polyhistor,* **13.1**
The Hister (Danube) rises from the German mountains which face the Rauraci tribe in Gaul. It receives about sixty rivers along its length and almost all are navigable. The Danube flows into Pontus (the Black Sea) through seven outlets. The first is Peuce, the second Naracustoma, the third Calonstoma, and the fourth Pseudostoma. The fifth and the sixth river mouths, which are the Borionstoma and Spilonstoma, flow slower than the other outlets. The seventh outlet is very sluggish and forms an expanse like a marsh. It does not have a name because it does not resemble a river. The first four outlets of the Danube are so large that the fresh water they discharge does not mix with the sea for a distance of 40 miles. (Men or animals) can therefore drink uncorrupted fresh water from the surface of the sea.

The Eastern Edge of Germany

039 Strabo, *Geography*, 7.3.1
The southern part of Germany extends east of the Albis (Elbe River). The land adjoining the river is occupied by the Suebi and their territories extend to the Getae (Dacians in Transylvania). The western part of Gaetic territory is narrow because it stretches along the river Ister (Danube) and is confined to the north by the mountainous edge of the Hercynian Forest. The land of the Getae includes part of these mountains. Eastwards, their territory broadens and extends north as far as the Tyregetae (a people on the Black Sea coast). I cannot be certain about the precise boundaries of this territory. Authorities are ignorant about these regions, or pay greater attention to mythical northern domains such as the 'Rhipaean Mountains' or the 'Hyperboreans'.

The Part-German Bastarnae

040 Strabo, *Geography*, 7.3.17
Inland from the Black Sea (between the Dnieper River and the Carpathian Mountains) are the people of the Bastarnae. Their country shares a frontier with the Tyregetans and the Germans. They are therefore said to be part-Germanic. The Bastarnae are divided into several tribes including the Atmoni and the Sidoni. Part of this nation also took possession of an island in the Ister River called Peuce and have become known as the Peucini (occupying the Danube Delta).

The most northern population in this region are the Roxolani (horse-mounted nomad Scythians) and they roam the plains between the Tanais (Don) and Borysthenes (Dnieper). We do not know for certain what people dwell beyond the Roxolani. As far as we know, the entire country extending from the north of Germany to the Caspian Sea is a vast plain.

041 Strabo, *Geography*, 7.3.2
At the present time the populations of this region are intermixed (eastern Danube). The Thracians have mingled with the Wagon-dwelling Scythians and Sarmatians, along with Bastarnian tribes. This occurred on both sides of the Danube River (north and south). They have also intermixed with Celtic tribes including the Boii, the Scordisci, and the Taurisci.

Where Germany becomes Scythia

042 Pliny, *Natural History*, **4.12**
Most of the people living beyond the outflow of the Danube are Scythian, but other populations occupy the Black Sea coasts. The Getae, known to Romans as the Dacians, inhabit this region (Transylvania). The Sarmatians, who the Greeks call the Sauromatae, also occupy the Black Sea territories. They include the Aorsi who are known as the 'Wagon-dwellers', the Scythians descended from slaves, the depression-dwellers, the Alani and the Rhoxolani.

The Sarmatian Iazyges occupy lands between the northern bend of the Danube and the Hercynian Forest. Their territory reaches to Carnuntum, which is the winter quarters of the Roman army in Pannonia. It extends across the plains and level country on the German frontiers (Hungry). The Iazyges have expelled the Dacians from this region and forced them back to the mountains, the forests, and the river Theiss (the Tisza).

The Iazyges are separated from the Suebi and the kingdom of Vannius by the river Marus or the Dora. The country opposite is occupied first by the Basternae, then by a sequence of other German tribes. Agrippa provides measurements for the entire Danube region extending to the sea. He reports that this region is 1,200 miles long and 396 across. It terminates near the river Vistula where the Sarmatian wildness begins (the Ukrainian Steppe east of Poland).

The Scythian name has spread in every direction, even reaching the Sarmatians and the Germans. But populations who still refer to themselves by this name, only exist in distant regions on the utmost margins of mankind.

Significance of the Black Sea

043 Pliny, *Natural History*, **4.12**
The Black Sea, formerly known as Axenus, is an enormous expanse that extends a great distance into the European continent. Its northern coasts bend southwards to create a vast arc in the shape of a Scythian bow. In the middle of its northern curve is the entrance to the Sea of Azov. The Straits of Kertsch separate the Black Sea from the Azov. The distance between the straits is 2½ miles. (…)

The river Don flows from the Riphean Mountains down to the Azov Sea. This river is the furthest boundary of Europe and divides the continent from Asia. The Don is said to be 1,406 miles long and some authorities say it stretches along a territory that is 1,125 miles in length. The distance between the outflow of the Don and the entrance to the Azov Sea is agreed to be 375 miles by using a straight line of measurement.

Routes into Germany

Hercynian Forest, Frontier Lakes

044 Strabo, *Geography*, 7.1.5
If there were straight roads to travel across Germania, the Rhine would be about 3,000 stadia (300 miles) from the river Elbe. But travellers must follow winding routes across the boglands and forests of this territory.

The Hercynian Forest is dense with large trees. It has such a wide extent that any clearings within the centre of it are fortified by nature itself. I have already described the territory (of the Suebi), which provides an excellent livelihood for these people. Near this region are the sources of both the Rhine and the Danube rivers. There is also a lake in the territory between the two river sources and there are marshes formed by the expanding Rhine (Lake Constance). There is a lake within the marsh that is more than 300 stadia long (30 miles). A passage by boat across this lake is nearly 200 stadia (20 miles). There is also an island in the lake which Tiberius (the commander and future emperor) used as a base of operations in a naval battle with the Vindelici.

This lake is south of the streams that form the Danube. It is also south of the Hercynian Forest. Therefore, when travellers journey from Celtica (Gaul) to the Hercynian Forest (in Germania) they must cross the lake region and pass over the Danube streams. From here the regions are easier to traverse for travellers approaching the forest. Tiberius (the general and future Emperor) had advanced only a day's journey from the lake when he himself saw the sources of the Danube.

The territory of the Rhaeti (an Alpine people) reaches the lake, but only for a short distance. The (Celtic) Helvetii and Vindelici have an extensive frontier abutting the lake. But the depopulated lands cleared by the (Germanic) Boii, form the greater part of the Lake perimeter.

There is another large forest in Germany called the Gabreta (Bohemia). It is in the western side of the territory held by the Suebi, whereas the Hercynian Forest is part of their eastern possessions.

The Helvetii and the Vindelici are the main population groups who inhabit the plateaus to the north of Pannonia. The countries of the Rhaeti and the Norici extend across the Alps and include passes that lead into northern Italy. They therefore border on the Insubri and Carni and are near the Roman legions stationed at Aquileia.

Internal Geography of Germany

Mela describes Germany and reveals the scale of the ancient Hercynian Forest. He probably took the figure of sixty days from the campaign reports of Julius Caesar.

045 Pomponius Mela, *Geography*, 3.29–30
Germany is difficult to cross because of its many rivers and its numerous rugged mountains. Large areas are impassable because of forests and swamps. The largest wetlands are the Suesia, the Metia, and the Melsyagum. The woodlands of Germany are named, but the largest and most well-known is the Hercynian Forest because it covers an area that requires sixty days to march across. The names of the German mountains are scarcely spoken by Roman people and the tallest mountains are Taunus and Retico. The rivers cross through the territories of other peoples. The most famous are the Danube and the Rhodanus (the river Rhône emerging from Switzerland). Other German rivers flow into the Rhine, the Moenis (river Main) and the Lupia (the Lippe). Certain other German rivers flow into the northern ocean including the Amissis (the Ems), the Visurgis (Weser), and the Albis (Elbe).

Roman Rhine Frontier

Germania between the Rhine and Elbe, Hercynian Forest, the Suebi, Marcomanni and Langobardi

046 Strabo, *Geography*, 7.1.3
The closest parts of Germany are next to the Rhenus (the river Rhine). This region extends from the source of the river as far as its outlet into the northern sea. The entire stretch of river-land forms the western flank of Germany. Some of the tribes who occupy this river-land were transferred by the Romans into Celtica (Gaul on the west bank of the Rhine). Other Germanic tribes migrated far into Gaul before the arrival of the Romans. One of these migrant German peoples were the Marsi. Only a small number of these migrant populations remain distinct, and they include part of the Sugambri tribe (a subdivision of the Ubii).

Beyond the river-land there are other German tribes occupying territories between the Rhine and the Albis (Elbe River). The Elbe flows almost parallel to the Rhine, and it extends northwards to the great ocean (North Sea coast). This river must have a similar length to the Rhine. In the land between these two major boundaries there are other navigable rivers. This includes the Amasias (the Ems) on which the Roman commander Drusus won an important naval victory over the Bructeri tribe. These rivers also flow from the south towards the north and empty into the ocean. This part of Germany is more elevated towards the south and there is a mountain range which connects with the Alps and extends eastwards. Some authorities claim that these mountains must be considered part of the Alps, due to their interlinked position and the fact that the same trees can be found on both ranges. However, the German ranges are not sufficiently high to be regarded as part of the true Alps.

The Hercynian Forest spreads across this region of Germany. Some of the tribes of the Suebi dwell within this forest, including the Coldui. Boihaemum is in their territory (ancient Bohemia and the homeland of the Boii tribe). The Germanic war leader Maroboduus had his domain in this region. His fellow tribesmen from the Marcomanni nation used to assemble here along with other peoples of the Suebi. As a young man Maroboduus was sent to Rome (as a political hostage) where he enjoyed the favour of the Emperor Augustus. The Romans promoted Maroboduus as a king and returned him to Germany as ruler of the Marcomanni state. This region of Germany is also occupied by large tribes called the Lugii, the Zumi and Butones (Gotones or Goths). There are also the Sibini and the Semnones tribes who have a large population that matches the Suebi in its size.

Some of the Suebi dwell inside the Hercynian Forest, but others live outside its boundaries. Those living beyond the forest share a frontier with the Getae (the Dacians in ancient Romania). The Suebi nation are the largest and most widely spread population in Germany. They extend all the way from the Rhine to the Elbe. Some of them also inhabit land to the east of the Elbe, including the Hermundori and the Langobardi. At the present time the Langobardi have been expelled from their western homelands and now only occupy territories to the east of the river.

Internal Rivers

047 Strabo, *Geography*, 7.1.3
In Germany the rivers Visurgis and Lupias (the Weser and Lippe) flow in the same direction as the Ems (south to north). The Lippe is about 600 stadia (60 miles) east of the Rhine and it flows through the territory of the Lesser Bructeri. The Salas River (the Thuringian Saale) is another river flowing through Germany. The Roman general Drusus Germanicus suffered a mortal injury while campaigning in this territory between the Rhine and the Salas. Germanicus had subjugated most of the tribes in Germany, including those inhabiting islands along the northern coast. He had even captured the island of the Burchanis (Borkum) by besieging the shore.

Chapter Five

German Habitats and Wildlife

Roman accounts provide information on habitats and wild animals found in Germany.

German Forests

048 Pliny, *Natural History*, **16.2**
The rest of Germany is crowded with formidable forests that augment the cold climate by placing the landscape under shadow. The tallest forests exist near the territories of the Chauci (northern Germany between the Ems and the Elbe). The highest trees can be found growing around the two main lakes in this region. They are oaks which grow to a great size and strength. These trees are sometimes uprooted by the encroaching sea and toppled by storms. When they fall, they tear up vast clumps of soil that are held firm by their roots. Thus, balanced and buoyant, the fallen trees can be swept out to sea with their enormous branches extending upwards like rigging. Our fleets have often been terrified by the sight of these objects, believing them to be the outline of approaching ships. Sometimes the sea seems to purposely propel these trees during the night into the bows of Roman vessels which are stationed at anchor. The crew will then be forced to engage in a sort of naval battle, but against trees (struggling to detach the trunk and branches from their ship).

This vast oak forest stretches across the entire northern region of Germany. The Hercynian Forest is as old as the world itself and has never been altered by mankind. This forest surpasses all other natural marvels in its almost limitless past and its unchangeable purpose (destiny). Other facts concerning this forest seem incredible, but are in fact verified and well known. It is confirmed that the vast roots extending between oak trees can collide and gradually raise up large hillocks of earth. If the soil is heavily eroded, then the conjoined roots will be exposed. Some of the exposed roots form arches that can rise up as high as branches and curve upwards like open gateways. Some of these arches are large enough to allow passage for entire cavalry squadrons (at least 7 feet high and 4 feet across). Virtually all these oak trees bear acorns, and this is the variety of oak which receives the greatest honour in Rome (as a tree sacred to the foremost god Jupiter).

Aurochs

The Romans describe Aurochs, a wild ancestor of modern cattle. They are now extinct.

049 Julius Caesar, *Gallic War*, 6.25
The width of this Hercynian Forest cannot be determined, for the Germans have no means to measure distance except journey-time. It takes as much as nine days for an unencumbered person to cross the forest. The forest begins in the territory of the Helvetii, the Nemetes, and the Rauraci (Switzerland and southern Rhine). It follows a line parallel to the Danube and extends to the frontiers of the Dacians and Anartes (Romania). Then the forest extends northwards beyond the river, reaching the frontiers of many nations (German tribes in the inner territories).

There is no man in Germany who claims to have reached the edge of the Hercynian Forest. Some might have travelled for up to sixty days through the expanse, but no one claims to know where it ends. It is known that many types of wild beasts live in the forest which are not seen in other places. The following are the most noteworthy because of their uniqueness.

There is an ox in these forests shaped like a stag (perhaps reindeer). A single horn, that is taller and longer than the horns we are familiar with grows from the forehead of this animal in the area between its ears (stags drop their antlers in spring – one horn after another, and these are found as singles). The top of these horns spread out in the shape of open hands. The male and female animals have the same appearance including the shape and size of their horns.

There are also animals (in the forest) called elks. They have dappled fur like goats, but they are larger and have stumpy horns. Their legs do not have flexible joints and they do not lie down to sleep. If some shock forces them to fall, they cannot easily raise themselves to regain a standing position. They therefore lean their weight against trees to rest themselves. When hunters spot their tracks, they undermine the trees in that area by cutting through the roots. The trees are left standing, but the weight of the elk leaning against it will cause both the tree and the animal to collapse.

A third animal is called the *ure-oxen* (aurochs). It is smaller than an elephant and in appearance, colour, and shape it resembles a bull. Ure-oxen possess great strength and speed. If they target a man or beast they will not relent (in their attack). The Germans zealously slay these creatures after capturing them in pits. The young men train and harden themselves in this form of hunting. Those who have slain the greatest number of these creatures bring the horns to a public place as evidence of their great skill and renown.

Even if they are caught very young, these animals (ure-oxen) cannot be tamed or accustomed to people. In bulk, shape, and appearance their horns are very different from the horns of our own oxen. The natives eagerly collect these horns and encase the tips with silver. They use them as drinking cups at their grandest banquets.

050 Pliny, *Natural History*, 8.15

Germany has few unique animals, but it does produce some remarkable breeds of wild oxen. This includes the 'maned bison' and an exceptionally swift and powerful creature called the *aurochaff* (aurochs). The ignorant masses call this animal a 'bison', but they are confusing this creature with the animal found in Africa (the African Buffalo). This African animal resembles a calf with the horns of a stag (a short robust body with large curving horns).

051 Solinus, *Polyhistor*, 20.4

Bison are extremely common in the whole northern region. These wild beasts resemble cattle but have shaggy necks and bristly manes. They can run faster than bulls and when they are captured, they cannot be tamed.

There are also aurochs in this territory, who ignorant people call '*bubali*'. But true bubali are native to North Africa (African Buffalo) along with a species of deer (gazelle). The creatures that we used to call aurochs can grow enormous bull-like horns. In the past the largest horns were cut off and made into drinking vessels for use at royal dining tables.

Elks in the Far North

052 Solinus, *Polyhistor*, 20.6

There is also a beast called the *alces* (elk) in these northern regions which resembles a mule. It has a long-extended snout and grazes by retreating backwards into its former footsteps (because of its horns?).

053 Solinus, *Polyhistor*, 20.7

The island of Gangavia, positioned north of Germania, has an animal resembling the *alces* (elk). But, like the elephant, this creature is not able to bend its hocks and therefore cannot lie down to sleep. It therefore slumbers while resting against trees. Men cut deep incisions into these trees so that they are quite easy to topple. Then, when the animal leans against the trunk, it collapses along with the tree. Its inflexible leg joints, which allow it to sprint at incredible speed, do not allow the animal to easily rise and regain its footing. The animals are thus captured while they are prone.

Gangavia is the largest of the Germanic islands, but there is nothing significant about the territory except for its dimensions (and its production of amber).

Strange Birds

054 Solinus, *Polyhistor*, 20.3

Birds are seen in the Hercynian Forest that have wings that shine and flash in the sunlight (light reflective feathers like a kingfisher). Their wings will even reflect light when in heavy shadows (forest shade) and in darkness (moonlight).

055 Pliny, *Natural History*, 10.35

There are also stories of strange birds seen in the Hercynian Forest of Germany. Their feathers are said to shimmer and shine like fires seen in the night. The other distant forests have no similar creatures, and their notoriety is a product of their extreme remoteness.

A speech survives written by the Emperor Julian to the people of Antioch (Eastern Romans).

056 Julian, *Misopogon*, 359

Consider the character of Cato and then do not be surprised at how I feel towards you. For I am less civilised than Cato. I am also fiercer and more headstrong. In the same manner that the Celts are fiercer and more resolved than the Romans. Cato was born in Rome and was cultivated amongst Roman citizens till he was on the verge of old age. But, as for me, from the moment that I was reckoned an adult, I had to contend with Celts and Germans in the Hercynian Forest.

Chapter Six

German Resources

Tacitus suggests that Germania possessed no significant reserves of gold or silver.

057 Tacitus, *Germania*, 5
The Germans have no natural silver or gold resources in their country. They have been refused this feature by the gods. But I cannot say if this was done in anger, or to confer some benefit upon them. I also cannot say for certain that gold or silver sources do not lie beneath the soil somewhere in Germany. After all, who would have made a thorough search of these territories?

Besides, the Germans seem to have little regard for precious metals. Roman envoys have presented their chiefs with costly silver drinking vessels, but only to find these gifts being used and abused like cheap clay pots. The tribes in the interior of Germany use the simpler and more ancient practice of barter to acquire and exchange commodities. But the border populations of Germany value gold and silver for their commercial utility. They are familiar with our coins and show a preference for certain coin issues (with a higher silver content). The frontier Germans prefer the older, more well-known coinage. They favour Roman coins with serrated rims (coins that cannot be easily reduced in weight by clipping off the edges). They also prefer the coin issues depicting a two-horse chariot (older Republican era denarii). The Germans would rather receive payments in silver than gold, but this is not due to any specific preference. It is simply more convenient for dealers in cheap and common products, to use large numbers of silver pieces to make their exchanges.

Roman Mines in Germania

The Roman military was able to open mines in territories beyond the imperial frontiers. Curtius Rufus, the governor of Germania Superior (southern Rhine) opened a mine in Mattium (Maden near Gudensburg). Rufus was in office from AD 79 to 84. The mineworks were 140 miles west of the Rhine.

058 Tacitus, *Annals*, 11.20
The emperor refused the war, but still awarded Corbulo the insignia of a triumph. This honour was also granted to Curtius Rufus who opened a mine in search of silver deposits near Mattium. The profits were slender and short-lived, and the legions suffered heavy losses when digging out the watercourses and constructing the underground mine works (the Romans redirected streams to erode soil and expose ores). These operations would have been difficult enough in the open (they were being conducted in the hills and woodlands of hostile territory, far beyond the frontiers). The legionaries were exhausted by their efforts and knowing that soldiers in other provinces faced similar hardships, they drafted a letter to the emperor in the name of the entire army. They begged him to award every general triumphal honours on achieving office (so the commander would not conduct unnecessary military operations in pursuit of further glory).

Further evidence comes from the map data compiled by Claudius Ptolemy in about AD 150.

059 Claudius Ptolemy, *Geography*, 10
There are iron mines to the south in the Luna Forest.

The Rhine Canal System

The Romans constructed a network of canals between branches of the Rhine close to where it flowed into the North Sea. This was an important network for military supply and riverine commerce. In AD 47, a Roman officer named Corbulo was made commander of the Roman forces in *Germania Inferior* (North Rhine).

060 Tacitus, *Annals*, 11.18
Corbulo had triremes (from the Classis Germanica fleet) brought through the Rhine Channel (the Fossa Drusiana Canal). Other vessels were sorted according to their drafts (hull depth), for conveyance through various suitable canals and estuaries. Reaching the sea, the Roman ships engaged and sunk the enemy vessels, expelling Gannascus and his piratical forces from this coast.

061 Tacitus, *Annals*, 11.19–20
To further occupy the troops, Corbulo ordered the construction of a 23-mile-long canal between the Meuse and the Rhine (for troop movements

and supply lines). This made it possible to evade the hazards of the North Sea (the difficult coastal stretch between the two river outlets).

In AD 40 emperor Caligula arranged for certain galleys active in the northern fleet to be brought to Rome. The ships might have been sailed or rowed up the Rhine and then dragged overland to the Rhône, which flowed down to the Mediterranean. The galleys were required for an imperial triumph, so a high cost was acceptable.

062 Suetonius, *Caligula*, 47
The emperor also ordered that certain galleys which had entered the ocean (North Sea) were to be conveyed to Rome. These vessels were brought a great part of the way by land (perhaps overland between the Rhine and the Rhône river systems, which offered a route through Gaul).

Economic Projects

The attitude and personality of the emperor could decide the outcome of economic projects (reign of Claudius, AD 56).

063 Tacitus, *Annals*, 13.53
Up to this time the situation had been quiet in Germany (the Rhine frontier provinces) and triumphal decorations (military awards) had become less prestigious. The Roman generals expected to obtain greater glory by the maintenance of peace (rather than conducting aggressive campaigns against the enemy).

Paulinus Pompeius and Lucius Vetus were in command of the army (the provincial governors of Germania Superior and Inferior in AD 56). To keep the soldiers active, they completed the construction of the embankment started sixty-three years earlier by Drusus. This earthwork was designed to confine the Rhine River to its existing stream (preventing overflow and keeping the river to a consistently deep and powerful course). Vetus also prepared the construction of a canal connecting the Moselle (a tributary of the Rhine) to the Arar (a tributary of the Rhône). This would allow troops arriving from the sea (the Roman Mediterranean) to be conveyed up the Rhône and Arar (to inner Gaul). They could then take the canal across to the Moselle and the Rhine and travel downstream to the ocean (the North Atlantic). All the difficulties involved in this route would be removed (facilitating troop movement, supply lines and trade). There would be a waterborne communication route between the seas to connect the western shores (of the Mediterranean) with the Far North (the Atlantic).

However, Aelius Gracilis, the governor of Gallia Belgica, discouraged this project. He did not want Vetus to send his legions to Gaul because that would increase his influence in the region. Gracilis said the project would incite the fears of the Emperor Nero (the concern that a regional commander was expanding his power and reputation). This is an accusation that often hinders and prevents large developments and praiseworthy undertakings.

German Cattle

064 Julius Caesar, *Gallic War*, 4.1
The Germans do not consume much grain, but subsist mainly on milk and meat from their herds. They are also heavily engaged in hunting. (...) They depend on the diminished and poorly shaped cattle breeds that are indigenous to their country. However, these native cattle are extremely hardy animals, due to frequent exercise.

Tacitus describes the terrain and agricultural resources of Germany.

065 Tacitus, *Germania*, 5
Germany has various territories, but most of the land is bristling with forests or sinking into reeking marshlands. There is more rainfall on the side of the country closest to Gaul. But it is bleaker and more exposed in the places approaching Noricum and Pannonia (Austria and the Balkans). Germany produces grain, but the climate does not favour fruit-bearing trees. The land is rich in flocks and herds, but these animals are generally undersized. The cattle breeds are not fine formed or attractive. The cattle are valued mainly for their quantity, rather than their appearance. Livestock are the main object of value in German society and often the only source of wealth available to the populace.

Waxed Tablet Receipt given to Frisian Herdsman

Receipt issued by a Roman solider to a Frisian farmer (AD 29). A silver denarius was equivalent to a day's pay for an unskilled labourer.

066 *Fontes Juris Romani Anteiustiniani*, 3.137
I, Gargilius Secundus, duly and in lawful manner purchased a cow for 115 pieces (of silver) from Stelus son of Reperius, Beosian, of the estate of Lopetius, with Cesdius, First Centurion of Legio V, and Mutus Admetus,

First Centurion of Legio I, as witnesses. Right to cancel and formalities of civil law are waived. Bought in the consulship of Gaius Fufius and Gnaeus Minicius, September 9. Proper delivery vouched for by Lilus Duerretus, veteran (list of witnesses follows).

Centurion and Trader

Roman gravestone on the Danube Frontier belonging to a businessman who might have conducted trade negotiations with the Quadi. The Fifteenth Legion was stationed at Carnuntum, headquarters of the Pannonian Fleet, from AD 90 to 138.

067 Roman Gravestone from Boldog, Slovakia
Quintus Atilius Primus, son of Spurio Tribune Votbrimus. Interpreter for the Fifteenth Legion, centurion and businessman. He lived eighty years, is buried here.

Oat Crops

Pliny records that the Germans generally grew oats rather than wheat grains, due to their damp climate and soils.

068 Pliny, *Natural History*, 18.43–44
Wheat crops will degrade into oat fields (unless they are properly cultivated and the soil replenished. Fields of cereal grasses with spike-seeds will be outperformed and replaced by hardier weed-like oats that have their seeds arranged in small florets). Barley crops will also degenerate into oat fields. In some regions oats are the primary crop and grown in the same manner as wheat (oats have more calories and protein, but the crop yields are smaller). The peoples of Germany grow oats as their main crop and live almost entirely on oatmeal porridge.

Oats are favoured in these territories due to the dampness of the soil and the moist climate. Wheat seed can often remain in the soil for too long before sprouting (the seed rots because of the lack of warm and dry conditions in the growing season). The wheat seed can also be spoiled with rot before it is sown (due to the damp environment). Wheat shoots are immediately recognisable once they break through the soil and most of its problems occur in sprouting (seed germination).

069 Pliny, *Natural History*, 17.3

Luxuriant pastures do not always indicate a rich soil underneath (for growing crops). For the meadows of Germany are the most famous pastures, but they are formed from a very thin layer of surface turf. Beneath this layer the soil is generally sandy (and unsuitable for growing crops with deep roots).

Material for Clothing:

Flax and Linen

Pliny describes how the Germans produced flax and linen. This material was probably reaching Roman markets.

070 Pliny, *Natural History*, 19.2

Flax is generally grown in sandier soils and requires only a single ploughing (to prepare the ground for the seed). No other plant grows as quickly as flax. It is sown in spring and plucked in summer and therefore does minimal damage to the soil and land.

Perhaps we should not criticise Egypt for producing flax (used for sailcloth and rope-rigging). This material allows Egypt to import merchandise from Arabia and India (via Red Sea trade fleets). Not even the Gallic provinces can produce revenue on this scale (to match import taxes on eastern imports). There are mountains between Egypt and the eastern sea (trails through the Eastern Desert). But they cross this obstacle to reach an ocean that is without limit (the Indian Ocean).

All the people of Gaul weave canvas for sailcloth. Even the most remote people in Gaul produce this material in abundance, including the Cadurci, Caleti, Ruteni, Biturigcs, and the Morini (regions from the Pyrenees and the Mediterranean to Atlantic coast facing Britain). At the present time, our German enemies beyond the Rhine are also growing flax to produce sailcloth.

Linen has also become one of the commonest dress materials used by Roman women. But this was not always the case and Varro records a custom of the Serrani family (a large influential family group) that women from these households would not wear linen dresses.

German women produce linen in underground chambers (perhaps the retting process where the plant fibres are broken down by decomposition into a more workable material). The same method is used in the Alia district of Italy between the Po and the Ticino. But this Italian linen is only considered to be the third best linen fabric produced in Europe.

Ox Hides

The Frisii occupied territories on the north coast of Germania beyond the Rhine. They were subject to the Romans until AD 28.

071 Tacitus, *Annals*, 4.72
Since they had limited resources (the Roman commander) Drusus had imposed only a moderate tribute on the Frisii. They were expected to provide ox hides for military purposes (an essential material for campaign tents, durable sacks for produce, flasks for water and wine, sandals for soldiers, bridles, saddles and straps for cavalry horses and pack animals).

No one had ever seriously considered the size or thickness of the ox hides required to fulfil this tribute, until Olennius, the leading centurion, was appointed to oversee the management of the Frisii. Olennius insisted that the hides of wild bulls (giant aurochs) should be the standard measurement for all future hides to be supplied (multiplying the size of the tribute). This imposition would have been difficult for most people, but it was intolerable for the Germans. The wild beasts in their forests are giant animals, while their domestic cattle are diminutive.

Rhine Salmon delivered to Rome (AD 530s)

072 Cassiodorus, *Letter*, 12.4 (senator, praetorian prefect to the Canonicarius of Venetia)
A well-furnished royal table is a credit to the state. A private person may eat only the produce of his own district, but a regent collects the delicacies of all lands at his table. So, let the Danube send us her carp, let the *anchorago* (salmon?) come from the Rhine, and let the efforts of Sicily furnish the *exormiston* (lamprey?).

German breed of Hunting Dogs – 'Swift Sicambrians'

073 Grattius, *Cynegeticon*, 202
Perhaps you favour a cunning style of 'light hunting' (a spontaneous hunt without extensive preparation). You want to hunt the deer or to follow the intricate tracks of the smaller hare. Then you should choose Petronian dogs ('Rock' dogs – perhaps hounds suited to craggy landscapes). Dogs with this reputation include swift Sicambrians and the Vertraha that have yellow markings (Celtic greyhounds). They run swifter than birds can fly.

They rapidly overtake the beasts they find. But they are less likely to find hidden prey (they were sighthounds with limited scent awareness). Their speed is the well-assured glory of the Petronians.

If only these dogs could restrain their eagerness until the completion of their sport. If they could approach without barking, so their prey was unaware, then they would surpass that *metagon* breed that you game trackers hold in such high regard.

Furs from Scandinavia

Jordanes mentions Suehan (Swedish) furs as a commodity supplied to Roman markets.

074 Jordanes, *Getica*, 3
Another population living in Scandza are the Suehans who possess splendid horses like the Thuringians (a tribe in northern Germany). They provide the blue-grey furs that the Romans acquire through trade. These furs are passed through numerous populations before they reach Roman markets. The Suehans are famous for the beauty of their dark furs. Though they live in apparent poverty, they are most richly clothed of all people.

Medical Herbs

Plants with medical properties were valuable and highly sought after in Roman commerce.

075 Pliny, *Natural History*, 25.6
It is not just animals that can harm mankind, as it seems water from certain regions can cause debilitating illness. Germanicus Caesar discovered this when he moved his military camps across the Rhine to occupy a maritime district of Germany with only one source of fresh water (Frisia in the Netherlands). Within two years the soldiers were suffering an illness that caused their teeth to fall out and their knee joints to fail.

Physicians used to call these conditions '*stomacace*' (stomach-ache) and '*scelotyrbe*' (partial paralysis). A remedy was found in the plant called '*britannica*', which strengthens the sinews (tendons) and is useful in treating diseases of the mouth (ulcers and abscesses). Britannica is also used to treat quinsy (pus forming around the throat and tonsils) and counteract snake bites (relief from the venom).

This plant has a gloomy colour, dark roots, and long leaves. The juice used to prepare the remedy is extracted from all parts of the plant including the roots. Its blossom is called *vibones*. Britannica is usually gathered just before thunderstorms (superstition and magical beliefs adding to its reputation). Once the remedy is prepared and swallowed, it is said to prevent quinsy for up to a year.

The afflicted Roman camp was in the territory of the Frisians who were a loyal tribe at that time. They therefore brought the britannica to the soldiers and made them aware of its healing properties.

I wonder why this plant is called britannica? Perhaps because it grows on the coast facing the British Ocean and Frisia is such a close neighbour of Britain. It has not received this name because it grows abundantly in Britain. Anyway, Britain at this time was an independent country (the Augustan era).

German Honey

In ancient times, honey was consumed as a food and the wax used for many purposes including the creation of temporary writing tablets or encaustic painting (mixing pigments with a heated wax medium).

076 Pliny, *Natural History*, 11.14
Some regions produce honeycombs that are valued for their wax, such as in Sicily and Abruzzi (southern Italy). In other places it is the quantity of honey that is valued as in Crete, Cyprus, and Africa. The honeycombs are significantly larger in the northern countries (northern Europe). A honeycomb was seen in Germany that was 8 foot long and entirely black within its hollow centre.

Salt as a Resource

Salt was a valuable preservative for meat and fish. The Hermunduri and Chatti fought over salt resources (AD 58).

077 Tacitus, *Annals*, 13.57
The same summer (in AD 58) a great battle was fought between the Hermunduri and the Chatti (major tribes in northern Germany). Both tribes claimed a river between their territories which produced large amounts of salt (an essential component in food flavouring and preservation). (…)

In other countries salt is made by drying up an overflow of water from the sea (natural evaporation in shallow pools), but in Germany salt is extracted using two opposite elements, fire and water. The salt is extracted when water is heated over a burning pile of wood (using metal pans to hold the water and capture the salt residue).

Hot Springs

Pliny describes naturally occurring hot springs near the Rhine frontier.

078 Pliny, *Natural History*, **31.17**
There are also hot springs in Germany in places across the Rhine. The hot springs of Mattiaeum (Wiesbaden) are so warm that pumice forms around the pools. Jars dipped into these pools will become boiling hot and their liquid contents (wine) will retain their heat for up to three days.

Goose Feathers

Pliny records that German goose feathers used to stuff pillows and cushions were a valuable product. An unskilled labourer could earn one denarius for a day's work. The price for a pound of goose feathers was five times this amount.

079 Pliny, *Natural History*, **10.27**
White geese produce a further profit when their feathers are sold. Their feather coats rapidly regrow and in some regions they are plucked twice a year. The plumage closest to the body is softer and the most valued variety is produced in Germany (Rhineland frontier or the lands beyond). These German geese have a bright white colour, but they are smaller than other breeds. The German word for this bird is '*Gans*' (English 'gander' – a male goose).

The Roman commanders in charge of the auxiliary cohorts put a price of five denarii per pound on these white German feathers. Consequently, officers have been reprimanded for sending entire cohorts away from their outposts and sentry stations to capture these birds. The pursuit of luxury and commerce has advanced to such an extent that now even our men cannot endure a night's sleep without a pillow of soft goose feather.

Roman Admiration for Fair Hair

Martial refers to the fair hair of German women in a poem about the death of a favourite slave girl.

080 Martial, *Epigrams*, 5.37
What could be valued more than this precious child? Not pearls from the Indian Ocean or polished Indian ivory. Not newly fallen snow or the untouched white lily. Her hair was softer than the fleece of Spanish flocks and finer than the braided hair of the Rhineland girls. It was the golden colour of the harvest mouse (autumnal auburn).

Hair Dye

German warriors dyed their hair in connection to certain battle oaths. But this dye also became a commodity in Roman consumerism.

081 Pliny, *Natural History*, 28.51
The Gallic provinces have also invented a substance for dying their hair red. This dye is made from suet and ash, but the most effective mix is made from beech ash and goat suet. It comes in two forms, a thick paste and a liquid. Both types of dye are used by the Germans and in their communities, men dye their hair more than women.

082 Martial, *Epigrams*, 14.26 'Verse to accompany a gift of Hair Dye'
This caustic substance reddens the hair of the Germans. Apply this and your hair will surpass the long tresses of your slave.

German hair dye may have come from Mattium, the leading settlement of the Chatti.

083 Martial, *Epigrams*, 14.27 'Verse to accompany Mattiac Dye'
Octogenarian you use this dye to colour your venerable hair. But why? Since you have no real hair left.

Martial suggests a Batavian origin for German dyes in a humorous verse that uses hyperbole to criticise the quality of a gilded cup received from his friend Paulus.

084 Martial, *Epigrams*, 8.33
Paulus! The gilded cup you sent me is thinner than a leaf in Praetor's crown (a laurel wreath). Is this a toy? Or a prop you took from the stage? When I put a dash of pale saffron water in the cup the gilding washed off! (…) The gilding is as thin as those frail hairnets that girls wear to contain their elaborate hair-do. It is thinner than the Batavian foam used to dye Roman hair (a hair-mousse preparation). (…) But maybe I am being too critical. Next time Paulus you will possibly send me a snail shell – or maybe nothing at all!

Fair Hair

The Romans imported cuttings of hair from India and Germany to make elaborate wigs and hair extensions.

085 Martial, *Epigrams*, 5.68 'To Lesbia – Hair from Germany'
Lesbia, I send you this hair from the northern regions. See how much lighter it is compared to your natural colour.

Ovid was writing in 16 BC in an era when Rome was about to conquer Germania between the Rhine and Elbe.

086 Ovid, *Amores*, 1.14
I said: 'Stop dyeing your hair!' or you will have no hair left to colour (…) you have subjected your hair to steel and fire (curling tongs) so it may move in waves or be twisted and tied in ringlets. I cried out: 'It's wicked to scorch your hair! It's fine as it is. Go carefully with the steel, use less pressure, you're singeing your hair' (…) now you look at what has been so cruelly destroyed and you sadly stare at yourself, silly girl, with a mirror in your hand (…) you have not been cursed by some Thessalian Witch using magic herbs or potions. It is not some tragic illness that has suddenly struck you, or an evil verse chanted to thin your once thick hair. You did this to yourself and now you are the subject of your own crime.
    So, you will send for the hair of some German prisoners (and have a wig made). You will be restored by the gift of some conquered peoples. But how often you will blush when someone praises your hair? For there is an extra cost to your purchase and you will think: 'Are they really complimenting me or the Sygambri (the Germanic girl)? For I am wearing her splendour (her attractive fair hair).'

A Frightening Mask

Martial wrote a short verse to accompany the gift of a Roman-made mask displaying grotesque 'barbarian' features. The later *Epigrams* were written after AD 86, but many readers may have remembered the Batavian Revolt of AD 69.

087 Martial, *Epigrams*, 14.76
The potter made this mask depicting a red-haired Batavian. You laugh at this object, but it will terrify children.

German War Captives

In 12 BC, the Roman general Drusus was engaged in campaigns to conquer Germania. He took prisoners from defeated armies and sold these captives as slaves.

088 Florus, *Roman History*, 2.30
The Germans had been so confident in victory that they had even reached agreement on how the plunder from their war was to be divided among the tribes. The Cherusci had chosen the horses, the Suebi claimed the gold and silver, and the Sugambri were allocated the captives. But the reverse occurred when Drusus defeated these nations. He seized their horses, herds, and precious necklets (Germanic torcs). This plunder was sold as the spoils of war alongside the captured prisoners.

Ethnic Appearance

The Emperor Caligula planned a campaign against the Germans, but the result was inaction (AD 40). He concealed his failure by holding an undeserved triumph in Rome.

089 Suetonius, *Caligula*, 47
The emperor (Caligula) gathered prisoners and deserters from barbarian armies in preparation for his triumph (in Rome). He selected men from all parts of Gaul who had the largest stature and seemed most suitable for the event. He arranged this with some of the Gallic chiefs and required the selected men to grow their hair long and dye it blond (to resemble the stereotypical German). These men were also required to learn German phrases and respond to names that were commonly used in that country.

German Slaves

In AD 374, the Emperor Valentinian crossed the Rhine frontier to conduct a campaign against the Quadi.

090 Ammianus Marcellinus, *Roman History*, 29.4
The Roman army encountered some merchants loading slaves intended for sale. But Valentinian was afraid that these men might run off and report what they had seen to the enemy. He therefore seized their merchandise (the slaves) and had all the traders killed.

Martial describes how a German slave obstructed a water fountain in Rome.

091 Martial, *Epigrams*, 11.96
The Rhine does not rise here, you German barbarian. This spring is coming from an Italian fountain. So why do you stand here at this source blocking the Roman boy and keeping him from the welcome water? This fountain belongs to the conquerors! The thirst of a captive slave should not exclude or even delay the immediate wants of a Roman citizen!

Martial also criticises a Roman woman named Caelia who refused his affections in favour of German men, perhaps freed slaves or custodes (imperial bodyguards).

092 Martial, *Epigrams*, 7.30
Caelia you grant your romantic favours to Parthians, to Germans and to Dacians. (...) You are a Roman girl, so why do you pay no attention to a Roman citizen who is so agreeable to you?

The Latin writer Ausonius composed poetry about a German slave girl named Bissula. She was captured during Roman victories against the Alemmani in AD 370.

093 Ausonius, *Bissula*, 3
Where Bissula was born and how she was acquired by her master.
    Bissula was born from the breed who live beyond the cold Rhine (the Germans).
    She knows the secret of where the Danube River rises.
    She was a captive maiden (a slave) who has been freed.
    She was a spoil of war (a captive) who now commands the emotions of her master.

She had no mother or guardian (as a slave) and now she is free from her mistress (the matron wife of the household).

Now she rules her master's house (overseeing domestic roles) which is no disgrace to her native land (Germania).

Her freedom was quickly granted, but Roman blessings have not changed her.

She remains German in her features – blue eyes and fair hair.

And she is now a maiden of either race or language (Roman or German).

To look at her you would think she was a daughter of the Rhine.

But she is first and foremost a child of Latium (Rome).

094 Ausonius, *Bussula*, 4

Darling, delightful favourite, beloved with joy!
  You are a barbarian by origin, but you surpass your Roman sisters.
  Bissula is a clumsy name for such a fine young woman.
  It is uncouth to strangers, but charming to your master.

Rhineland Zinc

Pliny mentions territories where the Romans were extracting copper and zinc. The Rhineland regions had become a significant source for zinc, an alloy used in the production of low denomination Roman coinage.

095 Pliny, *Natural History*, 34.2

I have described how copper deposits are mined and the ore is purified (metal extracted) by the application of fire. Copper is combined with another type of ore that the Greeks call *cadmea* (zinc for producing brass). This ore is held in very high regard and the best forms now come from overseas. It used to be found in Campania and some deposits are still produced in the territory of Bergamo on the farthest edge of Italy. It has recently been reported that *cadmea* ore has been found in the German provinces (Roman Rhine frontiers).

Copper was first discovered in Cyprus within an ore called *chalcitis*. But this resource became extremely low value when better copper deposits were found in other countries. These new deposits were used to produce *orichalcum* 'gold-copper' (shining brass – a copper-zinc alloy). For a long time this ore produced metals of outstanding quality and popularity. But now the extraction grounds for this ore have been exhausted.

The next quality ore extracted to meet our demands was the 'Sallustius Copper' found in the Alpine region of Haute Savoie. But this deposit lasted only a short time and soon the 'Livia Copper' discovered in Gaul became the dominant source for new metal. Both these varieties of copper were named after the owners of the mines. Sallustius was a friend of the Emperor Augustus and Livia was his wife (a mine owned by an imperial family and managed by its operatives). The Livia Copper was found to exist in only small deposits and the mine was quickly exhausted.

The best and most productive supply of this metal is currently 'Marius Copper' which is also called 'Cordova Copper' (a region in southern Spain). Marius Copper is almost as good as the Livia variety in absorbing *cadmea* (zinc) to produce *orichalcum* (shining brass). This metal is used to produce excellent sesterces and double-*aes* pieces (the main coins in the Roman monetary system). However, the single *aes* coin (the lowest denomination) remains a copper issue generally made from Cyprus copper (older recycled metals).

Precious Stones

Solinus describes a semi-precious stone found in Germany that might be feldspar.

096 Solinus, *Polyhistor*, 20.15
There are many types of *ceraunium*. The German variety is white, but it glitters with a blue tone. When exposed to sunlight it sparkles like the stars.

097 Solinus, *Polyhistor*, 20.14
The gemstone 'Gallaica' is found in Germania. It is valued more than the Arabian variety, for the German gem has superior qualities. The Arabians say that their varieties are only found in the nests of the rare birds they call '*melancoryphi*'. But no one accepts this story, since, although it is rare, this gemstone is also seen among the Germans. Gallaica is luxuriant with a pale green colour and nothing else makes gold jewellery look more delightful. Its appreciation and price therefore approach the value of emeralds.

098 Pliny, *Natural History*, 37.15
Metrodorus of Scepsis is the only authority I have read who claims that '*adamas*' (diamonds) are found in Germany. He records that they are found on the island of Basilia, which also produces amber. He also claims that these German diamonds are superior to the Arabian varieties. However, all his statements and claims on this subject are simply false and untrue.

Roman Traders in Germania

Julius Caesar describes conditions in the early phase of Roman expansion into Gaul.

099 Julius Caesar, *Gallic War*, 4.1–2
The Germans permit merchants access to their communities so that they can sell items captured in war. But they do not need any commodity that is imported by the merchants.

Roman Traders in Southern Germany

In AD 17, there was instability in the Marcomannic kingdom (southern Germania). The unrest was caused by a rival Germanic chief named Catualda.

100 Tacitus, *Annals*, 2.62
Catualda led a strong force of warriors into the territory of the Marcomanni. By using corruption, he induced many of the nobles to support him (probably bribes and pay-offs). They suddenly surged into the palace and the adjacent fortress and seized the long-accumulated plunder of this Suebic realm. They also captured camp followers and traders from our provinces (Roman merchants and civilians associated with the frontier military). These men had freely left their various home territories in the Empire to do business in enemy lands. They were originally attracted by profits and became neglectful of their Roman origins.

Ban on the Export of Weapons

In late antiquity the Empire tried to prevent the export of weapons to hostile foreign groups.

101 Code of Justinian 4.41.2 'Orders of the Emperor Marcian Augustus to Constantimis, the Praetorian Prefect' (AD 456)
Concerning foreign-born barbarians of any nation who come to this Most Sacred City (Rome). They may arrive under the guise of an embassy, or under some other pretext. Though they come from diverse places including cities, no one should sell them breastplates, shields, bows and arrows, long-swords, short-swords, or any other type of weapon. They are not to be sold hunting-spears, ordinary iron, or cast-iron items (from which they

could manufacture weapons). For these exchanges are dangerous to the Roman Empire. And it is close to treason to equip the barbarians with the materials that they lack. These exchanges provide them with weapons that increase their military strength.

Interdiction (intercepting and seizing illegal goods) is a product of piety. It applies to anyone who sells any type of weapon to foreign-born barbarians of any nation in any place. We decree that this person will have all his property immediately confiscated and assigned to the imperial treasury. The guilty person will then be subject to capital punishment.

Frontier Restrictions (Rhine)

During the Batavian Revolt of AD 69, the Ubii living in Germania sent envoys to their kinsmen settled on the Roman frontier (Colonia, west of the Rhine).

102 Tacitus, *Histories*, 4.64

Until now the Romans closed the river and land beyond to us (the militarised Rhine frontier). They did this to prevent free contact, exchange and converse between our peoples. They prevent us from meeting (as kinsmen). We are men born to bear weapons, but when we cross the frontier they force us to assemble unarmed. We are stripped of our weapons, watched by sentinels, and taxed for the right to converse with kinsmen (border taxes).

Frontier Restrictions (Danube)

103 Tacitus, *Germania*, 41

One of the nearest tribes to us is the Hermunduri who are loyal to Rome. Consequently, they are the only Germans allowed to trade on the Roman banks of the Danube. They are even permitted to travel further inland and visit the Roman colony that is flourishing in the province of Raetia (Switzerland). The Hermunduri are allowed to pass everywhere without a guard, while we display armed hostility to the other German tribes.

Peace Terms and Trading Rights (Danube Frontier)

During the Marcomannic War, the Emperor Marcus Aurelius imposed trade restrictions on defeated and subdued Germanic tribes (AD 166–180).

104 Cassius Dio, *Roman History*, 71.11

Other German tribes including the Quadi, asked for peace, which was granted to them. (The Emperor) Marcus Aurelius pursued this strategy in the hope that the Quadi could be detached from the Marcomanni (a powerful tribal confederacy in southern Germany). (…)

But the Quadi were not granted the right to attend Roman markets (to cross the river-frontiers and purchase Roman supplies). The Quadi had sworn not to receive the Iazyges and Marcomanni into their territory or allow them to pass through their lands. But the Romans were worried that people from these nations could easily mingle among the Quadi and present themselves as members of this tribe (due to their close cultural similarity). These individuals could reconnoitre the Roman positions and purchase provisions for their own purposes.

105 Cassius Dio, *Roman History*, 71.22

The Marcomanni fulfilled all the conditions that Marcus Aurelius had imposed upon them (after their defeat). So, when they sent further envoys to him, he grudgingly and reluctantly granted them further rights. Half of the neutral zone was restored to the Marcomanni so that they could now settle within 5 miles of the Ister River (the Roman frontier on the Danube). The emperor also designated permanent places where the Marcomanni could trade with Roman subjects (frontier towns or forts). Previously these sites had not been fixed (requiring special permission to arrange and set up). Under these new terms the Marcomanni also exchanged political hostages with the Romans.

Chapter Seven

Perceptions of German Origins and Character

Roman accounts outline perceived differences between the ancient Celts and the Germans. The Celts dominated Gaul, a territory comprising most of ancient France. Gaul was conquered by Julius Caesar in the 50s BC, but the new territory extended only to the Rhine. Beyond the Rhine was Free Germany.

106 Appian, *Gallic War*, 4.22

These Germans excel all other people since they are physically the largest and they are more savage and braver than other (nations). They do not fear death as they believe their spirit survives beyond this life. They are also capable of enduring extreme cold with the same forbearance as a warm environment. In times of scarcity, they can survive on simple herbs, while their horses graze from the (leaves) on trees. It seems that they have no restraint or patience in their battles. They do not fight in a strategic manner or form themselves into any regular order (disciplined unit formations). Instead, they fight in battles with the energy and spirit of wild beasts. But for this reason, they have been overcome by the strategies and endurance of the Roman army.

107 Strabo, *Geography*, 7.1.2

Europe extends eastwards beyond the Rhine, and the land of the Celts expands into the territory of the Germans. The Germans differ only slightly from the Celtic population, but they are generally taller, have fairer hair and are more savage. In all other respects the Germans are similar in appearance, actions, and customs to the Celts. I think the Romans may have given these people the name '*Germani*' to indicate that they were the 'original' Celtic stock. This is because it means 'genuine' in the Roman language ('*genu*' as in 'authentic' adjective: *germanum*).

108 Strabo, *Geography*, 4.4.2

Nowadays since they have been conquered by the Romans all the Gauls are at peace and live under Roman commands (the Augustan era). I am therefore taking this account of the Gauls from previous eras and from the shared customs still held by the Germans.

The Celts and the Germans have similar characteristics, and their governments (societies) operate in a similar manner. These people are kinsmen to one another, and they share a common boundary divided by the river Rhenus (the Rhine). Most of their territories are also similar. Southern Gaul can be likened to southern Germany and northern Gaul is comparable to northern Germany. However, the German lands extend further to the north (Frisia and Jutland). Migrations easily occur from these regions due to the shared characteristics of the people (solidarity, rapid action, and straightforward purpose). When these migrations occur, people move in massive crowds formed from numerous households and they bring with them an army. These movements occur when a population is expelled from their home territory by people who are stronger than themselves.

109 Plutarch, *Marius*, 11

The most prevalent conjecture is that the Teutones and Cimbri belong to the German peoples who occupy lands extending to the great northern ocean (Scandinavia). This conjecture was based on their large stature, their light-blue eyes, and the fact that the Germans call raiders 'Cimbri'.

Some authorities give an alternative origin for the Teutones and Cimbri. They suggest that Gaul was once large and wide enough to reach to the outer sea and the subarctic regions (of Scandinavia). From there, the territory extended eastwards to the Maeotic Sea in Pontic Scythia (the Azov expanse north of the Black Sea). Celtic territories therefore adjoined Scythia and in these regions, Celts and Scythians mingled. These mixed populations left their home and moved westwards. But they did not travel the distance in a single continuous journey. Instead, they pushed forwards each spring and fought to occupy new lands. Eventually they had crossed the entire continent. These people had many different names for their population groups, but they called their whole force by the common name of Gallo-Scythians (Proto-Germans).

110 Ammianus Marcellinus, *Roman History*, 15.9

The Druids claim that a portion of their people were indigenous to Gaul. But they state that other inhabitants swarmed in from islands on the coast (Scandinavia) and from districts across the Rhine (Proto-Germans). These populations were expelled from their former homelands by frequent wars, or by the inroads of fierce seas.

111 Diodorus Siculus, *Historical Library*, 5.32
The valour of the northern peoples and their savage manners are famous and widely known. Some authorities claim that they were the same people who, as ancient Cimmerians, overran Asia. Over time, 'Cimmerian' became corrupted to the (Germanic) name 'Cimbrians', by which these people are now known. It has always been their ambition to invade the lands of others to plunder. For they regard all other men with contempt.

112 Tacitus, *Germania*, 2
I believe the Germans are indigenous to their current homeland. They have not mixed with other peoples through immigration or other forms of foreign association (commerce, colonisation and conquest). In very ancient times, people emigrating to new lands would arrive by ship, rather than by land travel. The northern ocean is immense, but it is hostile to seafarers and is seldom entered by people from our part of the world (the Mediterranean). The perils of these rough and unknown seas would have prevented any population movement into Germany. Besides, who would leave Asia, Africa, or Italy for that country? Germany is a wild region with stormy skies, brooding manners, and a sullen aspect to its nature. Who would choose to live there except someone who was native?

113 Tacitus, *Germania*, 4
I agree with those who believe that German tribes have not intermixed with other nations. There is no trace of foreign elements in their population, and they appear to be a well-defined and distinct nation. They are unlike any other people, except themselves. The same distinctive physical characteristics can be identified across the vast German population. They have fierce blue eyes, red (or fair) hair, and huge physiques suited for sudden exertion. Their climate and terrain prepares them to endure cold and hunger. But they will not easily endure laborious work and will suffer from heat and thirst (in hot Mediterranean climates).

Celts in Germania

Tacitus writes about Celtic tribes who occupied the outer parts of Germany. Some northern tribes also possessed shared Celto-Germanic heritage.

114 Tacitus, *Germania*, 28
The highest authority in these matters is the great Julius Caesar. He reports that Gaul was once more powerful than Germany. Consequently,

we believe that Gauls could have crossed over into Germany in previous times. The river boundaries (Rhine or Danube) must have been only a minor obstacle to the ancient Gallic tribes as they increased in strength. They would have entered Germany to establish settlements in lands that were open to migration and not yet controlled by powerful royal chiefs. The Helvetii and Boii, who are both tribes of Gaul, entered Germany between the Hercynian Forest and the rivers Rhine and Moenus (Bavaria). The name 'Boiemum' still survives in this region to confirm its ancient traditions, although the population has been replaced.

The Aravisci tribe may have migrated into Pannonia from the Osi nation who are Germanic people. Or maybe the Osi entered Germany as an offshoot of the Aravisci nation (Celts). The historical situation is uncertain, but both nations still retain the same language, institutions, and shared (Celtic) customs. They must have migrated in an era when their population was unsettled and territories on both banks of the river had equal benefits and disadvantages. The Treveri and Nervii (Celtic tribes) are also eager to claim a German heritage. Their glorious origin distinguishes these tribes from the wider Gallic population who are losing their masculinity (through a reduction in warfare and independent warrior culture).

115 Julius Caesar, *Gallic War*, 6.24

There was a time in the past when the Gauls (Celts) were superior in valour to the Germans and conducted aggressive wars against them. These former Gauls had vast populations and due to a shortage of land they sent colonies across the Rhine (invasions to claim and settle Germanic lands). They seized the most fertile lands in Germany at the edge of the Hercynian Forest – this expanse was known to Eratosthenes and other Greeks writers who called it the 'Orcynian Forest' (in the third century BC). The land claimed in Germany was seized by the Volcae Tectosages ('Volcae', 'dwelling seekers'). Some of this nation still retains their settlements in Germany, along with the highest reputation for justice and success in war. However, they now live in the same impoverished condition as the Germans, experiencing hardship, eating the same basic foods, and enduring the same physical training (harsh exercise and exposure to the elements). In contrast, the Gauls who now occupy territories near our provinces have become familiar with foreign commodities, including lavish items of luxury (wines and soft clothing). Gradually they have grown accustomed to defeat, and after being conquered in many battles, they cannot compare themselves to German valour.

The Ubii at Roman Colonia: Capital of Germania Inferior

Germanic tribes also crossed the Rhine to occupy parts of Gaul that became frontier Roman territory. In 39 BC the Roman General Marcus Agrippa allowed a Germanic tribe called the Ubi to settle west of the Rhine. He established a military base in this territory called *Oppidum Ubiorum*. The site became an important urban centre and capital of Germania Inferior, Rome's northern Rhineland province. In AD 50, Agrippina the Younger, wife of the Emperor Claudius, arranged for the city, her birthplace, to receive the status of a *colonia* – city with Roman legal rights. The city then became known as *Colonia Agrippina* (Colony of Agrippina) – modern Cologne.

Ceaser describes the Ubii when they lived east of the Rhine.

116 Caesar, *Gallic War*, 4.3
Compared to the other Germans, the Ubii are more sophisticated because they border the Rhine and are visited more frequently by merchants. They are also more accustomed to the manners of the Gauls, due to their proximity to these neighbouring peoples.

117 Suetonius, *Augustus*, 21
Augustus forced the (hostile) Germans back to the far side of the river Albis. But the Suebi and Sugambri, who submitted to him, were accepted into Gaul and settled in lands near the Rhine.

118 Tacitus, *Germania*, 28
The Gallic banks of the Rhine are occupied by tribes that are undoubtedly German. This includes the Vangiones, the Triboci, and the Nemetes. The Ubii are also German, but they have earned the distinction of being recognised as a Roman colony. Consequently, they prefer to be called Agrippinenses, a name derived from their state-founder (Agrippina). This obscures their actual origin. The Ubii are said to have sailed across the sea in ancient times (possible Scandinavian origins). They occupied lands in Germania facing the Rhine, but due to an alliance with Rome they were permitted to settle on the west bank of the river (in Roman Gaul). They are seen as a force to guard the frontier, but they also need to be watched (in case of revolt).

Roman Frontier: Batavians, Mattiaci and Celtic Settlers

The Romans also incorporated the Germanic territory of Batavia into their Empire as a protectorate and source for military recruits. Ancient Batavia included the fertile Rhineland Delta (the Netherlands).

119 Tacitus, *Germania*, 29
The Batavi are foremost among the German tribes in terms of valour. They occupy a riverine island (coastal territory flanked by rivers) formed by the Rhine and a small portion of the opposite bank. The Batavi were once part of the Chatti tribe, but after internal quarrels they were forced to migrate to their present settlements. They later became part of the Roman Empire. They retain the honour of this ancient alliance and are not insulted by tribute payments or the oppressions of Roman tax gatherers. The Batavi are free from the usual burdens and state contributions imposed on imperial subjects. Instead, they are set apart for a military purpose. We keep them to serve us in our wars as though they were an armoury of weapons.

The Mattiaci tribe (on the east bank of the Rhine) are subject to these same obligations (troop levies). The greatness of the Roman people has therefore spread a reverence for our empire beyond the Rhine and our old territorial boundaries. The Mattiaci share our sentiments and purpose, though their settlements and lands are on the far banks of the river frontier. In all respects the Mattiaci resemble the Batavi, except their lands and climate are better suited for crops.

The cultivators of the tithe-lands (frontier settlers) are not considered part of the German tribes. Some of these people have settled on the far side of the Rhine and Danube, but they are not German. They are reckless adventurers from Gaul, who by necessity, have boldly occupied unclaimed lands. Over time, our frontier has advanced, and our military positions have been pushed further forwards. Lands that were once in obscure frontier zones have now become securely held parts of the Roman provinces.

120 Silius Italicus, *Punica*, 3.600
Now you (Domitian) shall outdo the exploits of your father and brother. You shall be conqueror of Germany, for even in boyhood the blond-haired Batavians feared you.

Types of German

121 Pliny, *Natural History*, 4.14
There are five German populations. The first are the Vandili (the Vandals – Scandinavians on the Baltic coast). Their population includes the Burgundiones (Burgundians), the Varini, the Carini, and the Gutones (the Goths).

The second German population is the Ingaevones (the Angles in the Jutland region). This includes the Cimbri, the Teutoni, and the tribes of the Chauci.

The third German population is the Istaevones (living near the Roman-controlled Rhine).

The fourth German people, known as the Hermiones, inhabit the interior of Germania. Their population includes the Suebi, the Hermunduri, the Chatti, and the Cherusci (occupying lands extending from Bavaria to Bohemia).

The fifth German population is the Peucini, which includes the Basternae. Their territory adjoins Dacia (a kingdom in Transylvania on the Danube frontier).

Germany has the following well-known rivers which flow into the northern ocean. These rivers are: the Guttalus (the Alle), the Vistillus or Vistula (the Elbe), the Visurgis (the Weser), the Amisius (the Ems), the Rhine, and the Mosa (the Meuse). There is a wooded mountain range in the interior of Germany known as the Hercynian Forest. This forest is superior to all other woodlands in its grandeur.

German Character

The Roman geographer Pomponius Mela summarised a Roman view of the Germans in about AD 43.

122 Pomponius Mela, *Geography*, 3.25–28
The western frontier of Germany extends along the banks of the Rhenus (Rhine) as far as the Alps and its southern edge connects to these mountains. Its eastern frontier extends to the Sarmatian peoples, and its northern limits face the ocean. The people who live in Germany are extraordinary in courage and physique. Due to their natural ferocity, they develop both these characteristics in themselves. They enhance their minds by practising warfare and their bodies are developed by habitual hard work and exposure to the cold.

German customs are so savage that they can eat raw flesh cut from newly killed animals. They also eat meat that has been frozen wrapped in the hides of cattle and wild creatures. They soften this meat by working it with their hands or pounding it with their feet.

Childhood is prolonged in their society, but their children do not wear (adult-style) clothing. The men dress in wool garments or clothing made from the bark of trees (bark cloth – a soft material made from the soaked and pounded inner bark of certain trees). This is what they wear, even in the harsh conditions of winter. The Germans are also strong swimmers and enjoy this exercise.

The Germans often wage war with neighbouring communities. They do not generally fight to enlarge their possessions. They provoke, then pursue these conflicts because they enjoy warfare. Any territories they already possess are not intensively cultivated, but they fight to devastate regions adjoining their homeland. The Germans believe that 'right lies in might' and they are not ashamed to engage in banditry (warrior warbands launching military raids). Nevertheless, they treat their guests well and accommodate anyone who comes to them as a supplicant.

German Reputation

During his Gallic campaigns Julius Caesar decided to attack a German population that had crossed the Rhine (58 BC). These Germanic settlers were led by their king, Ariovistus.

123 Julius Caesar, *Gallic War*, 1.38–40

Caesar remained in Vesontio for a few days to gather grain and other supplies. But a terrible panic suddenly seized the whole army and the courage and morale of everyone was affected. The soldiers started asking questions (about their opponents) and the Gauls and traders replied by describing the tallness and physical strength of the Germans. They said that the Germans were exceptionally brave and skilful with weapons. They claimed that those who had encountered the Germans in battle could not withstand their formidable appearance, or even the fierceness of their gaze.

124 Cassius Dio, *Roman History*, 38.35

Meanwhile, reports reached the Roman soldiers that Ariovistus was making vigorous preparations for war. It was reported that many other Germans had either already crossed the Rhine to assist him, or had gathered on the banks of the river to suddenly attack the Romans. The Roman soldiers therefore became deeply dejected. They were alarmed by the large stature of their enemies, their vast numbers, and their boldness. The soldiers felt that they were not being threatened by ordinary men. They were going to engage uncanny and ferocious creatures resembling wild beasts. The talk amongst the army was that this conflict was none of their business. The campaign had not been decreed by the Roman government, so they were deployed merely because of Caesar's personal ambition. Consequently, the soldiers threatened to desert their general if he did not change his course of action.

Roman Experience

Velleius Paterculus served with the future emperor Tiberius in his German campaign. His impressions come from personal experience.

125 Velleius Paterculus, *History of Rome*, 2.105–106

By the gods! A great volume could be written about our achievements that summer under the generalship of Tiberius Caesar (AD 5). All Germany was traversed by Roman armies. Populations that had been almost unknown to Rome, even by name, were conquered and the tribes of the Cauchi were once again subjugated. The best of their warrior youth assembled in a seemingly endless mass. Their huge stature was evident, and they were holding a strategically secure site. But all these Germans set down their weapons and were escorted by a gleaming line of our soldiers who took the flank and led them towards the tribunal of the commander. There they followed the example of their leaders and fell on their knees (surrendering to Rome).

126 Velleius Paterculus, *History of Rome*, 2.117–18

But the Germans possess a great ferocity combined with a scheming mentality. This attitude is difficult to understand, unless people are familiar with them. The Germans are a race of innate liars and under Roman occupation the tribes exaggerated a series of fictitious lawsuits against one another. They provoked each other with unnecessary legal cases and then feigned false gratitude when Roman justice intervened to settle the escalating disputes.

German Migration: Wagon Trains

Germanic tribes seeking new homelands to settle used wagon trains to transport their families and possessions.

127 Strabo, *Geography*, 7.1.3

It is a common characteristic of all the Germans that they migrate and can change territories with great ease. This is because they have a very simple livelihood, as they depend on growing crops and storing food. They generally live in small huts that are often temporary structures. They mostly subsist from their flocks in the same manner as nomads (mobile Scythian steppe dwellers). Like nomads, the Germans can load their entire households onto wagons and lead their animals to whatever lands they think will accommodate them. Other German tribes have even fewer possessions and a more primitive lifestyle. This includes the Cherusci, the Chatti, the Gamabrivii and the Chattuarii (also known as the Attuarii). Also, the Sugambri, the Chaubi, the Bructeri, and the Cimbri in their territories near the ocean. Other tribes include the Chauci, the Caulci, and the Campsiani.

128 Pliny, *Natural History*, 8.61

We have heard accounts of a dog that fought to defend its master from brigands. Although covered in wounds it would not leave his master's corpse and fought to keep away birds and other scavenging animals. Another dog, Epirus, recognised his master's murderer in a gathering of people and by snapping and barking at him, made him confess his crime. (…) When the Cimbri men were killed, their dogs still defended the wagons on which they had their homes.

Policy of the First Emperor Augustus (27 BC to AD 14)

129 Strabo, *Geography*, 7.1.4

All these Germanic tribes have become known to us through their wars against the Romans. In these conflicts the German tribes would often yield to Rome but would later revolt. Or else they would abandon their territory and migrate to new regions beyond Roman control. These nations would have been better known to us if the Emperor Augustus had allowed his generals to cross the river Albis (Elbe) in pursuit of those who were escaping Roman authority.

But perhaps Augustus reasoned that he could conduct his Germanic wars with greater success by keeping these conflicts within the boundaries of the Elbe. The Germans living beyond the Elbe had demonstrated no hostility to the Romans. Perhaps the emperor did not want to incite them and encourage these tribes to join with the other Germans in their enmity against the Empire.

German Endurance

130 Seneca, *On Providence*, 1.4
We can see the effect that endurance can have on people when we observe foreign nations who labour extensively, wear minimal clothing, and live with few necessities. Look at the nations that dwell north of the Roman Empire. I mean the Germans and all the nomad tribes (the Sarmatians) who wage war against us along the Danube. They suffer from extended winters and dismal climates. Their sparse soil only grudgingly gives them sustenance. They keep the rain off their dwellings with bundles of leaves or thatch. Yet they can sprint across the frozen marshes when hunting wild beasts for food. Do you think they are unhappy? There can be no unhappiness in performing a role that repetition has made part of nature and necessity. These populations have no secure homes and no resting-places, except those they themselves can provide through their own efforts. Their food may be basic and course, but they have sought it out themselves. Their climate is harsh and terrible, but their exposed bodies are accustomed to enduring these extremes. What you think of as hardship, is merely the usual mode of life of all these people (the northern Europeans).

Ancestral Populations, Origin of the Name 'German', War-Chants and Odysseus/Ulysses

131 Tacitus, *Germania*, 2–3 (AD 98)
The only way the Germans record or remember their past is through ancient songs. In the verses they recite, they honour an earth-born god named Tuisco and his son Mannus. They say that this god was the originator of their people and the founder of the German nation. The Germans claim that Mannus had three sons who gave their names to the three leading tribes. The Ingaevones were on the north coast, the Herminones inhabited the interior and the Istaevones occupied the remaining territories. But this distant past is subject to conjecture and some Germans assert that their god had further descendants who gave their names to other tribes. They claim that the Marsi, Gambrivii, Suebi and Vandilii all preserve ancient connections with their current names.

The Germans say that the name 'Germany' was only recently introduced to describe their homelands. The name appeared along with the first tribes of their nation who crossed the Rhine to expel the Gauls. These intruders, who are now the Tungrians, were called at that time 'Germans'. Their tribal name was adopted outside their kinfolk to describe the entire nation as 'Germans'. This was because the name created terror. Gradually the wider population called themselves by the self-adopted name of 'Germans'.

The Germans say that in ancient times the demigod Hercules once visited them. They therefore praise him in the verses that they sing, as first above all other heroes. (…)

It is also said that the hero Ulysses (Odysseus) found his way into the northern ocean on his legendary wanderings. Some believe he visited the German homeland and founded the settlement called Asciburgium on the banks of the Rhine (Asberg – 'Fort of the Ashwood'). This town is still inhabited (the site of a Roman auxiliary fort where the rivers Ruhr and Rhine meet).

They say that an altar dedicated to Ulysses was discovered at this site. This altar included the name of his father, Laertes. It is claimed that other monuments and tombs with Greek inscriptions have been found on the borders of Germany and Rhaetia. I have no proof of these statements, but I cannot refute them either. Therefore, every reader must either believe or dismiss these claims, depending on their views.

132 Tacitus, *Germania*, 33
It is commonly claimed that Hercules once visited this country, but we ascribe every great work of wonder to this ancient demigod.

Germanic Leader Remembered

133 Tacitus, *Annals*, 2.88
Arminius lived thirty-seven years and possessed leadership (among the Germans) for twelve years. He is still the subject of songs recited by the barbarian nations (Germanic verse narratives).

Verses Recited as Tribal History

A Gothic migration from Scandinavia to the Black Sea was preserved in verse. The Anglo-Saxons used similar methods to recall their ancestry (*Beowulf*).

134 Jordanes, *Getica*, 4
After this victory (in North Germany) the Goths migrated south through Scythia to the Pontus (northern Black Sea coast). This is the account of their past told in their early songs. These songs preserve information in a form that is almost historic. A famous chronicler of the Gothic race named Ablabius has confirmed these details in a trustworthy account.

Defiance until Death

Seneca the Younger was a stoic philosopher and stateman writing in the first century AD.

135 Seneca, *Moral Letters to Lucilius*, 70.20–21
It is not just great men like Cato who have the mental strength to smash the bonds of human servitude (...) even men reduced to nothing have escaped to safety through great determination or gained the right to die by their own means. They have snatched up whatever was near and by sheer strength of will turned harmless objects into the required weapons.

For example, there was a German captive held at a training school for gladiators who fought wild beasts. On the morning of the arena exhibition, the slave was allowed into the latrine unaccompanied – the only thing he was permitted to do in private without the presence of a guard. While there he seized the stick of wood tipped with the cleaning sponge and stuffed this vile object down his own throat. He blocked his windpipe and choked the breath from his body. (...) What a brave man. Surely, he deserved the right to choose his own fate, and how bravely he would have wielded a sword.

Saxon Slaves Kill Themselves

In AD 393, a group of Saxon captives chose to kill themselves rather than die as an exhibit in the Roman arena. Symmachus was a statesman living at a time when the emperors had converted to Christianity. By this era the ideals and attitudes of the Roman Empire had diverged from their early origins. But the Germanic peoples remained resolute and ready to die for their ancestral customs and beliefs.

136 Symmachus, *Letters*, 2.46
Symmachus sends greeting to his brother Flavianus. I am following the example of Socrates and trying to find the good in my misfortune, for

death has taken some of the Saxons I had acquired to entertain the people of Rome in the arena. So, I will tell myself that too many of these captives might have spoiled the show. After all, what private guards could have stopped this group of desperate men from harming themselves? Twenty-nine Saxons were found strangled without a noose on the first day of the Gladiatorial Games (group suicide). Therefore, I am not wasting my time on that lot. They are worse than Spartacus. I would gladly replace the spectacle of their death with a show of Libyan beasts for the emperor.

Chapter Eight

German Appearance and Reputation

In AD 66, the Roman client king, Herod Agrippa II, tried to persuade the Jews in Judea not to revolt against the Roman Empire.

137 Josephus, *Jewish War*, 2.16
'What do you hope for? Are you wealthier than the Gauls, stronger than the Germans, or wiser than the Greeks? Are you more numerous than any other population? What gives you the confidence to oppose the Romans? (…)

'Which of you have not heard how vast the German population is? You have certainly seen for yourselves how tall and strong the Germans are, since the Romans make use of them as captives in every place. These Germans occupy an immense country, and they have minds superior to their bodies. They have a spirit that despises death and a rage fiercer than wild beasts. But the Rhine is the limit of their enterprises, and they are held in place by eight Roman legions. The Germans who have been taken captive have become servants of the Romans. The rest of their nation have preserved themselves by fleeing conflict with Rome.'

Enemies of Rome

Martial mentions the Germans when criticising the work of another Roman writer.

138 Martial, *Epigrams*, 6.60 To Faustinus 'The works of a popular writer'. Pompullus has achieved fame with his poetry. Undoubtedly his reputation will spread throughout the whole world. It will be enjoyed by every nation that detests Rome. It will flourish among that fickle German race with their fair-hair. They call writings of Pompullus 'ingenious', but that is not enough to give immortality to a piece of literature.

139 Horace, *Epode*, 9
Savage Germany with its blue-eyed youth.

140 Lucan, *The Civil War*, 2.51
Let the Elbe, and the Rhine's unconquered outflow, release swarms of fair-haired Suebians from the Far North. Make Rome the enemy of every nation, but avert this civil war.

German Appearance

Juvenal mentions the distinctive hairstyle of German men. This included the 'Suebian knot'.

141 Juvenal, *Satires*, 13.170
Who among us is amazed to see a German with blue eyes and fair hair, coiling his greasy locks into a twist (the Suebian knot). No one marvels at this sight, because this person is acting according to their customs and nature.

Mistaken Identity

Parts of the Indus region was settled by Scythians and Sakas from the Eurasian Steppe. These people possessed European features (see the coins of Azes II and his predecessors). This explains why certain Republican Romans could mistake the Suebian knot for the Indian *Ushnisha* (topknot).

142 Pliny, *Natural History*, 2.67
Cornelius Nepos suggests that a northern circuit of the oceans is possible (east from the Indian Ocean to the North Atlantic). He records an incident that occurred when Quintus Metellus Celer shared the consulship with Lucius Afranius (in 60 BC). When Metellus was serving as a proconsul of Gaul, he was given some 'Indian' captives by the king of the Suebi. These men were probably on a trade voyage and were swept off course by storms around the coast of Asia to Germany. Thus, the sea must encircle the land on every side (forming Eurasia).

The Population of Sweden

Jordanes wrote in Late Antiquity. He possessed Swedish ancestry and could distinguish between Germanic 'types'.

143 Jordanes, *Getica*, 3
All the nations of Scandza (Scandinavia) surpass the Germans in physical size and resolute spirit. They can also fight with the cruelty of wild beasts.

Scandinavian Germans: Goths, Visigoths and Ostrogoths

Gothic populations emerged in Scandinavia, but over many generations they followed complex settlement and migration routes across eastern Europe.

144 Procopius, *Wars*, 3.1.2
All these Gothic nations are distinguished by their separate names, but in all other respects they are identical (appearance, language, and core culture). They all have pale bodies and fair hair. They are tall and handsome, use the same laws and practise a common religion – the Arian faith (a Christian doctrine). They also have one common language called Gothic. It seems that all these Gothic nations came originally from one tribe and took their names from the leaders of each sub-group.

German Fury

Seneca reveals Roman beliefs about character and climate.

145 Seneca, *On Anger*, 2.15
Your opponent may say, 'anger has some noble quality, just look at the unconquered nations, such as the Germans and Scythians, who are especially prone to anger'. But this is because determined and daring intellects are quick to anger before they are tamed by discipline. Some strong passions can imbed themselves on superior characteristics. In a similar manner, good land, when it has been laid waste, will produce strong brushwood. The tallest trees grow on fertile soil. Likewise, people with naturally bold dispositions are prone to irritability. They are fiery tempered and do not tolerate trivial matters. But their energy is misdirected when there is no training to control their natural mental advantages. Unless a courageous temper is constrained, it will lead to rash and reckless practices. (...)

All those nations which are free because they are wild, like lions or wolves, cannot command the masses because they cannot obey others. The strength of their intellect is not civilised, but fierce and unmanageable. No one can rule unless he is also able to be ruled. Consequently, world empires have almost always emerged from among those nations who enjoy a milder climate. People who dwell near the frozen north have an uncivilised temper. As the poet says, 'a people are modelled on their native skies'.

146 Galen, *Writings on Health*, 1.10
I am no more writing for the Germans, than for wolves and bears.

Concern with World Affairs

Martial criticised a friend who claimed to have exclusive knowledge of world events.

147 Martial, *Epigrams*, 9.35

Philomusus! You are constantly trying to secure invites to fancy dinner parties by displaying your made-up knowledge. You present these facts as true, but you have invented the accounts. You claim that you were informed of discussions at the royal court of the Parthian king Pacorus. Then you say you know the exact numbers of the German and Sarmatian armies (…) if you give us some respite from your 'knowledge', you can dine with me anytime. But only if you fulfil this one condition – no more news!

Germanic Attitudes and Stereotypes

Realistic wall paintings were displayed in the Roman Forum. The 'Old Shepard' was a popular motif in Classical art. The Roman elite placed enormous monetary value on these artistic works.

148 Pliny, *Natural History*, 35.8

The painting known as 'The Old Shepherd with his Staff' was also displayed in the Roman Forum. It was said that a Teuton envoy (from a Germanic tribe) was once asked what he thought of the work and its possible value. He replied that it was worthless, and he would not even accept the living shepherd as a gift!

Physical Similarity to Caledonians

149 Tacitus, *Agricola*, 11

It is not known for certain who the original inhabitants of Britain might have been, or whether the current populations are indigenous, or incomers. This is often the case among barbarian peoples. The British populations possess different physical characteristics and some conclusions can be made from these features. The inhabitants of Caledonia have red (fair) hair and large limbs, clearly suggesting a Germanic origin.

Chapter Nine

Germanic Society

Julius Caesar campaigned against the Germans and was the first Roman general to cross the Rhine. He provides a description of their customs and society in his campaign accounts.

150 Julius Caesar, *Gallic War*, 6.21–23
Their time is spent in hunting expeditions and military pursuits. From early boyhood they are eager for toil and hardship. Their society encourages youths to remain unmarried (Romans, including Caesar, were married in their early teens). The Germans see this as a way to increase the stature, strength and power of their populace (ensuring that children were born to young adults with mature bodies). The Germans regard it disgraceful for a man to have had sexual relations with a woman before his twentieth year (possibly the age of marriage). But there is no modesty among them, for both sexes bathe in the rivers and wear skins or small cloaks made from deer hide. The greater part of their bodies are therefore left bare.

The Germans have no eagerness for agriculture and most of their diet consists of milk, cheese, and meat. No man owns a definite quantity of land or claims his own estate. Every year the 'magistrates' and chiefs of the nation assemble the tribes and clans and assign them as much land as seems appropriate. Then after a year they compel these tenants to move to another location. The Germans give many reasons for this practice. They fear that continuous occupation may make them abandon their warrior zeal for settled agriculture. The more powerful people will also become eager to acquire larger territories and force their lower status kinsmen from essential land holdings. They know that the more they build on the land, the greater will be their intolerance of cold and heat (they will lose their endurance to severe weather). They fear that a passion for wealth will develop, causing competing factional disputes. The Germans therefore aim to keep common people in contentment, and this is achieved when each man sees that his own wealth is equal to that of the most powerful people in his society.

The tribal states of Germany believe that great praise is gained by devastating their frontiers so as wide a wilderness as possible exists around their territories. They think it is a sign of valour when neighbouring peoples are forced out of their lands, and no one dares to settle nearby. They regard this as a measure of safety since they have removed all fear of a sudden incursion by a hostile rival.

Germanic Settlements

151 Tacitus, *Germania*, 16

It is well known that the German nations have no cities and do not live in closely clustered dwellings. They live scattered and apart, and select somewhere where a spring, a meadow, or woodland has attracted them. Their villages are not arranged in our fashion with buildings connected and joined together. Every person surrounds his dwelling with an open space, either as a precaution against the outbreak of fire, or because they don't build in any other fashion. They do not use stone blocks or ceramic tiles in their buildings and employ timber for all required purposes. The crudely cut beams in their buildings are not carved for ornamental effect or selected for attractiveness. However, some parts of their buildings are decorated with colour. They will carefully plaster some timbers with a clay-like pigment to create a colourful, light-reflective surface like a painted panel.

The Germans also dig out subterranean chambers near their dwellings. These underground spaces provide a shelter in winter and a storage place for the annual harvests. The Germans pile great heaps of dung on top of these chambers to mitigate the extreme cold of winter. If an enemy does invade and plunder the country, they may not discover the underground chambers. Even if they know they exist, they may not be able to locate and unearth them in their searches.

German Houses

152 Herodian, *Roman History*, 7.2

There is a scarcity of stone and fired brick in Germany, but the forests are dense, and timber is so abundant that they build their houses entirely of wood. They fit and join the squared-off beams (to create solid structures).

153 Ammianus Marcellinus, *Roman History*, 16.2

These savages avoid towns as if they were tombs surrounded by nets (spiritually unclean and cursed sites where malevolent forces had to be restrained by physical barriers).

Condition of the Chauci (North Coast of Germany)

154 Pliny the Elder, *Natural History*, 16.1
I have already mentioned how many nations on the east coast of the ocean (North Sea/Baltic) exist in this impoverished condition (treeless). I myself have personally witnessed the circumstances of the Chauci located in the Far North, both the greater and lesser parts of this nation.

There is a vast tract of land in these (coastal) territories that is inundated twice each day and night by an outpouring of waves from the ocean (high tides). This raises a question that is repeatedly proposed to us by Nature. Should these regions be considered land or part of the sea?

A wretched race is found in this territory (the coastal Chauci). They inhabit either the more elevated portions of the land, or occupy artificially constructed mounds. From experience, they raise these mounds to a height that they know the highest tides will never reach and there they build their cabins. When the incoming waves cover a great extent of the surrounding country, they are like mariners on board a ship. Then, when the tide recedes, they emerge from their homesteads like shipwrecked men and pursue fishes escaping with the withdrawing sea.

These men do not keep livestock like the adjoining nations. They have no flocks to provide milk as sustenance and there are no wild beasts to be hunted. There are not even shrubs in their territory, as everything has been banished (destroyed or driven off by tidal inundations that contaminated any crop-raising ground with saline deposits).

These people make cords from sedge (grass-like freshwater plants) and the rushes in their marshes. With these cords they weave nets to capture fish. They also shape mud into blocks that are dried more by the wind than the sun (turf cut from peat bogs). They cook their food with these blocks, heating the entrails they consume. They are frozen by northern winds and their only drink is rainwater which they collect in pits dug at the entrance of their abodes.

And yet these nations, if they were conquered today by the Romans, would cry out against the slavery (of subjugation). Fortune is therefore kindest to those she means to punish.

Land, Clothing, Livestock and Trade

155 Julius Caesar, *Gallic War*, 4.1–2
Among the Germans there is no private land entirely separate from public ownership. People are not permitted to reside on the same site for more

than one year. The Germans do not consume much grain, but subsist mainly on milk and meat from their herds. They are also heavily engaged in hunting. From their youth, they are occupied in no other employment or profession, and they do nothing contrary to these habits. Consequently, due to their diets, frequent exercise, and manner of life, they increase their strength and become men of remarkable physical stature. They also have a practice that they themselves promote. Even in the coldest regions they wear minimal clothing except animal furs. A large portion of their body is consequently exposed, and they can endure bathing in cold rivers.

The Germans permit merchants access to their communities so that they can sell items captured in war. But they do not need any commodity that is imported by the merchants. The Gauls take great effort and pride in breeding cattle and will procure the best animals at a great price. By contrast the Germans will not use imported cattle for this purpose. They depend on the diminished and poorly shaped breeds that are indigenous to their country. However, these native cattle are extremely hardy animals, due to frequent exercise. (…)

Germans do not allow wine to be imported into their communities. They believe that wine will weaken their capacity to endure hard work and it will render their men effeminate.

According to their beliefs, the greatest praise a nation can obtain is that the lands surrounding their territories are unoccupied to a great extent. They think that this demonstrates the reputation and power of their people in overcoming nearby populations. Consequently, on one side of the Suebic territories, the lands are said to be desolate for about 600 miles.

Germanic Clothing

Tacitus describes Germanic clothing styles, including materials.

156 Tacitus, *Germania*, 17

The Germans wear a cloak which they wrap round themselves. It is fastened with a clasp, or if this is not possible, with a 'thorn' (perhaps a wooden toggle). Beneath the cloak their chest may be bare. Dressed in this fashion they can spend whole days sitting by their hearth fires. The wealthiest Germans wear tightfitting outfits which expose and exhibit their arms (jerkins or close-fitting jackets). These outfits are very different from the baggy and flowing costumes of the Parthians and Sarmatians (other martial enemies of Rome).

The Germans also wear the fur and hides of wild beasts. The tribes on the Rhine and Danube wear these furs in a rough state. But the interior tribes of Germany fashion these furs with greater care because they do not generally receive other forms of clothing from commerce. They strip the hides of certain animals and sew together the spotted skins of beasts. Parts of their clothing come from the outer ocean and seas that are not known to us (waterproof sealskins). German women generally have the same clothing as the men. But they also wear linen garments which they embroider with purple thread. This clothing does not extend down the arms so that the limbs and the side part of the bosom are left exposed (tabards).

German Hairstyles

Tacitus describes the distinctive 'Suebian knot'.

157 Tacitus, *Germania*, 38
The Suebi chiefs take elaborate care over their hair and hairstyling, but this is not to appear attractive. They have an unusual custom to twist and fasten their long hair on the side of their head with a knot (the Suebian knot). This hairstyle indicates that a man is freeborn and distinguishes the Suebi from the other Germans. They arrange their hair before battle, to make themselves seem taller and more intimidating. They are therefore adorning themselves for the eyes of the foe. Other tribes are adopting this practice due to some connection with the Suebic population, or to emulate their practices. But the custom is still occasional in other territories and is restricted to youths. The true Suebi will follow this practice throughout their lives and when they are old and grey, they will still gather their unkempt hair into the knot.

158 Juvenal, *Satires*, 13.170
Who among us is amazed to see a German with blue eyes and fair hair, coiling his greasy locks into a twist (the Suebian knot).

Warrior Distinctions:
Short-Hair, Ornaments and Old Warriors

Tacitus describes how certain Germans used their appearance to indicate status.

159 Tacitus, *Germania*, 31
There is a custom among certain Germans to indicate prowess as a warrior and this practice has become popular among the Chatti. These Germans

do not let their hair grow long, but when a boy reaches adulthood, he does not cut his hair or beard. This is a vow to valour and only after he has killed a foe does he alter his appearance. After the enemy is defeated and blood has been shed, the youth will declare that he has fulfilled the obligations of his birth. He has proved himself worthy of his country and of his parents. Then he trims his beard and cuts his hair. The coward and the unwarlike remain unshaven.

Men from the bravest German tribes also wear an iron ring (perhaps an arm ring or a metal collar). These objects are a mark of disgrace among other peoples (due to associations with shackles and slavery). However, for the German these objects are another form of their warrior vows, and they will not remove the iron ring until they have slaughtered a foe in combat. The Chatti relish these warrior customs. Even veteran warriors with greying hair will encourage these practices as marks of distinction. This is because, by their very appearance, proven warriors can clearly display their status to both enemies and kinsmen. These men have a duty to begin the battle and they form the front line, presenting a remarkable spectacle. But these warriors do not assume a less savage aspect in peace time. They have no home, no lands, and no other occupation. They are supported by whoever they visit, and they will readily consume the produce of others, but have no interest in gaining their own property. Eventually, the feebleness of old age diminishes and undermines their sternness and valour.

Customs and Practices:

Feuds, Hospitality, Meetings, Gambling and Slaves

160 Tacitus, *Germania*, 21–26

It is a duty among the Germans to continue the feuds and friendships of their father or kinsman. But these feuds can be resolved and even homicide can be repaid by a certain number of cattle and sheep. All kinsmen will accept that a feud has been resolved with the payment of a penalty. This system is of great advantage to the state, because feuds are dangerous if a population has a great deal of public freedom.

The Germans are generous in their hospitality and will entertain and indulge their guests more than any other nation, thinking it is impious to exclude a guest. The Germans do not discriminate between an acquaintance and a stranger when it comes to hospitality. Every German will strive to provide a visiting person with a well-furnished meal and if the host's stores are exhausted, he will become the companion of the visitor. Without waiting for an invitation, he will take his guest to a neighbouring house and make sure that hospitality is offered. The other householder will generously host and feed both men. A host will give the departing guest whatever he asks for and won't hesitate to ask for a gift in return from the guest. The Germans are fond of gifts, but they don't expect to gain from it or feel obliged for what they receive.

The Germans usually sleep until a late hour in the morning and this custom suits a country where winter is the dominant season (dark, cold mornings). When they wake, they often bathe in warm water. After their bath, the Germans take their meals at separate seats and tables before arming themselves and starting the day's business. They also carry their weapons to festival gatherings. In their society no one is disgraced if he spends the entire day and night drinking, but when they have been drinking, their quarrels rarely end with mild abuse. The infliction of wounds and bloodshed are common. Yet it is during their feasts that the Germans generally consult with one another about reconciling with enemies, forming matrimonial alliances, choosing chiefs, and deciding whether peace or war is preferred. This is because they believe that these gatherings permit a unity of purpose with noble ambitions. The Germans are a people without innate or acquired cunning or duplicity. They therefore debate and deliberate in a setting where they cannot easily pretend or mislead one another. Consequently, they will freely disclose their inner thoughts and feelings at these feasts. All participants will reveal their intentions so that when discussions are renewed the following day, the outcomes of each proposal are better understood. This is because they make their resolutions in circumstances where deception is impossible.

The German alcoholic drink is made from fermented barley or other grains, and it has a similar strength to wine. Populations living on the riverbank also purchase Roman wine (Rhine and Danube frontier). Their food is simple and includes wild-fruit, fresh game, and curdled milk. They satisfy hunger without resorting to delicacies or elaborately prepared meals. But they are not moderate in their drinking. If their passion for drinking is fully indulged, they are overwhelmed and subdue themselves, as if defeated in battle by an armed enemy.

The same event is always exhibited at every major German gathering. Naked youths take part in an athletic military drill that resembles a dance. They move nimbly amid drawn swords and spears that could injure them. This practice gives them skill, dexterity, and speed. They do not seek profit (prizes for performances) and payment for this training is never considered. It is reckless, but the risk is taken purely to impress spectators. It is strange that Germans make hazards and high risk into a game. Even when they are sober, they take risks in games involving gain and loss (gambling involving bets or dice games). When every other resource has been lost, a German can stake their own freedom for a final throw of the dice. The loser may be younger and stronger than his opponent, but he will allow himself to be bound and sold into slavery. Their stubborn persistence in this bad practice (the losing streak) will lead them into this situation and honour will make them submit. But this is a scandal for the victor who will dispose of this type of slave through commerce (the slave will be sold or traded to another community).

Other slaves owned by the Germans are not employed as we (Romans) do with distinct domestic duties assigned to them. Each slave manages his own house and home. The master requires a regular quantity of grain, cattle, and clothing from the slave. But these are the limits of subjection, and the condition of the slave therefore resembles a tenant farmer.

Most tasks and functions in the German household are performed by the wife and children. It is rare for a master to strike a slave or to punish him by confinement or hard labour. Slaves are often killed, but not through enforcing strict discipline (Roman style floggings). Slaves are often killed in anger and slain like an enemy combatant (struck down with weapons). The master acts with impunity in this matter (no legal, moral or sacred repercussions).

Freedmen (emancipated slaves) do not have a much greater status than slaves. They seldom have much influence in the family and are never important in state affairs unless the tribe is ruled by kings. In these instances, freedmen might enjoy positions greater than freeborn people and even nobles. But in other contexts, the inferiority of a freedman confirms the freedom of the state (the powerful cannot arbitrarily advance low status people to high-rank positions).

The Germans know nothing about lending money with interest and increasing the sum owed by compound interest. This ignorance is a more effective safeguard from corruption than state prohibitions. Territories are proportioned according to the number of people in a population, and they are occupied by the entire community. Lands are divided and allocated according to rank, but ownership is not permanent. A wide expanse of plains within these territories makes these partitions an easy task. Every year the Germans till fresh fields and there is always sufficient land for the community (fields left fallow to recover from harvests). Their soil is rich and extensive, but they laboriously plant orchards, enclose meadows, and water their gardens. The only produce they require from the earth is grain and consequently they do not need to divide the year into as many harvesting seasons as we (Romans) do. The Germans have a name and a purpose for winter, spring, and summer. But they do not recognise autumn as a truly distinct season or appreciate its many blessings (late harvests).

161 Julius Caesar, *Gallic War*, 6.26
The Germans do not think it is right to abuse a guest. Men who have come to them for any reason are sheltered from harm and regarded as under a sacred protection. They open all their houses to these individuals and freely share food with them.

Chapter Ten

Germanic Women and Families

Tacitus describes German attitudes to women, marriage, and families.

162 Tacitus, *Germania*, 25
Most tasks and functions in the German household are performed by the wife and children.

163 Tacitus, *Germania*, 18–20
The German marriage code is strict and is the most praiseworthy of their customs, for they are the only barbarians who are content with one wife. Only a very few men will have multiple wives, but this is not done for passion. Noble birth secures many offers of marriage alliance. The wife does not bring a dowery (marriage gift of wealth or property) to her husband, but the husband provides an offering to the prospective bride instead. The parents and relatives of the bride pass judgment on the marriage gifts which are not items for womenfolk, but goods such as oxen, a well-equipped horse, a shield, a lance, and a sword. With this exchange the wife is accepted by her husband, and she brings the gift of arms back into his possession.

The Germans regard marriage as the strongest bond of union within their society. The most sacred religious rites are assigned to this practice and the gods of marriage receive supreme recognition. The German woman does not think that she is separate from her husband in pursuit of noble deeds and contentions in war. The marriage ceremony instructs the wife that she is her husband's partner in both labour and danger. They are destined to suffer or prosper together in both peace and war. This fact is proclaimed by the yoked oxen, the harnessed steed, and the gift of weapons. She will live and die knowing that she is receiving properties that must be handed down undiminished to her children. One day, her future daughters-in-law will receive these items and pass them down to her grandchildren.

The virtue of German women is protected, and they are not corrupted by the allurements of public shows or the excesses of feastings. Men and women do not engage in clandestine correspondences. Even though the German population is vast, it is very rare for adultery to occur. The punishment is prompt and usually enacted by the husband. He cuts off the hair of the adulteress and strips her naked. She is expelled from their house in the presence of her kinsfolk and flogged as she walks through the whole village. There is no acquittal from this disgrace and neither beauty, or youth, or wealth will secure that woman another husband. In Germany, nobody laughs at vice or follows popular trends that lead them to practice immorality.

A state is in a better condition when maidens are married and devote their lives to one husband, in one union. Their hopes and expectations end with the family and do not extend into any further-reaching desires. Through this process they learn to love the condition of marriage even more than their husbands. The Germans do not limit the number of children produced in their families (infanticide by neglect or exposure). They regard it as reprehensible to kill surplus infants. In Germany good customs and good conduct therefore prove to be more effective than the benign laws of other countries.

The children found in every household are naked and unkempt, but they grow up to possess those same sturdy bodies and strong limbs that we admire. Every mother nurses her own new-born infants and this task is never entrusted to a servant or wetnurse. The future master is not distinguished from the household slave by being brought up with greater comforts. Both master and slave are reared together amongst the same flocks and lie on the same ground until the freeborn receive the honours brought by adulthood and are recognised by merit. The young men marry late, so their vigour for war is not impaired. The maidens are not hurried into marriage but are required to have a similar age and comparable prowess to their husbands. The Germans are well-matched and vigorous when they marry. Their offspring match the strength and potential of their parents.

A man will hold his sister's sons in as much regard as his own. Some Germans even regard this position to be more sacred and binding than the father-son bond. They therefore seek nephews as hostages (house guests) and believe this gives them a stronger hold on the affections of the kin group and a wider influence on the tribe. But in Germany a man's children are his heirs and successors. There are no wills and if a man doesn't have any children his brothers and uncles on either side may inherit his property. The more relatives a man has the more numerous his connections are in society and the more honoured he will be in old age. There are no advantages to being childless in their society.

Civilis and the Revolt of the Batavians

These social connections were evident during the Batavian uprising led by Civilis (AD 69).

164 Tacitus, *Histories*, 4.33
Civilis kept part of his forces in place (besieging the Roman camp). But he sent the veteran cohorts and the bravest of his German troops against Vocula (the Roman commander) and his army. This attacking force was commanded by Julius Maximus and Claudius Victor, who was his sister's son.

Women in Warfare

Tacitus describes how German women appeared on the battlefield to support the warriors.

165 Tacitus, *Germania*, 8
The warriors are accompanied by their families so that they can hear the shrieks of women, and the cries of infants who have come to witness their bravery on the battlefield. These are their revered observers and the applauders of valour. A warrior will display his fresh wounds to his mother or wife, and they will not flinch from counting the injuries or demanding greater heroism. These women will give essential sustenance and encouragement to the combatants. Tradition says that armies already wavering and withdrawing from the battlefield have been rallied by their women. The women will plead passionately, expose their bosoms, and recount the horrors they expect from defeat and captivity.

The Germans especially fear the capture and enslavement of their women and they have an appalling dread of this outcome. One of the strongest assurances a state can provide is to surrender maidens of noble birth alongside the other political hostages. The Germans believe that women possess a certain sanctity, and intuition (knowledge of future events?). Therefore, they do not dismiss or despise their advice, or ridicule their suggestions.

Women follow the German Army

Tacitus records how women accompanied Germanic armies to battle sites during the Batavian Revolt (AD 69).

166 Tacitus, *Histories*, 4.18
Meanwhile Civilis surrounded himself with the battle standards of the captured Roman cohorts. This reminded his men of their recent success and demoralised the Romans by displaying their defeat. Civilis now instructed his own mother and sisters, and the wives and children of all his men, to follow behind his army. From this position the women could encourage the menfolk to victory, or shame them if they faced defeat. The war-song of the men that dominated the battle lines was punctuated by the shrill cries of the women. An answering call came from the Roman army, but the legions and auxiliaries could only manage a less courageous cheer.

Resistance by Germanic Women

After their menfolk were slaughtered in battle, Teutonic women defied the Romans and resisted them from within their fortified wagon camp (the Battle of Aquae Sextiae, 102 BC).

167 Orosius, *History*, 5.16
The wives of the enemy showed great determination in their defeat. They informed the consul (Marius) that he should meet their requirements for surrender, or they would take their own lives. They insisted that their chastity should remain inviolate, and when taken to Rome they must be assigned duties serving the gods and the Vestal Virgins (the sacred priestess). When their requests were refused, they bludgeoned their infants to death on the rocks. Then they committed suicide using swords, or by hanging.

168 Plutarch, *Marius*, 19
The Romans slew everyone in their path until they advanced as far as the wagons surrounding the enemy encampment. The women in the encampments stood ready with swords and axes in their hands. They screamed at their fleeing warriors with furious shrieks calling them deserters. Then they tried to drive back their foes with fearsome cries. Women who became mixed up with the combatants, used their bare hands to tear away the shields of the Romans. Some grabbed the blades of the Roman swords with their unprotected hands, thereby suffering horrific wounds and mutilations. But their fierce spirits remained unvanquished to the end.

Rome defeats the Cimbri at the Battle of Vercellae (101 BC)

Resistance of the Women

The women of the Cimbri also resisted the Romans when their menfolk were defeated at the battle of Raudian Plain (Vercellae).

169 Florus, *Roman History*, 1.38

After the battle there was a severe struggle with the barbarian womenfolk. They had used their wagons and carts to form a barricade and clambering on top of this defence they prepared to fight with axes and pikes. But first they sent a delegation to Marius requesting, that if their lives were spared, they would willingly become servants of the priestesses (slaves of the Vestal Virgins in Rome). Marius refused, since this request could not lawfully be granted (as he held a military command and not a religious office). In response the women strangled all the infants in their camp or bludgeoned them to death. They fought as fiercely as their men and their death was as honourable as their resistance. They died fighting the enemy, or from wounds inflicted on one another. Some made ropes of their own hair and hanged themselves on trees, or the upward jutting yokes of their wagons.

170 Orosius, *History*, 5.16

The women fought a conflict that was perhaps more severe than the main battle. The enemy wagons had been drawn up in the form of a fortified camp, so that the women defended themselves from an elevated position. They managed to keep the Romans from entering this compound for a long time. But they finally became terrified by the method that the soldiers employed to kill the defenders. When they dragged women down from the barricades, the Romans scalped them in full view. The soldiers then left the exposed and mutilated corpses in sight for the defenders to witness their shameful and horrific wounds. After this, the women began to commit suicide using the very weapons they had employed against the soldiers. They slaughtered their own children and helped to kill each other. Some women cut each other's throats. Some tied cords to the legs of horses and put the end of the nooses round their own necks. When the horses were driven forwards, the women were dragged along and choked to death. Others hanged themselves with nooses suspended from wagon poles raised high in the air. One woman was found who had slipped nooses over the necks of her two sons, and then bound the ropes to her own ankles. She died by hanging with her two sons suspended from her lower limbs.

171 Plutarch, *Marius*, 27

There the Romans witnessed a tragic sight. The Cimbri women were dressed in black garments, and they stood at the wagons killing any of their menfolk who fled the battlefield. They slew their husbands, brothers, or fathers (flinging themselves at exhausted and panic-stricken men fleeing the enemy). Then they strangled their little children and placed babies to be crushed beneath the wheels of wagons, or the hooves of cattle. Finally, they cut their own throats.

It is said that one woman was found dangling from the tip of an upturned wagon-pole (noose around her neck). She had hung herself with the dead bodies of her two small children tied to each ankle (also hung). The men would have hung themselves from branches, but there were no suitable trees at the site. So, they fastened their nooses to the necks, horns, or hind legs of cattle. Then they goaded the beasts forwards and were dragged or trampled to death as the cattle dashed away.

Fate of the Cimbri Women

Writing in AD 409, the Christian leader Jerome mentioned the fate of the Cimbri women.

172 Jerome, *Letter*, 123.8 'Appeal to the Widow Ageruchia'

The Teutones came from the remote shores of the Germanic Ocean. They overran Gaul, and slaughtered several Roman armies, before Marius finally defeated them at Aquae Sextiae. As a condition of their surrender, 300 of their married women were to be handed over to the Romans. When the Teuton matrons heard of this arrangement they begged the consul (Marius) that they might instead serve in the temples of Ceres and Venus (Roman goddesses associated with harvests and fertility). When they failed to obtain their request, they were silenced by the Lictors (official agents of the consul). So, they slew their little children and next morning they were all found dead in each other's arms, having strangled each other in the night.

Settlers Resist Caesar

Similar scenes occurred when Julius Caesar engaged the Germanic settlers west of the Rhine (Battle of Vosges in 58 BC).

173 Julius Caesar, *Gallic War*, 1.51

Caesar deployed the Romans in a triple line adjacent to the enemy's camp. (…) There were wagons and carts in the German lines, so the fighters would be unable to flee. Their women took position on board the wagons. They watched with tearful eyes, as the men marched forwards. The women called out, not to allow their families to be taken into Roman slavery.

174 Cassius Dio, *Roman History*, 38.50

Many Germans were instantly slain with a single sword thrust (to the face or throat). They were dead before they fell, but they were kept upright in the tightly packed closeness of their defensive formations. Most of the Germans died during this engagement, but some were driven back to their wagons. These men died with their wives and children.

175 Julius Caesar, *Gallic War*, 1.53

(The Germanic chief) Ariovistus had two wives. One was a Suebian who had accompanied him from his homelands in Germany. The other was a woman from Noricum (a territory in the Celtic Alps). She was the sister of King Voccio and had married Ariovistus in Gaul (a political alliance). Both wives were killed in the rout. One of his daughters was also slain, but the other was taken prisoner by the Romans.

Women of the Usipetes and Tencteri

In 55 BC, Julius Caesar attacked a large group of Usipetes and Tencteri who had crossed the Rhine with their families.

176 Julius Caesar, *Gallic War*, 4.14

The Roman soldiers, agitated by the treachery of the preceding day, rushed into the enemy camp. Those Germans who were able to arm themselves resisted our men for a short time, fighting among their carts and baggage wagons. Since the Germans had left their homeland and crossed the Rhine with their entire families, the camp included infants and women. So, these people began to scatter and flee in every direction. Caesar therefore sent the cavalry to pursue them. When the German fighters heard the noise to their rear, they realised that their families were being slaughtered. They cast down their weapons and abandoned their battle standards. They fled out of the camp in the direction of the nearby river where the Meuse and the Rhine converge. A great many of the Germans were killed and those that reached the river threw themselves into the current as they despaired of any other escape. Overcome by panic, fatigue, and the turbulence of the river, they drowned.

Response of the Suebi

The Suebi prepare for a Roman attack on their territory (55 BC).

177 Julius Caesar, *Gallic War*, 4.19
The Suebi had been informed by their scouts that the Romans were building a bridge across the Rhine. They had held a council according to their custom and sent orders to all parts of their state. The people were instructed to evacuate their settlements and transfer all the women and children into the woodlands, along with their possessions. All the men capable of wielding weapons were then to assemble in a single location. The chosen location was close to the centre of the territories held by the Suebi. The men had resolved to meet the approaching Roman army in this place and engage them in battle.

Marcomannic Wars

In AD 169, Germanic forces breached the frontiers and surged towards Roman Italy (the Marcomannic Wars).

178 Cassius Dio, *Roman History*, 71.10
Meanwhile, many Germans (from other tribes) surged across the Rhine and advanced as far as Italy. They inflicted great damage upon the Romans before they were forced back by the emperor. During this campaign, two Roman commanders were distinguished for their ability. They were (Tiberius Claudius) Pompeianus and (Publius Helvius) Pertinax, who later became emperor. It is said that the bodies of women wearing armour were found among the corpses of the barbarians.

Women Hostages

179 Suetonius, *Augustus*, 21
Augustus tried exacting a new kind of political hostage from the barbarians. These were women and girls, since he realised that the barbarians would disregard pledges secured by male hostages.

Women Prisoners

The Emperor Caracalla conducted military operations against the Alemanni in AD 213.

180 Cassius Dio, *Roman History*, 78.14
During this conflict the Romans managed to capture some of the German women. Caracalla asked them if they wanted to be sold as slaves or killed. They chose death, but the emperor ignored their wishes. When these women were sold, they all took the opportunity this presented to slay their children and kill themselves.

Thusnelda, Wife of the War Leader Arminius, is Captured (AD 15)

181 Tacitus, *Annals*, 1.57
Among the German captives were some high-status women including the wife of Arminius (Thusnelda), who was also the daughter of Segestes. It was found that she exhibited the spirit of her husband, rather than the sentiments of her father (she was anti-Roman). She was not reduced to tears and did not speak in the tones of a suppliant. She folded her arms across her bosom and cast her eyes down towards her offspring (she was pregnant with the child of Arminius).

Chapter Eleven

Germanic Religion

Julius Caesar suggests that Germanic worship lacked deities equivalent to Roman gods.

182 Julius Caesar, *Gallic War*, 6.21
The Germans are different from the Gauls. They have no Druids to regulate their divine worship and no great interest in sacrifices (organised by officials). They only value the gods that they can observe and those that offer them clear assistance such as the Sun, the Firegod, and the Moon. They have not heard of the other deities, even through rumours.

Germanic Priests

Caesar was writing in the 50s BC. Tacitus composed his *Germania* in AD 98. He contradicts Caesar by describing a Germanic priest class who could reprimand warriors.

183 Tacitus, *Germania*, 6
The priests are the only ones who can command a warrior to be reprimanded, imprisoned, or flogged. This is because the Germans believe that only the dictates of the gods can inspire, or reprimand, a warrior.

The Germans carry certain figures and images removed from their sacred groves into battle with them.

Germanic Gods

Tacitus gives an account of the Germanic gods by using Roman equivalents to explain their character and attributes. He also describes German practices for foretelling the future.

184 Tacitus, *Germania*, 9–11
The chief deity worshipped by the Germans is Mercury (the divine messenger of the gods). They even deem it right to sacrifice human victims

to this god on certain days. They present more legitimate offerings to Hercules and Mars (the demigod hero and the war god). Some of the Suebi also sacrifice to Isis (an Egyptian goddess who assisted worshippers in the afterlife). I have not discovered how this foreign rite might have reached Germany, but images of Isis displayed on light galleys confirms the existence of an imported cult (her cult was associated with ships and solar discs).

The Germans do not think that their grand celestial beings should be confined within temple walls the way our gods are housed. They also do not believe that divine entities assume human form. The Germans therefore consecrate woods and groves, and also give the name 'deity' to abstract concepts that exist in spirit form.

The Germans practise augury (foretelling events by observing the behaviour of birds). They also engage in divination by casting lots more than any other people. They have a simple method for this. A small branch is cut off a tree and cut into small pieces. These pieces are distinguished by certain marks or carvings (runestones with sacred symbols). They are then scattered randomly over a white garment to foretell events. When these events concern a community, the state priest will act like the father of a family and invoke the gods. With his eyes fixed towards heaven he will take up and cast the pieces three times and find the meaning in the mark carved on them. If the cast is unfavourable, there is no further consultation about the matter that day. However, if the cast goes well, then the matter is sanctioned. But a confirmation of augury is still required.

The Germans are familiar with the practice of consulting the sounds and the flight of birds to foretell future events. However, they also have a unique practice involving horses and seek omens from the behaviour and movements of these sacred animals. There is a breed of pure white horses maintained at the expense of the community in sacred woods and groves. The horses are kept free from earthly labour. They are yoked to a sacred vehicle and accompanied by the priest and the king, or chief, of the tribe. The priest will note how the horses will neigh and snort as an indication of future events. The Germans trust this more than any other method for discerning the future. It is trusted in full, not only by the general populace, but also by the nobility and the priests. The priests regard themselves as the ministers of the gods and the horses as intermediaries who are acquainted with the divine will.

The Germans have another method of observing auspices when they want to learn the result of an important war. They use whatever means they can to take a prisoner from the hostile tribe and force him to fight a chosen man from their tribe. Each combatant uses the weapons of their own country, and the victory of either man is taken as an indication of the outcome of the war.

The German chiefs deliberate over minor issues, but more important matters involve the entire tribe. But even when the final decision is made by the general populace, the affair is always thoroughly considered and discussed by the chiefs. The Germans assemble on certain fixed days, but meetings can be convened if there are sudden emergencies. The assemblies follow a schedule dictated by the moon, with gatherings occurring at either the new, or the full moon. These times are considered auspicious for transacting business. The Germans do not reckon the passage of time by days as we do, but count and allocate time by nights. This is because, in their minds, night brings the onset of day. The Germans use this system to arrange both ordinary and legal meetings.

185 Tacitus, *Germania*, 33
It is commonly claimed that Hercules once visited this country, but we ascribe every great work of wonder to this ancient demigod.

Emperor Julian

The last pagan emperor of Rome was influenced by Germanic culture (Julian, Caesar of the West AD 355 to 360 and Roman emperor AD 361 to 363).

186 Ammianus Marcellinus, *Roman History*, 16.5
Julian secretly prayed to (the god) Mercury. The (pagan) theologians state that Mercury possesses the swiftest intelligence in the Universe and can arouse this activity in the minds of men.

Influence of Foreign Cults

Germanic chiefs were held as political hostages in Roman territory. Some were inducted into foreign cults.

187 Ammianus Marcellinus, *Roman History*, 16.12
Mederichus had been kept as a political hostage in Gaul for a long time and he had been inducted into the Greek mysteries (a secretive religious cult). He therefore changed the name of his son from the native Agenarichus to Serapio (in honour of Serapis the Greco-Egyptian god worshiped in underworld cults).

Afterlife

The Celts had strong beliefs in an Afterlife. Appian suggests that the Germans shared these ideas.

188 Appian, *Gallic War,* **4.22**
The Germans do not fear death as they believe their spirit survives beyond this life.

Human Sacrifice in Sacred Groves

Tacitus describes the religious customs of the Suebi in central Germany.

189 Tacitus, *Germania,* **39**
The Semnones say they are the most ancient and renowned branch of the Suebi and their great antiquity is attested by their religion. At a stated time, all the tribes of this nation send representatives to a sacred grove, consecrated by the worship of their forefathers. It embodies a terrifying ritual venerated since immemorial times. They publicly slaughter a human victim in the sacred grove and acclaim this barbarous rite. They show other reverence in this ritual space. Everyone entering the grove must be bound with a chain to acknowledge that he is inferior to the presiding deity. If anyone should trip and fall, he will not be allowed to stand and no one may assist him to his feet and he must crawl about on the ground (since they believe the deity has cast him down). These rituals suggest that this place is the origin of the Suebi nation. The entire tribe is subject and obedient to this sacred authority, so they must have originated in the place where their supreme deity is worshiped. The good fortunes of the Semnones strengthens this belief. They occupy a territory containing 100 districts and have a vast community. This permits the Semnones to regard themselves as the head of the Suebic race.

Roman Rescue

Julius Caesar rescued a Roman envoy from the Germans (Battle of Vosges, 58 BC).

190 Julius Caesar, *Gallic War,* **1.53**
Gaius Valerius Procillus had been bound with a threefold chain (restraints on his wrist, ankles and waist) and was being dragged along by his captors

as the Germans fled. Caesar himself was leading the pursuing cavalry that overtook this group of fleeing Germans. His rescue of Procillus gave Caesar as much pleasure as the victory itself. A most distinguished member of the Roman Province of Gaul had been saved and someone who was a close friend and guest of Caesar himself. This demonstrated to Caesar that his good fortune remained intact and consistent. Procillus said that on three occasions the Germans had cast lots in his presence to decide whether he should be immediately burnt to death, or saved for a later sacrifice. So Procillus owed his safety and salvation to the favour of the gods.

Invoking the Celestial Gods

In AD 58, a Germanic chief named Boiocalus requested settlement rights on abandoned land near the Roman frontier.

191 Tacitus, *Annals*, 13.55
Boiocalus said he was adding further merit to fifty years of loyalty (to Rome) by bringing his tribe, the Ampsivarii, under imperial domination. He stated:

> (…) Once these meadows belonged to the Chamavi; then to the Tubantes and then to the Usipii (earlier German tribes). As heaven is for the gods, so earth is for mankind. All empty lands can be taken by anyone.

Then Boiocalus looked up at the sun and invoked the other aspects of the sky (the moon, the planets and the stars). He addressed these heavenly bodies as though he stood in front of the gods themselves. He demanded:

> Do you want to behold a vacant land empty of people? It is better to submerge such a place beneath the sea than see it taken by those who plunder.

Sacred Groves

The plot that launched the Batavian uprising against Rome was conducted in a sacred grove (North Rhine, AD 69).

192 Tacitus, *Histories*, 4.22
Civilis arranged for a feast to be held at one of the groves that were sacred to the Batavians. The chiefs of the nation attended, along with the boldest

and most influential members of the lower classes. When they were worked up by this raucous occasion, Civilis began speaking about the reputation and glory of their nation. He listed the wrongs and the oppressions which they had recently endured and called these the 'evils of slavery'.

Speech by War Leader Arminius (AD 15)

193 Tacitus, *Annals*, 1.59
'The Roman standards which I hung up to the gods of our country can still be seen in the groves of Germany.'

Worship of 'Mother Earth'

Tacitus describes German religious practices east of the Elbe.

194 Tacitus, *Germania*, 40
The tribes beyond these regions are confined by forests and rivers. None of them have any noteworthy features, except that they all engage in the worship of Ertha, 'Mother Earth'. They believe that this goddess interposes in human affairs and visits the nations in a chariot. There is an island in the ocean containing a sacred grove and within that grove there is a consecrated chariot and a garment prepared for the goddess. Only one priest is permitted to touch this sacred object and only he can perceive the presence of the goddess in this sacred recess. He walks with the utmost reverence by the side of her sacred chariot as it is drawn along by heifers (young cows that have not birthed calves).

Whenever the chariot travels, this sacred group is welcomed and there is great rejoicing and festivity among the communities they visit. At these times, the people of the region do not go into battle or carry personal weapons. All armaments are locked away so that peace and quiet endure while the goddess travels. Finally, the goddess will become weary of humankind and the priest will restore her to the sacred grove. Afterwards the chariot and the vestments are purified in a secret lake, and it is believed the goddess also enters these same waters. The slaves who perform these purification rites are instantly swallowed by the sacred lake (ritual drowning). The ritual possesses a mysterious terror, and most people are in pious ignorance of what occurs, since only men doomed to die will observe the ceremony.

Worship of the Twin Gods

Tacitus described the worship of twin gods in the eastern part of Germania. The Anglo-Saxon divine ancestors Hengst and Horsa embodied similar traits.

195 Tacitus, *Germania*, 43
In the territory of the Nahanarvali, there is a forest grove with an ancient sanctuary. A priest in female garments oversees this sacred space. The gods that preside over the grove are described as the Roman deities Castor and Pollux (the Dioscuri – twin horse-riding gods with a youthful appearance). They have the characteristics of the Dioscuri, but are known by the name 'Alcis'. There are no images of Alcis and no evidence of foreign rites in the worship. Nevertheless, the deities at this site are worshiped as brothers and youths.

The War God (Tyr)

The Cimbri and Tuetones invoked the war god when they requested lands to settle (113 BC).

196 Florus, *Roman History*, 1.38
The Cimbri, Teutones and Tigurini were fugitives from the extreme parts of Gaul (Germany, northern Europe). The ocean flooded their territories, so they sought new places to live. But their settlement in Gaul was opposed and their progress into Spain was halted. They therefore descended upon Roman Italy. They sent representatives to the headquarters of the Roman commander Silanus and offered a message to the Senate. They requested that 'O, Romans, followers of the war god Mars, grant us land as payment and use our manpower and weapons for any purpose you wish.'
But what land could the Roman people give them? They were involved in their own disputes about land shortages and agrarian legislation.

Batavian Revolt

During the Batavian uprising of AD 69, a Germanic people called the Tencteri (living east of the Rhine) tried to incite the Ubii to revolt. The Ubii had German ancestry, but they were peaceably settled in Roman territories west of the Rhine. The Tencteri spokesmen invoked the war god.

197 Tacitus, *Histories*, 4.64
'We give thanks to the gods that you have re-joined the united German nation. We thank the gods that we worship in common and we praise Mars (the war god) who is the chief of our divinities. We congratulate you, because you may now live as free men among free men.'

Gothic God

The Goths worshiped a Nordic war god before their full conversion to Christianity in the fourth century AD.

198 Jordanes, *Getica*, 5
The Goths had always worshiped Mars with cruel rites and captives were slain to him as sacrificial victims. This was because they thought that the lord of war ought to be appeased by the shedding of human blood. They devoted the first share of their plunder to him and weapons stripped from the enemy were hung from trees in his honour. They had a deeper belief in this god than any other people, since it was their ancestral custom.

Equating the Gods

The Anglo-Saxons who settled in Britain during the fifth century AD renamed the weekdays to honour their own Germanic gods.

Tuesday – Latin *Martis*, the day of the war god Mars was renamed in honour of Tyr.

Wednesday – Latin *Mercurii*, the day of the artisan god Mercury was renamed in honour of the chief Germanic god Woden.

Thursday – Latin *Jovis*, the day of the ruler god Jupiter was renamed in honour of the Germanic warrior god Thor, who commanded thunder and lightning.

Friday – Latin *Veneris*, the day of Venus, the goddess of passion, was renamed in honour of Fria, the wife of the chief god Woden.

These Germanic gods are described in later Norse mythology.

Divine Ancestors and Heroes

199 Tacitus, *Germania*, 3
The Germans honour an earth-born god named Tuisco and his son Mannus. The say that this god was the originator of their people and the founder of the German nation. (...) The Germans also say that in ancient times the demigod Hercules once visited them. They therefore praise him in the verses that they sing, as he is the first above all other heroes.

Sacred Bronze Bull of the Cimbri

200 Plutarch, *Marius*, 23
The Barbarians attacked and captured the Roman strongholds located north of the Atiso River (securing mountain passes through the Alps). The Roman garrisons demonstrated extreme bravery in defence of their country. The enemy so admired these soldiers that they allowed them to depart the forts without further harm (a truce while the Romans evacuated their positions). But first they made the soldiers take an oath on their bronze bull (a tribal idol). This object was subsequently captured by the Romans (when the Cimbri were defeated). It is said that it was taken to the house of Catulus as the main prize of his victory (at the Battle of Vercellae in 101 BC).

Germanic War Totems

201 Tacitus, *Germania*, 6
The Germans carry certain figures and images removed from their sacred groves into battle with them.

Batavian Revolt

During the Batavian Revolt of AD 69, a Rhine military base was besieged by a Germanic army carrying war totems. The battle standards of Batavian soldier mutineers were carried alongside these Germanic emblems.

202 Tacitus, *Histories*, 4.22
Civilis led from the centre of his army with his force of elite Batavian troops. He presented a terrifying military display with his German allies lining both banks of the Rhine. Meanwhile his cavalry galloped about the plains and the captured fleet manoeuvred along the river. Civilis displayed the

battle standards of his veteran cohorts (banners and insignia). But images of wild beasts had also been carried out of the woods and the sacred groves (Germanic totems and religious emblems). These were the various objects that each tribe followed into battle. Germanic totems were mingled with Roman battle standards so that the besieged troops were confounded by the sight of their imperial emblems alongside the symbols of foreign warfare.

Sacred Vows and Red Hair Dye

The Batavian war leader Civilis performed a ritual before rebelling against the Empire (AD 69).

203 Tacitus, *Histories*, 4.61

Then Civilis (the Batavian rebel commander) fulfilled a vow often made by barbarians. The day he took up arms against the Romans, he let his hair grow long and coloured it with a red dye. Now, after the legions had been destroyed, he cut his hair short. It was also said that he set up some of the Roman prisoners as targets for his little son to shoot at with child-sized arrows and javelins.

Warband Ritual

In AD 366, the Roman general Jovinus ambushed a German warband engaged in a similar ritual.

204 Ammianus Marcellinus, *Roman History*, 27.2

The Romans advanced slowly along a valley concealed by a thick growth of trees. They saw the barbarians bathing in the river. Some of them were reddening their hair according to their national custom (using red hair dye) while others were drinking.

Acclimation of a War Chief

The Canninefates selected a war leader when they joined the Batavian Revolt (AD 69). The battle host raised their new leader, Brinno, on a shield.

205 Tacitus, *Histories*, 4.15

A man named Brinno was renowned among the Canninefates for his steadfast bravery and distinguished nobility. (…) Following their national custom, they raised him up on a shield, balanced on the shoulders of the bearers. Brinno stood on this platform to be proclaimed as their general.

A Sacred Resource

Salt was a vital food preservative but also a sacred substance in ancient Germanic society. Tacitus describes a war between the Hermunduri and Chatti (AD 58).

206 Tacitus, *Annals*, 13.57

That summer (AD 58) a great battle was fought between the Hermunduri and the Chatti (major tribes in northern Germany). Both tribes claimed a river between their territories which produced large amounts of salt (an essential component in food flavouring and preservation). It was their tradition to settle these disputes by warfare, but the site was also subject to profound superstitions. The Germans believe that such sites have a greater proximity to heaven and mortal prayers made at these sacred locations will be more attentively heard by the gods. They believe that salt is produced in the rivers by a divine power that occupies the forests.

Sacrifice After Battle

In 105 BC, the Cimbri gained a major victory over two Roman armies and thereby captured a vast quantity of war gear.

207 Orosius, *History*, 5.16

Having gained possession of both military camps and a vast amount of booty, the enemy acted in a strange and unusual manner. As though performing a curse or a sacrifice they utterly destroyed everything they had captured. They tore the Roman clothing into pieces and had it strewn about the landscape. The captured gold and silver were cast into the river. The Roman breastplates were hacked to pieces and horse trappings were deliberately destroyed. The horses they seized were drowned in whirlpools and the captured soldiers had nooses fasted around their neck before being strung up to die on trees.

Germans Capture and Crucify Roman Officers

The Germans sacrificed captured Roman officers to their deities.

208 Florus, *Roman History*, 2.30

On his next campaign Drusus simultaneously attacked the powerful tribes of the Cherusci, Suebi and Sugambri (12 BC). These tribes had begun hostilities against Rome by capturing and crucifying twenty centurions. They performed this ritual in an oath-making ceremony to unite their people into a common cause against the Romans.

Mutilation of Roman Captives

After the Battle of the Teutoburg Forest, Roman captives were mutilated (AD 9). Note: in Norse mythology the trickster god Loki had his lips sewn shut as punishment for oath-breaking and duplicity involving misleading wordplay.

209 Florus, *Roman History*, 2.30

The slaughter that took place in the marshes and woods of Germania was unsurpassed. The retaliations inflicted by the barbarians were horrific and there were unbearable abuses. They directed the most severe punishments against the legal pleaders (those who practised or participated in Roman law). The Germans gouged out the eyes of some victims and cut off the hands of others. One captive had his tongue cut out and his mouth sewn shut. The barbarian held the severed tongue in his hand and cried out, 'Now viper – you have ceased to hiss!'

The Teutoburg Massacre Site

In AD 15, Roman forces reached the site of the Teutoburg massacre and saw the remains of Germanic sacrifices.

210 Tacitus, *Annals*, 1.61–62

The soldiers located the remains of the first camp which Varus had established on his march into the forest. From its circumference and dimensions, they determined that this had been a base for all three legions. Further on, Roman forces discovered a partially fallen rampart encircled by a shallow ditch. This must have been where some shattered remnant of the army had made their final stand against the attacking enemy. The whitening bones of men could be seen in the centre of this clearing, revealing where individual soldiers had stood their ground or attempted to flee. Bones were strewn everywhere between the camps or piled into heaps. Fragments of weapons and the decayed limbs of horses were visible within the remains. Human heads had been nailed to tree trunks in a prominent display of savagery. Near the battle site the Germans had dedicated sacred groves around barbarian altars. They had sacrificed Roman captives at these sites. In these ceremonies, tribunes had been immolated and first-rank centurions consumed in the flames.

Survivors of the disaster accompanied the soldiers. These were men who had escaped from the battle or the captivity which followed. They pointed out locations where their officers had been killed or some other major event had transpired. This place was where an eagle (battle standard) was seized by the enemy, that location was where Varus received his first wound, here is where the commander surrendered to fate and killed himself. They pointed to the rising ground where Arminius had appeared, urging his warriors onwards to fiercer action. The survivors showed where numerous gibbets had hung from trees to suspend Roman captives. They showed the pits and explained how Roman prisoners had been crammed into these confines. (...)

So, six years after the disaster, the Roman army once more stood on the site of this battle. Consumed by grief and anger, they began to collect the bones of the three legions for burial. Each man did not know whether he was interring the remains of a relative, or of a stranger. But he knew that those he looked upon were the bodies of his kinsfolk and people who shared his blood. The wrath of the army rose higher than ever against the enemy.

Germanicus began this task and deposited a clod of soil on the first burial mound that the army was raising. This was a welcome honour for the dead and all present shared their common sorrow.

Sacrifices to 'Mars and Mercury' (Tyr and Woden)

Outcome of a war between the Hermunduri and Chatti (AD 58).

211 Tacitus, *Annals*, 13.57
The war (over the salt resources) was a success for the Hermunduri and a disaster for the Chatti. This was because the Chatti had promised the victory to their gods Mars and Mercury (the Roman equivalent to the Germanic Gods of War and Craft – perhaps forerunners of Tyr and

Woden). They promised these gods that when the Chatti obtained victory, the slain enemy army would be presented to them as a sacrificial offering. They vowed that everything on the vanquished side would be offered up for destruction, even the Hermunduri horses. But this violent fate recoiled back upon themselves (they became the sacrificial battlefield offering of the Hermunduri).

Sacrifices prior to War (Augustan Era)

212 Cassius Dio, *Roman History*, 54.20
It was reported that the Sugambri, Usipetes, and Tencteri had seized some Romans in their territories and crucified them.

213 Florus, *Roman History*, 2.30
On his next campaign Drusus simultaneously attacked the powerful tribes of the Cherusci, Suebi and Sugambri. These tribes had begun hostilities against Rome by capturing and crucifying twenty centurions. They performed this ritual in an oath-making ceremony to unite their people into a common cause against the Romans. They had been so confident in victory that they had even reached agreement on how the plunder from their war was to be divided among the tribes. The Cherusci had chosen the horses, the Suebi claimed the gold and silver, and the Sugambri were allocated the captives.

Sacrificed and Slaughtered Romans

The revolt of the Frisii involved further massacres that may have involved sacred rituals (north coast of Germania, AD 28).

214 Tacitus, *Annals*, 4.73
When their angry objections and protests increased and the Romans still offered no respite, the Frisii sought a solution in war. The soldiers appointed to collect the tribute were seized and gibbeted (nailed dead or dying to gallows in a public execution). (…)

Soon afterwards, the Romans learned from deserters about other killings (that had occurred during the uprising). It was reported that 900 Roman soldiers had been slaughtered in a wood called the Braduhenna. These men had resisted and fought for two days before being massacred.

Sacrifices conducted by the Saxons (AD 480)

Sidonius wrote a letter to his friend Namatius, who was trying to counter seaborne raids by the Saxons.

215 Sidonius, *Letters*, 8.6.15 'Letter to his friend Namatius'
The Saxons have a custom that they enact before they set sail from the continent, even before they drag their firm-holding anchors up from the enemy's shore (Gaul). Before they begin the homeward journey, they abandon every tenth captive to a slow and agonising death by drowning (sacrifices). They cast lots to determine who in the doomed crowd will suffer this unjust death sentence.

These customs are more deplorable because they are prompted by sincere beliefs. These men (the Saxons) are constrained by religious vows that must be paid in victims. They believe that this horrific killing is a religious act, and they must extract anguish from the prisoner in place of a ransom (sums paid to release the captives). In their view this polluting sacrilege is an absolving sacrifice.

A Sacred Battle Trophy

In AD 15, Roman forces recovered a captured legionary battle standard from a sacred grove. It was one of the lost eagles taken in the Teutoburg massacre.

216 Tacitus, *Annals*, 2.25
Germanicus himself invaded the lands of the Marsi with a larger army, since Mallovendus, the chief of this nation, had recently surrendered to Rome. Mallovendus claimed that one of the eagle (battle standards) belonging to Varus' legions had been concealed in nearby woods (probably a sacred Germanic site). According to reports, the eagle was guarded by only a small hostile force. Germanicus immediately sent troops to the location to engage this enemy. Some of the soldiers appeared in front of the wood and others assembled at the rear before entering the trees. (The goddess) Fortuna favoured both divisions and they successfully recovered the eagle.

Sacred Swords (AD 69)

The revered 'Sword of Julius Caesar' was kept at the Temple of Mars in Colonia Agrippina (Cologne). Colonia Agrippina was founded by the Romans for

German tribesmen resettled on the west banks of the Rhine. When the Rhine commander Vitellius was declared emperor, he was given this 'Sword of Caesar'.

217 Suetonius, *Vitellius*, 8
The soldiers hailed Vitellius as emperor. Then he was carried about the main population centres holding the drawn sword of the Deified Julius. Someone had taken this sword from the Shrine of Mars and handed it to him when he was first acclaimed (as emperor).

Trophies for the Mars Temple at Colonia Agrippina

Roman Civil War (AD 69)

Vitellius inspected the battlefield where his imperial rival Otho had committed suicide. His Rhineland forces included numerous Germans.

218 Suetonius, *Vitellius*, 10
Vitellius finally visited the battlefield. Some shuddered with horror at the rotting corpses. But Vitellius encouraged them with a bold and repulsive comment. He said, 'the odor of dead enemies is sweet, but the odor of fallen fellow-citizens is even sweeter.' Then he openly drained a great draught of unmixed wine to withstand the awful stench. He distributed similar wine draughts to the troops. With equal bad taste and arrogance, Vitellius gazed upon the stone inscribed to the memory of Otho. He declared that Otho deserved such a Mausoleum (a simple, makeshift grave marker). Then he sent the dagger with which his rival had killed himself to the Colony of Agrippina. There the blade was dedicated to Mars (placed in the temple).

Savage Rites

Juvenal mentions the Cimbri in connection to human sacrifice rumoured to be practised by distant savage peoples.

219 Juvenal, *Satires*, 15.100
The ritual practices performed in Egypt are more savage than anything that occurs on the Maeotid altar (human sacrifices near the Azov Sea). If the stories told by the Greek poets are true, then the Egyptians slay their victims, then partake in that accursed Tauric rite (cannibalism). (…) No dreaded Cimbrians, feared Britons, savage Scythians or monstrous Agathyrsians ever raged like this unwarlike and worthless rabble (the Egyptians).

Animal Sacrifice

Account of sixth-century pagan practices among the Alemanni (Germans) settled in Frankish Gaul. Agathias was a Byzantine scholar.

220 Agathias, *The Histories*, 1.6
The Alemanni follow the Frankish system of government and public administration (a Christianised post-Roman state). But they maintain their own religious observances. They worship certain trees, streams, hills, and mountain valleys. They sacrifice horses, cattle, and many other animals to honour these natural features. These animals are beheaded, and by this means the devotees believe they are performing an act of piety.

Germanic Priestesses

221 Strabo, *Geography*, 7.2.3
Earlier writers report the customs of the Cimbri (Greek and Roman authors). It is recorded that Cimbri were accompanied by their wives on their expeditions (mass migrations). They were also attended by priestesses who were seers (able to foretell the future). The seers were grey-haired, clad in white, with flaxen cloaks fastened onto their shoulders with clasps. They wore girdles decorated with bronze, walked barefoot, and carried swords in their hands.

These priestesses moved about the Cimbri camp seeking the prisoners of war (captive Roman soldiers). They crowned some of the captives with wreaths and led them to a giant bronze vessel which had a capacity of about twenty amphorae (a cauldron able to hold 100 litres). The priestess stepped onto a platform raised above the cauldron. The prisoners were brought forwards while the priestess stooped down to cut the throat of each captive. These priestesses predicted the future from the blood which flowed from the victim into the cauldron. Other priestesses cut open the corpse to inspect the entrails (like an animal sacrifice). From these observances they could utter a prophecy of victory for their own people.

During their battles, the priestesses would rhythmically beat on animal hides that had been stretched across the wicker frames of their wagons (a reverberating beat like a giant drum). This produced a fearsome and unearthly noise.

Sacred Cauldrons

222 Strabo, *Geography*, 7.2.1
The Cimbri still live in that country (Jutland) and have recently presented the Emperor Augustus with a sacred cauldron (diplomatic gift). This object was given with a plea for friendship and a request that their earlier offences against the Roman state be forgiven. Their petition was granted, and the Cimbri returned by ship to their homeland (a sailing from the Rhine to Jutland).

Women Augurs

Women had a special status in Germanic religion. Female augurs in the German forces warned their warriors not to fight Julius Caesar until the new moon (Battle of Vosges, 58 BC). This delay would have given the German cavalry time to return to the settler camp. The divine signs were revealed by the casting of runestones or scrying (gazing into a medium such as water).

223 Julius Caesar, *Gallic War*, 1.50
The Romans questioned some German prisoners to discover why Ariovistus did not fight a decisive action. From these reports Caesar discovered the reason. It was a custom among the Germans for their women to make divinations by casting lots to determine whether to engage an enemy force, or not (*sortes* – pieces of stone or wood marked with sacred signs). The women declared that if the Germans fought a battle before the new moon, some divine force had forbidden them to gain a victory.

224 Cassius Dio, *Roman History*, 38.48
While the two armies were encamped opposite one another, the barbarian women conducted divinations (foretelling the future by interpreting natural phenomena). Due to their predictions the women forbade the (German) men to engage in any battle before the appearance of the new moon. Ariovistus always paid great heed to these pronouncements whenever he had to make decisions. Consequently, he did not attack the Romans immediately with his entire force, even though the Romans were already challenging him to battle.

225 Plutarch, *Julius Caesar*, 19
The German war spirit was also diminished by the dire prophecies of their sacred women. These women were able to foretell the future by observing

the currents and eddies in river streams. They saw the signs amid the whirling water and forbade any German to join battle before the new moon cast its first light.

226 Polyaenus, *Strategems*, 8.23.4
Caesar learned that the German augurs (who foretold the future) had forbidden their warriors to fight before the new moon appeared. He therefore seized the first opportunity to advance his army and attack the enemy. This is because he reasoned that the Germans would fight with less eagerness and ferocity if they were acting against the instructions of their augurs.

227 Frontinus, *Stratagems*, 2.1.16 'Choosing the Time for Battle'
When Julius Caesar was in Gaul, he learned that it was a custom and ruling of the German king Ariovistus never to fight when the moon was waning. Caesar therefore chose that time to engage the enemy in battle and he conquered them while they were constrained by superstition (thus proving the belief to be true!).

Prophecies of Veleda: Germanic Priestess

Germanic tribes east of the Rhine were inspired to join the Batavian uprising by the prophesies of a high priestess named Veleda (AD 69–70). Tacitus also mentions a seeress named Aurinia who might have been the holy woman encountered by Drusus at the Elbe River.

228 Tacitus, *Germania*, 8
The Germans believe that women possess a certain sanctity, and intuition (knowledge of future events?). Therefore, they do not dismiss or despise their advice, or ridicule their suggestions. During the time of the Emperor Vespasian, many of the Germans regarded the priestess Veleda as a divinity. In former times, the Germans also venerated Aurinia and many other women. But this worship did not involve servile flattery or sham deification.

229 Tacitus, *Histories*, 4.61
According to ancient custom the Germans believed that many of their women had prophetic powers. This superstition grew in strength until some women were regarded as possessing actual divinity. Veleda was a maiden of the Bructeri tribe who had extensive influence over her people. The authority of Veleda had now reached its height because she had foretold

the success of the Germans and the destruction of the legions. A captured legate (senior commander) of one defeated legion, named Munius Lupercus, was sent along with other trophies to Veleda (a Germanic priestess). But Lupercus was murdered on the journey to reach Veleda (perhaps an attempted escape, failed rescue, or Roman ambush).

Power of the Priestess

During the Batavian Revolt, the Ubii (Germans settled on the Roman frontier) reached a political agreement with the Tencteri (kinsmen living in neighbouring Germania). The priestess Veleda was named as an arbitrator in any disputes (AD 69).

230 Tacitus, *Histories*, 4.64
(The Ubii declared):

> Civilis (the Batavian commander) and Veleda (the priestess) will act as arbiters in any disputes between us. Under their sanction our treaty shall be ratified.

The Tencteri were appeased by this statement and ambassadors were sent with gifts to Civilis and Veleda. Everything was therefore concluded satisfactorily for the inhabitants of the colony.

But they were not allowed to approach or directly address Veleda, who dwelt in a high tower. They were prevented from seeing her in order to enhance the respect and reverence in which she was held. One of her relatives was appointed to convey messages to her. This messenger acted like the representative of a god, conveying questions, and returning with divine responses.

A Valuable Offering

During the Batavian War, the Germans managed to capture the flagship war galley of the Rhine River Fleet (AD 69–70).

231 Tacitus, *Histories*, 5.22
In full daylight, the enemy rowed the captured Roman vessels back to their own territory. But they towed the praetorian trireme up the river Lupia as an offering to Veleda (the Germanic priestess).

Scene of warriors fighting bulls on the Gundestrup Cauldron, found in northern Denmark. The silver panels display Celtic-style artwork and may date to about 100 BC.

A warrior youth fights a bull. Inner base of the Gundestrup Cauldron.

Roman relief depicting a northern European fighting a legionary, second century AD (found in the Forum of Trajan, currently in the Louvre, Paris).

Germans depicted on the Portonaccio Sarcophagus, AD 180 (Museo Nazionale Romano).

Head of a Suebic German depicted on the Mušov Cauldron – a Roman bronze cauldron found in the grave of a Germanic chief, from the second century AD.

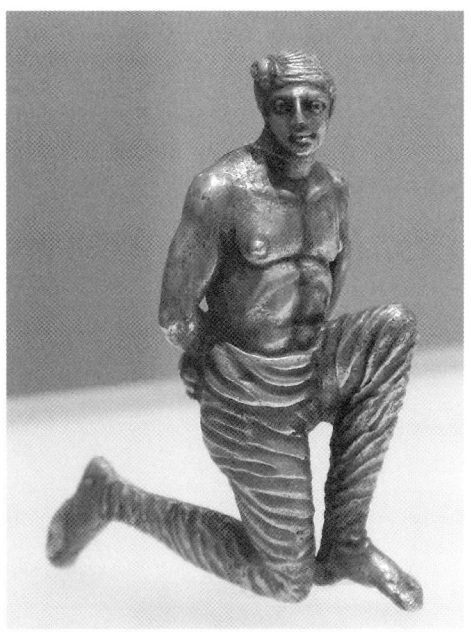

Bronze figurine of a Germanic warrior (National History Museum of Romania).

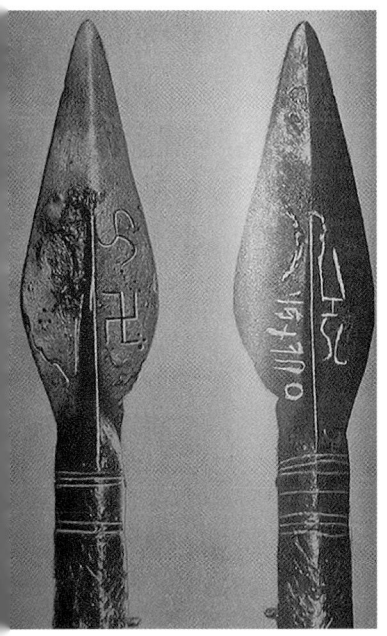

German spear carved with the sacred image of a fylfot and triskele, first century AD.

Gravestone of a Roman cavalryman named Titus Flavius Bassus (Cologne).

Roman gate pillar depicting Germanic captives (Landesmuseum, Mainz).

Roman Triumphal Arch of Orange, depicting captured North European war gear including shields and animal standards, 27 BC–AD 14.

Silver denarius of the Emperor Augustus: Germanic Surrender, 12 BC.

Silver Roman cavalry helmet found in Batavian territory at Waal, near Nijmegen (Valkhof Museum).

Roman silver drinking cup depicting King Priam of Troy appealing to Achilles for the return of his son Hector's body. Found in a Germanic chieftain's grave at Hoby, Denmark, from the first century BC. The Greek champion Achilles is depicted as Augustus and the cup was possibly a diplomatic gift.

Germanic chiefs depicted on Trajan's Column, AD 113.

Germanic warriors depicted on Trajan's Column.

A Roman attack including Germanic warriors, depicted on Trajan's Column.

Roman auxiliary cavalry, perhaps Batavians, depicted on Trajan's Column.

Germanic bodyguard on Trajan's Column.

Capture of Veleda

The Germanic seeress Veleda was taken into Roman custody by Rutilius Gallicus, governor of Germania Inferior (North Rhine) (AD 76–78).

232 Statius, Silvae, 1.4.89–93
'To Rutilius Gallicus on his Recovery from Illness'
There is insufficient time to describe how the northern armies repelled the Rhine (Germanic attacks). The latest and greatest glory has been the prayers of the captive Veleda.

Fate of Veleda

Veleda may have been detained in Ardea, near Rome. She was possibly employed as an oracle delivering prophesies at a temple sanctuary. A fragmentary Greek inscription was found at temple ruins in the town, probably a satirical verse. The emperor, or some other concerned authority, poses a question to the oracle:

233 Greek Inscription, *L'Annee Epigraphique*, 1953.25
'What should be done concerning the tall maiden whom the Rhine dwellers worship? For they shudder at the thundering of her golden voice.'

Germanic Seeress

The Emperor Domitian was visited by a Germanic seeress (AD 81–96).

234 Cassius Dio, *Roman History*, 67.8
Domitian was visited by Masyus, the king of the Semnones, and Ganna, a maiden priestess from Germany. Ganna had succeeded Veleda (as chief seeress east of the Rhine). After being honoured by Domitian they returned home.

A Supernatural Warning

According to Cassius Dio, the Roman general Drusus halted his conquests at the river Elbe when he saw a supernatural female figure who commanded him to halt. Drusus suffered a mortal injury and died shortly afterwards (9 BC).

235 Cassius Dio, *Roman History*, 55.1–2

But Drusus paid no heed to these warnings. Instead, he invaded the country of the Chatti and advanced as far as the territory of the Suebi (tribes in inner Germany). It was difficult to traverse these territories and the Romans only defeated the attacking Germans after much bloodshed. From there Drusus entered the country of the Cherusci and crossed the Visurgis River (the Weser). The Roman army plundered everything in the region as it advanced as far as the Albis (the Elbe). The Elbe rises in the Vandalic Mountains (*Riesengebirge*) and becomes a mighty river before it empties into the northern ocean. Drusus wanted to cross this river, but he failed in the attempt. It is said that a woman of superhuman size approached Drusus at the river and commanded:

> Drusus, where are you rushing to reach with such eagerness? It is not your fate to see lands beyond here. Depart from this place, for your efforts and your life are nearly at their end.

The Emperor Acknowledged as a Divinity

The imperial prince Tiberius reached the Elbe when he campaigned in Germania (8–7 BC). The German tribes east of the Rhine may have ascribed divine aspects to the imperial household. Velleius Paterculus was a direct eyewitness to these events.

236 Velleius Paterculus, *History of Rome*, 2.107

These were indeed great events, but I must mention a small incident. When we were encamped on the western bank of the Elbe, we could see the weapons of the enemy warriors glinting on the far side. It seemed that they might flee with every unexpected movement or manoeuvre of our vessels. Then one of the barbarians, who was very tall and elderly, approached the river. To judge from his clothing, he was of high status. This man climbed into a canoe, made in the German manner from a hollowed log. On this strange craft he embarked from the far riverbank and manoeuvred out to the middle of the stream. From there he asked permission to land without harm on the shore which was occupied by our troops. He wanted to see Tiberius Caesar and he was granted this request. The German beached his canoe and was brought before Tiberius. He stared at the commander for a long time in complete silence. Then he said:

Our young warriors must be insane. When you are absent, they venerate you as a divine being. But when you are present, they fear your armies, instead of invoking your divine protection. With your permission I will speak, and I will say, Caesar – today I have seen the gods that I once merely heard about. And in my life thus far, I have never hoped for, or experienced, a happier day.

The German asked for, and received permission, to touch the hand of Tiberius Caesar. Then he went back to his canoe and began his return crossing. All the way across he continued to gaze back at Caesar until he had landed on his own bank (on the far side of the Elbe).

German Participation in the Imperial Cult (AD 9)

Segestes was a young German hostage from the Cherusci nation. He was detained by Roman authorities near Cologne (Oppidum Ubiorum, Rhine frontier).

237 Tacitus, *Annals*, 1.59

Among the envoys was Segestes, son of Segimundus, but the youth was reluctant to engage with the Romans due to his shame and guilt. For when the revolt occurred in Germany (AD 9), Segimundus had been serving as a priest at the altar of the Ubii (a site devoted to the Imperial Cult on the west bank of the Rhine). But when he heard about the uprising, he had torn apart the sacred garlands and fled to the rebels.

Death of Domitian Foretold

The death of the Emperor Domitian was foreseen by a Germanic seer. The Romans believed that dreams could forewarn people of danger.

238 Suetonius, *Domitian*, 16

(The night before his death) at about midnight, Domitian leapt from his bed in terror. The next morning, he conducted the trial of a soothsayer sent from Germany. This man had been consulted about lightning strikes and announced that these events signalled a change of rulers. Domitian therefore condemned him to death.

239 Cassius Dio, *Roman History*, 67.16

No event of such great magnitude occurs unforeseen, and various unfavourable omens signalled the fate of Domitian. (…) The most remarkable circumstance was the following. In the province of Germany (the Rhineland) a man named Larginus Proculus had publicly proclaimed that the emperor would die on a certain day (a possibly seditious action requiring state investigation). He was sent to Rome by the provincial governor and when he was brought before Domitian he made the same declaration. He was therefore condemned to death, but his execution was postponed so that he might die after the emperor had escaped the danger (the predicted day having passed, and the prediction shown to be false). But Domitian was killed on the predicted day and Proculus was therefore spared. He received 400,000 sesterces from Nerva (the succeeding emperor, who recognised his talent as a seer).

The Hanged Man

Herod Agrippa encountered a German prisoner who foretold his fate. The image of a man hanging from a tree appears in Germanic paganism and the owl is sacred to the Greek goddess Athena.

240 Josephus, *Antiquities*, 18.5.5; 18.6.7

Herod Agrippa (the Jewish prince) had a strong friendship with Caligula (the imperial heir). Once, when they were riding in a chariot and discussing matters, Agrippa uttered a prayer to God that, 'Tiberius might die soon and leave the Roman government to Caligula, who was truly worthy of this role.' This comment was overheard by a freedman of Agrippa named Eutychus (leading to the arrest of Agrippa). (…)

Agrippa stood bound in chains in front of the imperial palace along with many other prisoners (men accused of disloyalty, war captives and criminals). In tiredness and grief, he leaned heavily against a tree. Then an owl landed in the branches. One of the other prisoners was a German, and when he saw the bird he turned to the soldier he was chained to and asked, 'Who is that man dressed in purple?' (the royal colour). He was told that the man was a Jew named Agrippa, one of the principal men of his nation. The German asked the soldier holding his chains if he could approach Agrippa and speak directly to him about his country. The soldier agreed and the German spoke to Agrippa through an interpreter. He said:

> Youth, you have suffered a great adversity with this sudden reversal of fortune. And so, you will not believe me when I foretell your fate. Your grief will soon end. You are protected by a divine providence which

will preserve and provide for you. I therefore appeal to the gods of my homeland (the Germanic deities) and the enslaving gods of this place (the Roman Pantheon) for you to accept my message. My words are not given for reward, flattery, or to give you hope without cause. For futile hope causes greater grief and bitterness when expectations fail. But I must put myself at risk and tell you the prediction of the gods (as revealed by the owl omen).

You will not be held in chains for long. You will soon be released and promoted to the highest dignity. You will have power and authority that will be envied by all who now pity your misfortune. You will be blessed and happy until your death. Your future children will inherit your good fortune. But remember. When you see this bird again (the owl) you will have only five days left to live. This is foretold by the god who has sent the bird to you as a sign. It is unjust for me to withhold this prediction from you. For this knowledge of future good fortune will allow you to endure your current hardship. But when you receive these rewards, do not forget the misery that I am suffering and deliver me from my captivity.

(Possibly a reference to *Genesis* 40:14 – 'When all goes well with you, remember me and show me kindness; mention me to Pharaoh and take me out of this prison.')

When the German had said this, Agrippa laughed at his comments (a dismissal). But later, these words proved worthy of great admiration.

241 Josephus, *Antiquities*, 18.8.2

When King Agrippa had reigned in Judea for three years, he visited Caesaria. (…) He entered the theatre (a Greek venue) in the early morning so that his garment could be illuminated by the rising sun. The radiant light made people look away from his awe-inspiring form and amid the crowd, flatterers cried out that he was a divine being. (…) Agrippa did nothing to rebuke their impious flattery (blasphemies against the true God). But when he looked up, he saw an owl perched on a rigging rope high above his head. He immediately realised that this bird was the messenger of misfortune, just as it had earlier foretold good tidings (when he was a captive in Rome). Agrippa fell into the deepest sorrow when a severe and violent pain struck his stomach. (…) he was carried into the royal palace as word spread that his death was imminent, and inevitable.

Reverence for Leaders

Attempted Killing of Gaius Marius by a German Slave (88 BC)

In 88 BC, the Roman general Gaius Marius supported a political faction that seized power in the Roman state. When the rival general Sulla marched his legions on Rome, Marius fled, but was detained at Minturnae (a town in southern Italy).

242 Velleius Paterculus, *History of Rome*, 2.19
Marius had held six consulships and was now more than 70 years old. Pursued by the cavalry of Sulla, he hid in the reed marsh at Marica with only his head above water. But he was dragged from this hiding place naked and covered with mud. Then a rope was fixed around his neck, and he was detained at Minturnae in the custody of its *Duumvir* (leading town magistrate).

A public slave of German nationality was given a sword and told to put Marius to death. This man had been taken prisoner by Marius when he was commander in the Roman war against the Cimbri. When the German recognised Marius, he was indignant and uttered a loud outcry concerning the plight of this great man. He immediately threw away his sword and fled from the place.

243 Plutarch, *Marius*, 39
The magistrates and councillors of Minturnae debated what should be done with Marius. They decided that he should be immediately put to death, but none of the citizens would undertake the task. It is said that a horseman, either a Gaul or a Cimbrian, received a sword and was sent into the room where Marius was being held. Marius was lying in the shadows of a poorly lit cell. As the barbarian approached, his prone form suddenly appeared wakeful. His eyes gleamed with light and a loud voice called out, 'Do you dare kill Gaius Marius?' The barbarian fled the room, throwing his sword down upon the ground as he dashed from the building. He uttered only one cry as he fled: 'I cannot kill Gaius Marius.'

Emperor or Priestess?

Towards the end of the Batavian Revolt, the Rhineland population began to doubt their allegiance to the priestess Veleda (an embodiment of Germanic religion). Instead, they started to speak in favour of the emperors (a return to imperial allegiance).

244 Tacitus, *Histories*, 5.25

'Consider the Rhaetians and Noricans (subject nations in the Swiss Alps and Austria). Think of the burdens endured by the other allies of Rome (as taxpayers). We are not subject to tribute requirements, except a payment of manhood and valour (military recruits). This is the closest we will come to liberty, and if we must choose between masters, it is more honourable to select the emperors of Rome, rather than some German women (the priestesses).'

These were the words of the lower classes, but the Batavian nobles used fiercer language.

Funerals

245 Tacitus, *Germania*, 27

The Germans display no great pageantry or pomp in their funerals. It is their custom to burn the bodies of esteemed men with certain kinds of wood. They do not dress the dead in expensive garments or heap great quantities of expensive incense on the funeral pyre (Roman customs). Only the weapons of the dead man and sometimes his horse are consumed by the fire. The Germans mark the grave site with a mound which serves as a tomb. They do not erect large and elaborate funeral monuments for the deceased (a Roman practice). They regard these monuments to be somehow oppressive to the dead. They soon cease from tears and lamentations (acts of public sorrow), but genuine grief and sorrow is slow to leave them. The Germans think it is appropriate for women to lament the deceased, but men should honour the dead through solemn remembrance.

Lamentations

Battle of Aquae Sextiae (102 BC)

246 Plutarch, *Marius*, 20

The Ambrones who had survived the battle had joined the main host (the Tuetones) and their cries of grief could be heard all night. Their lamentations did not resemble the mournful groans of ordinary men (Romans in grief). The Ambrones howled and bellowed like wild beasts, while uttering threats and cries of sorrow. The sound came from such a vast multitude that it echoed among the surrounding hills and reverberated down the river valley. The whole plain was filled with this terrible sound which provoked great fear among the Romans.

Chapter Twelve

Germanic Politics and Law

Julius Caesar gave an account of Germanic politics based on direct experience.

247 Julius Caesar, *Gallic War*, 6.23
When the tribal states engage in war, either to attack or to resist a hostile enemy, they appoint military leaders to direct the conflict. These leaders have the power of life and death (they can execute kinsmen).

248 Julius Caesar, *Gallic War*, 6.26
In peacetime there is no general officer of state (a supreme magistrat). But the chiefs of districts and cantons impose justice among their followers and settle disputes (the role of judges). Those who commit acts of brigandage outside the borders of their states do not suffer disgrace (impunity for raids). In fact, the Germans affirm that these actions are necessary to give the young men military practice and discourage idleness.

Any one of the chiefs can declare in a Public Assembly that he will be their leader. He will announce, 'Let those who will follow me give their approval.' Then all who approve his cause will stand and declare their service, promising their assistance and guaranteeing the general praise of the populace. Anyone who does not follow the new leader after this popular ascent is reckoned to be a deserter or traitor and all trust is denied to them (social exclusion).

Tacitus describes German councils that decided political affairs, confirmed status and determined punishments.

249 Tacitus, *Germania*, 11–13
The German attitude to liberty has its disadvantages, as the masses do not meet simultaneously when they are required. Instead, two or three days are wasted in delays as the populace gradually assembles. When the multitude have gathered in sufficient numbers, they set down their weapons. Then priests who keep order at these meetings will proclaim silence. Each king or chief will speak according to age, nobility, distinction in war, or eloquence. Their status is due to their influence and persuasive force, rather than their

power to command (state titles and official positions). If the crowd reject the sentiments in the speeches, they will express their displeasure with murmurs. If they are satisfied and agree, they will take up their weapons. The greatest form of assent and approval is made when the men brandish their spears.

German councils decide verdicts in criminal cases involving the death penalty. Penalties are selected according to the offence and traitors and deserters are hanged on trees. Cowards, unwarlike men and male homosexuals are plunged into the bogland (areas of boggy or muddy ground). They are held down with wicker hurdles (death by drowning). This difference in execution is because the Germans believe that some punishments must be exposed to public display, but certain shameful acts must be concealed, even when being punished.

People convicted of lesser offences can be given more lenient sentences, including a fine involving a number of horses, or cattle. Half of the fine is paid to the king or to the state, and the other half is received by the person who has been wronged or their relatives. The Germans also elect their chief magistrates in these councils. These men administer law in the tribal districts and settlements. Each of these magistrates has 100 associates chosen from people who will support him with advice and influence.

The Germans transact every public and private business while armed. However, it is not usual for a man to carry a weapon before the state has recognised and approved his permission to use them. This occurs in the presence of the council when a young man is equipped with a shield and a spear by one of the chiefs, or the young man's father, or some other kinsman. These weapons are what the 'toga' is for us (a symbol of free citizen status and rights). The weapons are the first independent honour which a German youth receives. Until this moment he is considered part of a household, but afterwards he becomes a member of their shared commonwealth.

If the father is of noble birth or has rendered great services for his tribe, then he may secure the rank of chief for his son. These youths attach themselves to men of well-advanced power and long-standing valour. It is not shameful in their society to be seen as followers of these men. There are gradations of rank among those who escort the chief, and some men are selected for higher positions. The followers contest fiercely against one another to determine who will have the highest rank. The chiefs also compete against one another to decide who has the bravest and most numerous followers. Any chief who is surrounded by a large body of elite youths possesses great honour and at the same time maintains a strong reserve of fighting strength. These attendants are ornamental in peace and a defence in war.

German Chiefs and Warfare

Tacitus explains the role and duties of German chiefs.

250 Tacitus, *Germania*, 14–15

The renown and glory of a chief is recognised by his own tribe and in neighbouring states. Consequently, such a leader is sought out by embassies and honoured with gifts. The prestige of his name being attached to a dispute will often settle a war. When the Germans go into battle, it is a disgrace for a chief to be surpassed in valour. It is also a disgrace for his followers not to equal the valour of their chief. Followers who witness the death of their chief, and leave the combat with his death unavenged, will suffer ignominy and lifelong reproach. The height of loyalty is to defend and to protect the chief and add their own brave deeds to his great renown. The chief fights for victory and his followers fight for their chief.

Sometimes, after a prolonged peace, a German state will develop a lack of interest in war. On these occasions the noble youths will voluntarily seek out tribes that are waging war because inaction is offensive to the German people. The youths reckon they can easily win renown by confronting threats and dangers, so chiefs realise that to maintain a numerous and vigorous following, they too must engage in violence and warfare.

Warriors depend on the generosity of their chief to provide their warhorse and the cavalry spear that they will hold aloft in bloodstained victory. The chiefs provide great feasts and entertainments that are not elegant (by Roman standards), but well furnished with plentiful offerings. These gatherings are the only pay and reward the followers receive. The feasts are the bounty provided by war and plunder. These warriors are not easily persuaded to plough the earth and wait for the next year's produce to emerge. They would rather challenge an enemy for the produce he has gathered and earn the honour of being wounded in the process. These warriors think it is foolish to toil in the fields for what they can acquire through bloodshed.

When they are not fighting, the Germans spend much of their time hunting, or devote time to sleeping and to feasting. The bravest and the most warlike men perform no other tasks. They surrender the management of their entire household, both home and land, to women, old men, and the weakest members of their family. They enjoy leisure, but in a strange combination of motives, they abhor peace.

It is the custom for the German states to voluntarily gift cattle or grain to the chiefs. This is accepted as an honour and supplies the needs and requirements of the chief. Chiefs are especially pleased when they receive gifts from neighbouring tribes, either from individuals or from adjoining states. The gifts include select steeds, armour, neck-chains (torcs) and other symbols of rank. We have also taught them to accept Roman money.

Diplomatic Gifts to the Germans

In about AD 55, Pliny the Elder saw a Roman governor transporting a large quantity of fine silverware to his provincial command in Germania Inferior (North Rhine frontier). Some of these items might have been intended as gifts to Germanic chiefs.

251 Tacitus, *Germania*, 5
Roman envoys have presented their chiefs with costly silver drinking vessels, but only to find these gifts being used and abused like cheap clay pots.

252 Pliny, *Natural History*, 33.50
Pompeius Paulinus was the son of a Roman *equites* (the lesser nobility) from Arelate (Arles, in southern Gaul). On his father's side he was descended from a tribe who wore simple animal hides. But when I saw Paulinus he was transporting 12,000-pound weight of silver tableware to his posting (as governor of Germania Inferior). He brought this consignment on military service, alongside an army tasked with confronting the most ferocious tribes.

Chapter Thirteen

Germanic Chiefs, Warlords and Kings

In about 60 BC, the Germanic king Ariovistus crossed the Rhine and settled his followers in eastern Gaul. In this era, the Roman Empire only controlled the southern part of Gaul as a province (Gallia Narbonensis). But the Senate tried to bring the Germans into their network of allies by granting Ariovistus status as a 'friend' of Rome.

> **253 Cassius Dio, *Roman History*, 38.34**
> Ariovistus was the ruler of these Germans (settled west of the Rhine) and his authority had been fully confirmed by the Roman state. During his consulship, Julius Caesar had even formally acknowledged Ariovistus among the political 'friends' and allies of Rome. But this status had to be compared with the glory and power that could be derived from war. The general therefore dismissed previous considerations and used existing arrangements to provoke a quarrel with the barbarian (chief). Caesar did not want to be seen as the aggressor, so he required an excuse for the conflict.
>
> Caesar summoned Ariovistus, pretending that he wished to have a conference with him. But instead of obeying, Ariovistus replied:
>
>> If Caesar wants to say something to me, let him come to me in person. I am not inferior to him in any way. If a man needs the help of another, he should go himself to that person.

Caesar's Plans

Cassius Dio presents Caesar's intentions.

> **254 Cassius Dio, *Roman History*, 38.35**
> (Caesar spoke): 'We can also gain further confidence from what we know about Ariovistus. He has never united his people or unified their armed forces. Even now he does not expect a serious war and he is utterly unprepared. His countrymen (Germans east of the Rhine) will not assist him even if he makes them tempting offers. Who would choose to be his ally and fight against us, when they have suffered no injury from us?

Instead, they should cooperate with us. They could remove a despotic ruler on their very borders and obtain a share of his territory from us.'

Royal Captives

Ariovistus escaped the battle, but the Romans captured members of his family (Battle of Vosges, 58 BC).

255 Orosius, *History*, 6.7
Ariovistus seized a small boat and escaped across the Rhine to Germany, but he abandoned his two wives and both daughters, who were captured by the Romans.

Augustan Policy: Envoys Detained

The Emperor Augustus oversaw the Roman conquest of Germany (12–8 BC). Envoys were detained and the sons of subdued chieftains sent to Rome as political hostages to be indoctrinated into Roman customs.

256 Cassius Dio, *Roman History*, 55.6
After a second period of ten years in power, Augustus launched a further campaign against the Germans. He himself remained in Roman territory, while Tiberius crossed the Rhine (entering Germania). All the barbarians, except the Sugambri, became afraid and requested peace. But their offers were declined since Augustus refused to finalise a truce with any of them until the Sugambri conceded.

The Sugambri had sent envoys, but the negotiations were so far from completion that Augustus arrested all the German representatives. Numerous distinguished envoys from Germany were sent to various Roman cities and many of them died during detainment. This is because the detainees became so greatly distressed at their confinement that they committed suicide. Afterwards the Sugambri remained subdued for a time, but later they gained revenge on the Romans for this misfortune.

Arminius

Arminius was the son of a Cherusci chief raised in Rome. But he retained his national identity and plotted against imperial rule. His time for action came at the Battle of Teutoburg Forest when his coalition of free Germans ambushed and annihilated three Roman legions (AD 9).

257 Velleius Paterculus, *History of Rome*, 2.118

At this time a royal leader emerged from among the German nation. He was a young nobleman named Arminius, the son of Segimer. Arminius was courageous in action, mentally alert and possessed an intelligence far superior to ordinary barbarians. These attributes were clear from his appearance and mannerisms for his eyes glimmered with a fierce intellect.

Although still a young man, Arminius had accompanied and assisted the Roman forces on many military campaigns. He had therefore been granted equestrian status (an award of second-rank Roman nobility). But he used his position, and the negligence of the Roman commander, as an opportunity for treachery. Arminius astutely realised that an unwary man is quickly overpowered and defeated. Most disasters begin when a victim, with a full sense of security, encounters an unseen danger.

Flavus and Arminius

Other Cherusci nobles remained loyal to Rome and fought in the Roman campaigns to recover Germania (AD 15).

258 Tacitus, *Annals*, 2.8–11

The Visurgis River (the Weser) flowed between the Roman position and the Cherusci (the leading enemy tribe). On its banks stood Arminius (the enemy war leader) with the other Cherusci chiefs. Arminius asked whether Germanicus had arrived and when he received verification he asked to speak to his brother, surnamed Flavus, who was with the Roman army. Flavus was famous for his loyalty to Rome. He had even lost an eye when wounded a few years earlier while fighting in the service of Tiberius.

Flavus received permission to approach Arminius. Arminius had his guards move some distance away. He also required that the Roman bowmen arrayed across the far bank should move out of range. Then Arminius saluted his brother and the two men met (with the river between them). Arminius asked his brother about the scar which disfigured his face. Flavus told him about the injury and the battle site in which he had received the wound. Arminius asked him what reward he had received for this military service. Flavus spoke of increased pay, a necklet, a crown, and other military decorations (awards for gallantry). Arminius jeered at his brother for accepting such a meagre recompense for voluntary slavery.

A disagreement ensued. Flavus spoke of the greatness of Rome and the immense resources commanded by Caesar Germanicus. He said that the vanquished would soon suffer a dreadful punishment, but mercy was available to those who surrendered. He told Arminius that his wife and son (still held captive in Rome) were not being treated as enemies. In response Arminius reminded his brother of his duty to his fatherland and his ancestral freedom. He called upon the gods and homesteads of Germany. He spoke of the mother who shared his hope that Flavus would not desert and betray his people. Flavus might still rule amid his relatives and kinsfolk (as a free German).

Bitter words were spoken, and an argument began. The outraged Flavus called for his weapons and horse. He might have charged across the stream to fight his brother, if Stertinius had not dashed forwards and put his hand on his shoulder to reassure and restrain him. Meanwhile Arminius faced him across the river, making menacing gestures and challenging him to combat. Much of what he said was in Roman speech (the Latin language) since Arminius had served in our military camps as leader of his kinsmen (Germanic auxiliaries).

Royal Captives: Triumph in Rome

Strabo was writing while these campaigns were ongoing. He was not aware that Roman efforts to recover Germania would be permanently abandoned by Tiberius (AD 17).

259 Strabo, *Geography*, 7.1.4

The Romans believe that distrust is the best tactic for dealing with the German tribes. For good faith and trust has caused the Romans the greatest harm. As an example, the Cherusci and their subjects violated their treaties with Rome. Three Roman legions, including their general Quintilius Varus, were destroyed in an ambush by these tribes.

But, they all paid the penalty for this action when the younger Germanicus won a great military campaign against them. Their renown people were captured and led in triumph through Rome. This included the chief of the Cherusci, Segimuntus son of Segestes. It also included Thusnelda the wife of Armenius, the Germanic war leader who violated the treaty against Varus. Thusnelda's 3-year-old son Thumelicus was also paraded in the triumph. Armenius still leads the war against Rome. Other captives included a leader of the Cherusci named Sesithacus, son of Segimerus and his wife Rhamis. A daughter of the Chatti chief Ucromirus appeared in the triumph, along with a Sugambri chief named Deudorix (Theodoric), the son of Baetorix who was the brother of Melo.

Segestes, the father-in-law of Armenius, opposed his kinsmen when they decided to launch a war against Rome. At an opportune moment he deserted them to support the Empire. Consequently, he was guest of honour at the Roman triumph that celebrated the capture of his kinsfolk.

Prisoners from other plundered tribes were led in the procession including captives from the Caulci, Campsani, Bructeri, Usipii, Cherusci, Chatti, Chattuarii, Landi and Tubattii. A priest of the Chatti named Libes was also led captive in that triumph.

Tiberius Abandons Conquest Plans

In AD 17, the Emperor Tiberius instructed the Roman commander Germanicus to halt his German campaigns. The military operations of AD 16 had involved fleet transports and Tiberius refers to severe storms that had inflicted high-level losses on the campaign forces.

260 Tacitus, *Annals***, 2.26**
'You have now had sufficient success and enough disasters. You have fought victorious battles on a great scale. But consider the losses which the winds and waves have inflicted. They are not your fault as a general, but they are still grievous and shocking.

'I, Tiberius, was sent nine times into Germany by the Emperor Augustus (as a military commander). But I achieved more from political diplomacy than from military operations. I secured the submission of the Sugambri by negotiation. By similar means I compelled the Suebi with their king Maroboduus to accept peace terms. The vengeance of Rome has now been satisfied (revenge for the Varus disaster). The Cherusci and the other insurgent tribes can now be left to their own internal feuds.'

The Marcomannic Kingdom

The Marcomannic kingdom dominated southern Germany and endangered the Danube frontier. The Romans were able to install a Germanic ruler in the territory who had been raised in Rome.

261 Strabo, *Geography***, 7.1.3**
As a young man Maroboduus was sent to Rome (as a political hostage) where he enjoyed the favour of the Emperor Augustus. The Romans promoted Maroboduus as a king and returned him to Germany as ruler of the Marcomannic state.

Conquest Plans

The Romans were planning to fully conquer the Marcomannic kingdom in AD 6, but the build-up of troops caused the Great Illyricum Revolt (AD 6–9). Then the Teutoburg massacre expelled Roman forces from Greater Germania.

262 Velleius Paterculus, *History of Rome*, 2.108

Nothing remained to be conquered in Germany except for the Marcomannic population (Bohemia, southern Germany). Their leader Maroboduus had instructed his people to leave their settlements (near the Danube frontier) and head inland to the clearings that were protected by the Hercynian Forest. Maroboduus was from a noble barbarian family. He was physically powerful and courageous, but he also had a superior intelligence (possessing an aptitude for strategic political thinking). He exploited internal disorders that occurred among the Marcomanni.

Either by chance, or the impulsiveness of his subjects, Maroboduus gained a position among his people that exceeded that of an ordinary chieftain. He began to conceive an idea that he could form a definite empire and assume royal powers. To fulfil this ambition, he moved the Marcomanni far away from Roman power (the Danube frontier). He thought that by escaping the reach of the Roman military, he could develop his own population into an all-powerful regional force. Moving the Marcomanni northwards (to the Hercynian Forest), Maroboduus used warfare to reduce all the neighbouring tribes into subjugation, or else he brought them under his sovereignty by treaty.

Maroboduus also developed a company of guards to protect his new kingdom. Due to constant training, these men almost reached the Roman standard of discipline. Their existence placed Maroboduus in a position of exceptional power and made his kingdom a threat to our empire. His policy towards Rome was to avoid provoking any war, but at the same time he made it clear that he had the power and will to resist any aggression brought by the Empire. The envoys who Maroboduus sent to the Caesars sometimes presented him as a suppliant and at other times spoke as though he was their equal (holding royal power equivalent to an imperial prince). Soon individuals and entire tribes who revolted from Rome found a safe refuge in his domains. So, his kingdom became a rival of Rome, but with little concealment of its character. Maroboduus increased his army to include 70,000 infantry and 4,000 cavalry. He trained this army through constant wars against neighbouring tribes, and it seemed that he was developing this force for some greater undertaking.

After Teutoberg

The Marcomannic king Maroboduus chose not to support Arminius in his revolt against Rome. He rejected the severed head of Varus, the Roman commander defeated in the Teutoburg Battle by Arminius (AD 9).

263 Velleius Paterculus, *History of Rome*, 2.119
The partially burned body of Varus was retrieved by the enemy. They further mutilated and mangled the corpse. Finally, they severed its head and sent it as a prize to Maroboduus (the king of the Marcomanni in Bohemia). Maroboduus (who was still allied to Rome) sent the remains to Augustus. Though Varus had caused a great disaster, the emperor ensured that the remains were interred with honour in his family tomb.

Roman Interference

Emperor Tiberius, AD 18

In AD 18, the son of the Emperor Tiberius, Drusus Julius Caesar, was holding a military command in Illyricum (territories south of the Danube). He lent his support to an uprising against Maroboduus.

264 Tacitus, *Annals*, 2.62–63
Drusus gained further glory by creating political discord among the Germans. He urged them to complete the destruction of Maroboduus, who was already gravely weakened (as ruler of the Suebic Marcomanni – a powerful South German tribe). Maroboduus had forced a young dissident nobleman named Catualda into exile. He had taken refuge among the Gotones (a Germanic tribe living east of the Vistula River) and now that fortunes of the king were declining, Catualda decided to return and seek his revenge.

Catualda led a strong force of warriors into the territory of the Marcomanni. By using corruption, he induced many of the nobles to support him (probably bribes and pay-offs). They suddenly surged into the palace and the adjacent fortress and seized the long-accumulated plunder of this Suebic realm.

Former Roman Soldiers as Adversaries

In AD 47, the Roman general Corbulo had to deal with a German warlord who had served in the Roman military.

265 Tacitus, *Annals*, 11.18
The Chauci raided the province (Germania Inferior, North Rhine) under the leadership of Gannascus. Gannascus was of Canninefate ancestry (German allies in the Rhine Delta) and he had served as an auxiliary in the Roman army. But he had deserted and gathered a piratical fleet of light vessels to raid the coast of Gaul, as he was well acquainted with these peaceful and prosperous regions (west of the Rhine).

Romanised Kings

In AD 47, a Roman citizen of Germanic origin became king of the Cherusci, with the approval and support of the Emperor Claudius.

266 Tacitus, *Annals*, 11.16–17
That same year, the Cherusci tribe asked the Romans for a king (from the political hostages retained in Rome). The other noblemen had been killed during their internal conflicts and only one single member of the royal household remained. This was Italicus ('the Italian') who was residing in Rome (as a citizen). He was a son of Arminius' brother Flavus, while his mother was Actumerus, chief of the Chatti. He was handsome, skilled with weapons and well-practised at horsemanship, in both Roman and native (Germanic) traditions.

The Emperor Claudius granted him money (finances) and provided a retinue (a team of guards and advisors). He urged Italicus to accept the honour of his heritage with confidence. Other people who were living in the city as political hostages (client princes) had taken power in foreign kingdoms. But Italicus was the first person born in Rome to leave the city and ascend to a foreign throne (independent of the client system).

Initially the Germans greeted the arrival of Italicus with joy. He had not been involved in their earlier disputes (factional conflicts) and could therefore enjoy the support of the entire population. Admirers crowded around this prince who sometimes engaged in inoffensive displays of courtesy and moderation (acting like an ordinary tribesman). But he often engaged in the drunken and lustful behaviour that the barbarians value.

As his reputation spread, those who mistrusted him went to neighbouring tribes for support (dissidents seeking aid from rival communities). They said that the Germans had always thrived through mutual affiliation (Germans prioritised their own people). But this right was being denied to them by a king (a 'foreign' imposed leader) who was expanding Roman power.

They asked, 'is there no man of native soil who can fill the highest place (in our tribe)? Why is this offspring of Flavus, a (foreign) spy, raised above all others? They invoke the name of Arminius in vain (the famous rebel leader). This is no son of his that has returned to rule (the Chatti). They don't fear him because he doesn't seem corrupted by a taste for strange foods, foreign clothing, or a submissiveness to Roman power. He seems unaffected by foreign things (Roman influence). But this Italicus keeps his inner character hidden. He is a product of his father Flavus, who (under Roman command) exhibited unparalleled enmity when he fought against his homeland (of Germania) and its gods.'

By using these appeals the dissidents gathered a large force. But Italicus also presented a compelling case. He reminded his followers that he had not invaded an unwilling country. He had been called upon to rule because he possessed a high hereditary status. So, let his courage be tested (in battle) to see whether he was worthy of his uncle Arminius and his grandfather Actumerus (both renowned German warlords). He was not ashamed of his father. He had never pledged a loyalty to Rome (in military service) so he had no prior political commitments to renounce. He was free to pledge himself entirely to the German cause. The word 'liberty' (used by the dissidents) was only a pretext used by ignoble characters who threatened the nation with civil war.

The host loudly acclaimed his speech and the king proved victorious in the ensuing battle, which was a large engagement for a barbarian conflict. But later, overcome with success, Italicus lapsed into arrogance (failing to maintain support and overlooking political threats). He was expelled from the territory and only restored to power by Langobard forces (tribal allies). For the Langobard are a scourge to the Cherusci, both in their good fortune and in their adversity (they were opportunists ready to support internal factions, fighting for or against the tribe).

Roman Interests

Emperor Claudius, AD 50

267 Tacitus, *Annals*, 12.29–30

Around this same time, Vannius, the ruler of the Suebi (a central Germanic tribe) was expelled from his kingdom (in about AD 50). Vannius had been installed in power by Drusus Caesar (as a Roman client king in AD 17). At the start of his rule Vannius had been well respected and popular amongst his countrymen. But he became a tyrant (dictatorial) and provoked neighbouring tribes who encouraged insurrection in his territory. This led to his downfall. The revolt was orchestrated by Vibillius, king of the Hermunduri (another inner German tribe). Vibillius allied with Vangio and Sido, sons of Vannius' sister (nephews of the king) and they led the insurrection in Suebic territory.

Vannius repeatedly asked the Emperor Claudius for Roman military assistance, but the emperor refused to intervene in conflicts between barbarians (occurring far beyond imperial territory). He simply promised Vannius a safe refuge in the event of his expulsion from power.

Meanwhile, Claudius sent written orders to Publius Atellius Hister, the governor of Pannonia (the Danube Frontier). He instructed Hister to assemble his legions along with some specially selected auxiliaries from the province (in a force of up to four legions). This army encamped on the riverbank (the frontier) as a show of Roman support for Vannius and a warning to the victorious insurgents who were becoming elated by their success. This Roman military display discouraged any impulse these Germans might have had to disturb the peace that was maintained in the Empire.

Furthermore, the Romans learned that an immense host of Ligii (an East Germanic tribe located near the Vistula River) was advancing towards the territory of Vannius (the Suebic homelands). The Ligii were joined by many other German tribes who had heard about the great fame of this wealthy realm and knew that Vannius had gathered a vast fortune in plunder and tribute during his thirty-year rule. Vannius' own native force was infantry (Suebic warriors) and his cavalry was gathered from the Iazyges of Sarmatia (allies from the nearby steppe). This army could not hope to match the size of the invading force. Consequently, Vannius decided to place his supporters in fortified positions and prolong the war (either to exhaust the enemy or await Roman intervention).

But the Iazyges could not tolerate a siege (as steppe cavalry) and they therefore dispersed throughout the surrounding country. This made an engagement inevitable, as the Ligii and Hermunduri rushed to attack the available targets. In response, Vannius and his supporters left their strongholds and assembled for battle. They were defeated, but Vannius gained respect for bravely fighting in person and receiving wounds across his chest. He then fled to the Danube, where the Roman river fleet was waiting to receive him. Many of his supporters and adherents soon followed and each was granted land and permission to settle in Pannonia (the Roman province south of the Danube).

Vangio and Sido divided the Suebic kingdom between them (the two original usurpers). But they remained admirably loyal to us (successfully performing the role of Roman client kings). They were popular among their Seuvic people when they were seeking power, but when they became rulers, they were despised because their despotic character was revealed.

Political Payments

Emperor Domitian (AD 81–96)

268 Cassius Dio, *Roman History*, 67.10
Chariomerus, the king of the Cherusci, was expelled from his kingdom by the Chatti due to his friendship with the Romans (alliances). He gathered some companions (German allies) and successfully returned to power. But he was deserted by these new followers when he sent further political hostages to the Romans (confirming his imperial loyalties). He therefore became a suppliant of Domitian (a Roman client king), but he received money (financial backing) rather than military support (from imperial troops).

269 Tacitus, *Germania*, 42
Up until our era, the Marcomanni and Quadi were ruled by kings of their own nation. These kings were noble descendants of Maroboduus and Tudrus. But these tribes now submit to foreign rulers and their monarchs depend on the Romans to maintain power and influence. Occasionally we will support the rulers with military interventions, but it is more common to give them financial assistance. The gift of money has proven as effective as force is to maintain royal authority.

Marcomannic Wars (AD 166–180)

Emperor Marcus Aurelius

The Emperor Marcus Aurelius conducted a series of large-scale campaigns to subdue and conquer southern Germania. The Roman Empire was impeded by a lethal pandemic, which was probably an ancestral form of smallpox (Antonine Pandemic AD 165–180).

270 Cassius Dio, *Roman History*, 71.10
A force of 6,000 Langobardi and Obii (Germanic people) crossed the Danube frontier. But the Roman cavalry commanded by Vindex, and the infantry commanded by Candidus, met them. Together these Romans routed the barbarian intruders. The barbarians were so dismayed by this outcome that they sent envoys to Iallius Bassus, the governor of Pannonia. The envoys included Ballomarius, the king of the Marcomanni, and ten other chiefs, one from each of the tribes in their alliance. These representatives made formal peace with Rome which they ratified with oaths, before returning home.

271 Cassius Dio, *Roman History*, 71.11
After this conflict, Marcus (Aurelius) Antoninus remained in Pannonia to better receive the many embassies that the barbarians sent to him (from chiefs and hereditary rulers). Some of the Germans were under the leadership of Battarius, a 12-year-old boy who promised an alliance. Marcus gave Battarius a gift of money and his followers managed to restrain a neighbouring chieftain named Tarbus. Tarbus was leading his forces into Dacia (a Roman province north of the Danube). Once there, he was demanding money (from the Roman authorities) and threatening war (to plunder the region).

272 Cassius Dio, *Roman History*, 71.14
The Iazyges sent envoys to Marcus Aurelius requesting peace, but they did not obtain their objective. This was because the emperor still regarded this (steppe) population to be untrustworthy. The Quadi (Germans) encouraged these concerns and deceived the Romans because they wanted to see the Iazyges annihilated (as a political force). The Quadi had fought alongside the Iazyges on earlier occasions and during the war with Rome they received many fugitives from both the Iazyges and Marcomanni.

But when peace was restored the Quadi refused to meet their obligations to Rome and surrender the refugee population. The few captives that they did return to the Empire were too physically weak to be sold as slaves or employed in any useful labour. When the Quadi did surrender men in good physical condition, they retained their families so that these individuals had a strong incentive to leave (and escape back across the frontier). The Quadi also expelled their king Furtius and appointed Ariogaesus as their new ruler (without Roman approval). They offered to deliver 50,000 captives to the Romans if the former treaty was renewed. But the emperor refused to acknowledge Ariogaesus as a legally constituted king and dismissed the existing peace terms.

Marcus Aurelius was so embittered by this conduct that he issued a proclamation saying that anyone who brought him Ariogaesus alive as a captive would receive 1,000 aurei (gold coins). The man who slew him and brought his head to Roman authorities would receive 500 aurei. This was unusual because Marcus Aurelius always treated even his most stubborn foes humanely. For example, an eastern satrap named Tiridates had provoked disturbances in Armenia and had killed the king of the Heniochi (a Colchic tribe under Roman protection). Then, when the Roman authorities condemned his actions, Tiridates waved a sword in the face of Publius Martius Verus (the governor of Cappadocia). But Marcus Aurelius did not have Tiridates executed for this insult; instead he had him banished to Britain. This reveals how incensed the emperor had become towards Ariogaesus. But when the Quadi king was captured and brought to Marcus, no harm was done to him. He was merely sent to Alexandria (to be detained far from the European conflict).

273 Cassius Dio, *Roman History*, 71.22
The Iazyges also agreed terms with the Roman Empire after their defeat. Their king Zanticus even appeared in person as a suppliant before Antoninus (Marcus Aurelius). This was remarkable because the Iazyges had previously imprisoned a king named Banadaspus, because he had considered terms with Rome. But now all their leading men came with Zanticus to accept the Roman dictates. The Iazyges received the same terms as the Quadi and the Marcomanni. But they were required to remain twice as far away from the Danube as these Germanic tribes (the Iazyges were steppe horsemen, so a wider neutral zone was needed).

Payments for Peace

Emperor Severus Alexander (AD 235)

In AD 234, Germanic armies breached the Rhine and Danube frontiers. The Emperor Severus Alexander tried to restore peace and order with payments to the hostile nations. This might have avoided the cost and risk involved in large-scale military campaigns, but the Roman soldiers mutinied.

274 Herodian, *Roman History*, 6.7
While the Emperor Alexander was engaged in this campaign, he thought it wise to send an embassy to the Germans to discuss the possibilities of a peaceful settlement. He promised to give them everything they asked for, including a large amount of money. The rapacious Germans are susceptible to bribes and are always ready to sell 'peace' to the Romans in return for gold. Therefore, Alexander managed to buy a truce, rather than risk the hazards of further war.

German Chiefs in the Late Roman Army (AD 374)

By the fourth century AD, large numbers of barbarians were being drafted into the Roman army to serve in distinct units. German chiefs were also being awarded senior positions in the Roman army.

275 Ammianus Marcellinus, *Roman History*, 29.4
Valentinian made Fraomarius king of the Bucinobantes, a tribe of the Alemanni dwelling opposite Mogontiacum (Mainz). But soon afterwards, when an invasion had utterly devastated this territory, he transferred him to Britain with the rank of tribune. There he gave him command of a troop of the Alemanni which was distinguished for its numbers and military strength.

Valentinian gave other chiefs of this nation commands in the Roman army, including Bitheridus and Hortarius. But Hortarius sent written messages to Macrianus and other barbarian chiefs containing information detrimental to Rome. His actions were discovered and reported by Florentius, the Roman commander in Germany. After torture, Hortarius was put to death by burning (a form of execution that the Romans had now adopted).

Commanders and 'Kings'

Batavian kings fought as unit commanders at the Battle of Argentoratum (Rhine frontier, AD 357).

276 Ammianus Marcellinus, *Roman History*, 16.12
In response the Batavians advanced quickly to assist their comrades. They were led by their 'kings' (native officers awarded 'royal' status in the imperial system).

German 'Arrogance'

277 Suetonius, *Claudius*, 25
The Emperor Claudius allowed envoys from the Germans to sit in the front rows of the auditoriums. The Germans were led to upper seats occupied by the common people, but they saw the position of other envoys. Representatives from the Armenian kingdom and the Parthian Empire were sitting with the senators in the front rows of the theatre. The Germans therefore acted with natural self-confidence and began making their way down to join them, loudly protesting that their merits and rank made them inferior to no one.

278 Tacitus, *Annals*, 13.54
The two Frisian leaders (Verritus and Malorix) travelled to Rome and waited for an audience with the Emperor Nero. But Nero was occupied with other engagements and the barbarians were therefore given a tour of the city to witness its astonishing sights. They were taken into Pompey's theatre so that they might behold the vastness of the Roman people (the theatre had a capacity of more than 20,000 spectators and seating was allocated according to social class). The Germans found no amusement in the theatre entertainment, but they did take advantage of this leisure time to ask their guide questions about the crowds who sat on the benches. They asked about the distinctions between the senior social classes (the nobility). Who exactly were the *equites*? Where were the senators? Then they saw some people in foreign costumes sat on the seats among the senators and asked who they were. They were told that this honour was granted to envoys from foreign nations that were distinguished for their bravery and for their friendship to Rome. The Frisii cried out that no men

on earth surpassed the Germans in their military valour or their loyalty. Then they scrambled down through the Roman crowd and took their seats among the senators.

The spectators recognised this undertaking as a good-natured act. They understood that it was due to the impulsiveness of a primitive people who upheld an honourable rivalry. Nero gave both rulers the Roman franchise (an endorsement to rule as subject representatives of Rome). Then he ordered the Frisii to withdraw from the contested territory (on the imperial frontiers).

Authority of Kings

279 Tacitus, *Germania*, 6
The Germans choose their kings from those who possess royal heritage, but generals are selected according to individual merit. The kings do not have unlimited or arbitrary power, and the generals achieve more by example, rather than authority. The generals fight in the front ranks, and they are therefore admired if they are energetic and prominent. But they cannot impose punishments on the men they lead. The priests are the only ones who can command a warrior to be reprimanded, imprisoned, or flogged.

Tuetonic Kings in Battle

German kings were expected to lead and fight on the battlefield. This was attested at the Battle of Aquae Sextiae in 102 BC, when the Romans defeated the Tuetones.

280 Florus, *Roman History*, 1.38
Now, Teutobodus, the king of the Tuetones, had previously demonstrated his physical prowess by vaulting over four or six horses at a time. But when his need for strength came, he could scarcely find a single mount able to carry him in his escape. He was captured in a nearby forest and displayed in the triumphal procession held in Rome. Teutobodus had great stature with extraordinary height and bearing and even in defeat he towered over the other trophies of battle. Thus, the Teutones were destroyed, and the Romans could direct their attention to the Cimbri.

Germanic Kings of the Cimbri

The Romans defeated the Cimbri at the Battle of the Raudian Plain (101 BC).

281 Florus, *Roman History*, 1.38
Their king Boiorix died fighting with great fury in the forefront of the battle, after he had inflicted many vengeful injuries upon his foes. (...)

The enemy suffered many wretched forms of death. It was reported that two chieftains attacked each other with drawn swords, each inflicting killing blows on his comrade. The kings Lugius and Boiorix were both killed on the battlefield, while the royal commanders Claodicus and Caesorix were captured.

Arminius Leads

The rebel leader Arminius was also seen at the forefront of the fighting during the Battle of Teutoburg (AD 9) and later efforts to resist Roman invasions (AD 15).

282 Tacitus, *Annals*, 1.61
Survivors of the disaster accompanied the soldiers. (...) They pointed to the rising ground where Arminius had appeared, urging his warriors onwards to fiercer action.

283 Tacitus, *Annals*, 2.21
Arminius was less active in this combat. This was either because the Germans faced severe peril in the battle, or Arminius had been partially disabled by his recent wound. In contrast, Inguiomerus (another chief) was seen on many parts of the battlefield dashing here and there (to encourage the fighters or escaping danger). He retained his courage until the fortunes of war had overcome the Germans.

Germanic Leadership in the Late Era

Ammianus describes the Battle of Argentoratum when the western Caesar Julian fought the invading Alemanni led by King Chonodomarius (Rhine frontier, AD 357).

284 Ammianus Marcellinus, *Roman History*, 16.12
Meanwhile, King Chonodomarius was creating a great disturbance throughout the enemy force. He was seen everywhere boasting about the

dangers he had faced, and the many successful military actions he had led against the Romans. He said he had fought the previous Caesar Decentius on equal terms and defeated him (AD 353). Then his forces had overrun Gaul without further opposition, plundering and destroying many wealthy cities. He had also recently routed a Roman general who possessed a superior military force. These arrogant claims strengthened the confidence of the enemy. The Alemanni had also seen the emblems on the Roman shields (the defenders of Argentoratum). They realised that these same soldiers had retreated in earlier encounters against minor raiding warbands.

285 Ammianus Marcellinus, *Roman History*, 16.12

All these warlike and savage tribes were led by Chonodomarius and Serapio. They were kings possessing greater authority than the other Alemanni leaders (the seven royal chiefs) Chonodomarius was in fact the notorious instigator of the whole conflict. He rode along the left wing of the Alemanni army (the infantry line) full of boldness and bravery (reviewing his forces). He wore a flame-coloured plume on his helmet. He owed his position as leader to his mighty muscular strength (physical prowess). He was a huge figure and the mouth of his steed foamed under his great weight and power (his horse was overexerted). Chonodomarius carried a lance-like spear of formidable size and was easily spotted due to his gleaming armour which made him even more conspicuous. He was a steadfast soldier and a more skilful general than the other leaders.

The Alemanni right wing (cavalry and ambush infantry) was led by Serapio. He was still a young man without a grizzled beard, but his great ability far surpassed his youth. He was the son of Mederichus, who was the brother of Chonodomarius. Mederichus was a man who had demonstrated the utmost treachery through his life (duplicity and consistent opposition to Rome). He had been kept as a political hostage in Gaul for a long time and he had been inducted into the Greek mysteries (a secretive religious cult). He therefore changed the name of his son from the native Agenarichus to Serapio (in honour of Serapis, the Greco-Egyptian god worshiped in underworld cults).

The Alemanni army included another five kings of lesser authority (royal chiefs) and ten princes (leaders with royal connections?). There was a large gathering of nobles and the army comprised about 35,000 fighters.

286 Ammianus Marcellinus, *Roman History*, 16.12

Julian now deployed the greater part of his army opposite the forefront of the savages. But suddenly an outcry was heard among the German warriors.

They shouted in unison for their princes (royal leaders) to dismount and join them as infantry in the oncoming battle. The warriors were afraid that their mounted leaders might flee the battlefield if the Romans seemed to be winning the combat. In response, Chonodomarius immediately jumped down from his horse and the other German leaders followed his example. But some were hesitant and slow to dismount, as if they now doubted that a victory could be achieved (the ambush strategy had failed, and the Roman infantry was resolute).

Fate of Royal Exiles and Captives

In AD 18, the long-reigning Marcomannic king was exiled from his kingdom by a rival Germanic chief.

287 Tacitus, *Annals*, 2.62–63

Maroboduus was now utterly deserted by his supporters and had no recourse but to seek the mercy of the emperor (Tiberius). He crossed the Danube where it flows past the province of Noricum (the Roman frontier near Switzerland). Then he wrote to Tiberius, not like a fugitive or a suppliant, but as someone who recalled his past greatness. In former times Maroboduus had been a famous king who received offers of alliance from many foreign powers. But he had preferred the friendship of Rome and he still maintained this allegiance. Tiberius replied that he would be granted a safe and honourable home in Italy. He could remain there as long as he pleased and if future interests required his departure, then he was free to leave under the same protection by which he had come (a return to Germania).

However, the Senate disagreed (contradicting the emperor). It was argued that Maroboduus had been as dangerous to Rome as King Philip of Macedon had been to the Athenians (fourth century BC). He had been as formidable as King Pyrrhus (of Epirus) and matched the threat that the Seleucid King Antiochus presented to the Roman people (serious threats to Roman lives and power in the third and second century BC). This speech is still extant (a record of the senatorial debate). It magnifies the political power that Maroboduus held and stresses the ferocity of the tribes under his rule. It emphasises the proximity of his former realm to Italy and describes the events that led to his overthrow and ousting.

As a result, Maroboduus was detained at Ravenna (a strategic imperial city in northern Italy). His possible return to power was used to threaten and menace the Suebi, if they failed to obey Roman dictates. But Maroboduus never left Italy and after eighteen years he was reduced to an old man. He had clung to his hopes too long and lost his former renown.

288 Tacitus, *Annals*, 2.62–63
Catualda had a similar downfall and did no better in the refuge he sought after defeat. Soon after he seized power (in the Marcomannic kingdom), he was attacked by an overwhelming force of Herunduri (a tribe from the Elbe region) led by (their ruler) Vibillius. Expelled from his homeland, Catualda was received by the Romans and sent to Forum Julii, a Roman colony in Gallia Narbonensis (southern Gaul).

The barbarians who followed these two rulers into exile received a different treatment. It was thought that these Germans might create disturbances if they were allowed to remain in the Empire and mingle among the Roman population. Therefore, they were resettled beyond the Danube between the rivers Marus and Cusus. This land was in the territory of a ruler named Vannius of the Quadi (a Germanic tribe on the mid-Danube that was still allied to Rome).

Fate of Defeated Kings

The Alemannic King Chonodomarius fled defeat at the Battle of Argentoratum (AD 357). But he was later caught in an outcrop of trees as he searched for a safe route of return across the Rhine.

289 Ammianus Marcellinus, *Roman History*, 16.12
Chonodomarius was overcome with fear and surrendered of his own accord. He came out of the trees alone. Three of his remaining attendants, his closest friends, also surrendered since they thought it was a disgrace to survive their king (they wanted to share his fate). A further 200 of the enemy were taken prisoner with him (followers and fugitives in the woods).

These savages are by nature arrogant in success, but meek when they suffer adversity. Chonodomarius was now subservient to another power. He was dragged along pale and ashamed, dumbstruck by the knowledge of his crimes against Rome. His character was now vastly different from the man who had committed such savage and distressing outrages. Chonodomarius had once trampled upon the ashes of Gaul and threatened immense destruction on the Empire. (…)

Julian gave orders that Chonodomarius should be brought before him (for judgement). The king bowed down and then humbly prostrated himself upon the ground (grovelling). He begged for forgiveness in his native language (Germanic, not imperial Latin). In response, Julian instructed him to take courage (he was to be spared execution).

A few days later, Chonodomarius was conveyed to the court of the Emperor Gratian (in Ravenna) and then sent to Rome (for public display). He was detained at the Castra Peregrina (a military barracks for provincial troops) on the Caelian Hill. And in the end, he died of senile decay (dementia after long-term confinement).

Chapter Fourteen

Germanic Warfare and Military Threat

The first major contact between the Romans and the Germans occurred in about 113 BC, when Cimbri and Teutones migrated from Jutland into Gaul. These Germanic migrants were joined by a Celtic tribe called the Ambrones as they approached Gallia Narbonensis, the southern part of Gaul under Roman control.

290 Plutarch, *Marius*, 11
Soon afterwards reports reached the Romans concerning the Teutones and Cimbri. Information regarding the numbers and strength of the invading hosts were at first disbelieved, but afterwards these details were found to be accurate. The reports said that 300,000 fighting men carrying weapons were advancing on Italy and far larger hordes of women and children accompanied these warriors. These people were searching for lands to support a vast multitude and for cities in which to settle and live. The circumstances resembled the earlier Gallic invasion of Italy. These new invaders had learnt how the Gauls had seized and occupied the best part of Italy from the Tyrrhenians and they planned to do likewise. Both tribes (the Teutones and Cimbri) therefore descended upon Gaul and Italy like a vast cloud.

Unrest in 60 BC

In about 60 BC, a Celtic tribe called the Sequani allied with a large force of Germans and invited them to settle west of the Rhine.

291 Orosius, *History*, 6.7
Later, the Sequani (a powerful Celtic tribe in eastern Gaul) threatened warfare by inviting a vast number of German warriors into the country. They were led by King Ariovistus who boasted that he might subjugate all the Gallic tribes with his invading forces. But Caesar was determined to overcome and defeat this threat. The Roman army was terrified by the vast numbers and ferocity of the invading Germans, but the enemy refused opportunities to fight for a long time.

The (Germanic) army commanded by Ariovistus included the Harudes, Marcomanni, Triboci, Vangiones, Nemetes, Sedusii and Suebi (a wide alliance of Germanic tribes).

Disturbances in 55 BC

In 55 BC, other Germanic tribes took refuge in Gaul when threatened and expelled from their homelands east of the Rhine.

292 Cassius Dio, *Roman History*, 39.47

During this season, the German tribes known as the Tencteri and Usipetes crossed the Rhine and invaded the country of the Treveri (a Celtic tribe centred on Trier). These Germans made the crossing because they were expelled from their homelands by the Suebi (a rival Germanic tribe), but they were also invited into the region by some of the Gauls (hoping to increase their manpower or political position).

Scale of Threat

Julius Caesar estimated the military potential of the Germans in this era (during the Roman conquest of Gaul, 58–52 BC).

293 Julius Caesar, *Gallic War*, 4.15

Now the Romans had been alarmed by the prospect of a great a war, for it was reported that these Germans possessed a nation of 430,000 people.

The Suebi

In this era, the largest Germanic nation was a tribal coalition called the Suebi.

294 Julius Caesar, *Gallic War*, 4.1

The Suebi are by far the largest and the most warlike Germanic nation. They are said to possess 100 districts and each year every one of these territories sends 1,000 men with weapons to participate in their wars (potentially 100,000 warriors). The kinsmen who remain at home can maintain their own households and provide (sustenance) for their absent comrades on expeditions. The following year they themselves will take up arms to fight while their returning comrades remain at home (managing communal resources and producing food). Consequently, their herds are not neglected, and their skill and practice in war are continually maintained.

Conflict against the Suebi

In 55 BC, Julius Caesar defeated the Germans west of the Rhine (Tencteri and Usipetes) then crossed the river boundary to confront the Suebi.

295 Orosius, *History*, 6.9

After constructing a bridge, Caesar crossed into Germany and saved the Sugambri and Ubii (allied Germanic tribes) from a siege of their territories (by the Suebi). His arrival brought terror to the entire country and especially intimidated the Suebi, who were the largest and fiercest German tribe. According to information confirmed by many people, the Suebi possessed 100 cantons and districts (large territorial units). Caesar then destroyed the bridge over the Rhine and withdrew to Gaul.

The Marcomanni

Another large coalition of Germanic tribes called the Marcomanni occupied southern Germania (Bohemia). They could therefore attack the Empire across the Danube frontier.

296 Velleius Paterculus, *History of Rome*, 2.108

Maroboduus increased his army to include 70,000 infantry and 4,000 cavalry. He trained this army through constant wars against neighbouring tribes, and it seemed that he was developing this force for some greater undertaking. His kingdom was to be feared because of its (geographical) position. (Greater) Germany was to the north and the main Marcomanni settlements faced this region. Pannonia (the Roman province) was to the south (across the Danube frontier). While Noricum was to the rear (Roman Austria, positioned to the south-west). The Marcomanni might suddenly attack in any one of these directions, so the kingdom of Maroboduus was dreaded (by all surrounding states). Even Italy was concerned by the growing power of Maroboduus, since the boundary summits of the Alps were less than 200 miles from Marcomannic territory.

Engaging the Enemy

In AD 366, the Roman commander Jovinus ambushed some Germans who had crossed the Rhine and were roving through Gaul. This was a raiding force of warriors.

297 Ammianus Marcellinus, *Roman History*, 27.2
The Roman army advanced to attack a second predatory force (raiders). Trusted scouts reported that, after plundering nearby farmhouses, the enemy were resting near the river (the Moselle). The Romans advanced slowly along a valley concealed by a thick growth of trees. They saw the barbarians bathing in the river. Some of them were reddening their hair according to their national custom (using red hair dye) while others were drinking. The commander gave the signal to attack and the clarion calls were sounded. The Romans charged into the enemy camp while the Germans shouted and yelled vain threats. They could not gather up their scattered weapons, or rally themselves to resist. Most of them were killed, pierced by spears and swords, except for those that ran and fled through narrow winding paths.

Wagon Trains

German migrations involved entire communities with warriors protecting settler families. In 102 BC, the Tuetones and Cimbri tried to cross the Alps and invade Italy.

298 Florus, *Roman History*, 1.38
It seems incredible, but the Cimbri had already crossed the Alps during the winter when the mountain heights are more inaccessible. They therefore descended from the Tridentine ranges into Italy like an avalanche. Their first obstacle was the Atesis River (Adige), which they did not attempt to cross using a bridge or boats. Instead, with the stupidity of barbarians, they tried to swim the river against the strong current. Finally, they reduced the river current by casting trees into the stream and using their shields to block the water flow. This allowed their force (including wagons) to ford the river.

Battle of Aquae Sextiae (102 BC)

The Tuetones were met by a Roman army under the command of general Gaius Marius. The Battle of Aquae Sextiae began with Roman forces approaching the enemy camping grounds, which included fighting men and their families.

299 Plutarch, *Marius*, 19
When Marius ordered that the river should be seized, the soldiers reluctantly obeyed. Only a few of the enemy engaged them at first. Warm streams

emerge from the ground near this site and the main enemy host were some distance away taking their meals after bathing in these warming pools. The Romans were surprised by the number of barbarians who were engaged in this activity and enjoying the pleasant environment of the plain.

Rome Fights the Tuetones

300 Plutarch, *Marius*, **21**
Marius sent officers to all parts of the Roman line to ensure that the soldiers stood firmly in their ranks. As the enemy rushed forwards the Romans launched their javelins. They drew their swords and began to crowd forwards and batter the Barbarians back with their shields. The enemy were on treacherous ground (a downward slope) so their blows lacked force and their shield walls could not lock together with sufficient strength. The uneven ground disrupted the enemy battle line as shields were flipped and turned. (…)

As instructed, the Romans had awaited the enemy's charge. They closed the distance, withstood their upward rush, and by crowding them back, pushed them down, little by little back onto the plain. Here the foremost Barbarians could at last form battle lines on level ground. (…) The enemy broke formation and fled.

Battle of Vercellae: Rome vs the Cimbri (101 BC)

301 Plutarch, *Marius*, **25–27**
The Cimbri infantry advanced slowly from their defences. The depth of their ranks was almost equal to the length of their battle line, which extended over more than 3 miles. Meanwhile, a force of Cimbri horsemen, including 15,000 cavalry, rode forth in a splendid display. Their helmets were crafted to resemble the jaws of terrifying wild beasts or the outline of strange animals. Towering crests of feathers (large plumes) made the fighters appear taller than they really were. These warriors were equipped with iron breastplates and carried gleaming white shields. Each man was equipped with two lances and a large heavy sword for close-quarter combat.

The Cimbri horsemen did not charge directly towards the Romans. They swerved to the right and tried to draw the left part of the Roman battle line out of position, to be caught between themselves and their advancing infantry. The Roman commanders perceived the strategy, but they could not restrain their units on the left flank. One of the soldiers yelled that the enemy was fleeing, and they all rushed forwards in pursuit.

Meanwhile, the barbarian infantry surged forwards to attack, like a vast sea set in motion. (...)

The Romans had the advantage in this contest. Sulla says that the sun was shining in the faces of the Cimbri, exposing them to greater glare and heat. They sweated profusely, breathed with difficulty, and were forced to hold their shields before their faces (to provide shade and avoid sunstroke and heat exhaustion). By Roman reckoning the battle was fought just after the summer solstice, three days before the new moon in August in the month previously known as 'Sextilis'. The dust also assisted the Romans and gave them encouragement, since they could not see the vast numbers of the enemy. Instead, each man avoided this terrifying sight and concentrated only on the enemy he engaged in immediate hand-to-hand combat.

According to Catulus, his soldiers were so supremely fit and well trained that they barely sweated or panted with effort as they fought in the great heat. They had even run into combat, but scarcely felt the effects of this added effort. Anyway, this is what Catulus wrote in praise of his soldiers. Most of the Cimbri army was soon cut to pieces by the Romans, including their best fighters. Their leading warriors had bound themselves together with long chains passed through their belts. This ensured that their ranks would never break. But the other fighters were forced back from the battlefield towards their own entrenchments (the outer defences of their camp).

Attack on Ariovistas

In 55 BC, Julius Caesar attacked the Germanic king Ariovistas, who had settled his followers west of the Rhine. Caesar provides a first-hand account in his campaign diaries.

302 Julius Caesar, *Gallic War*, 1.51

Leading the legions himself, Caesar deployed the Romans in a triple line adjacent to the enemy's camp. At last, compelled by necessity, the Germans began moving their own forces out of the encampment. They formed up in their tribal groups with an equal interval (between the nations). These tribes included the Harudes, Marcomanni, Triboces, Vangiones, Nemetes, Sedusii and Suebi. There were wagons and carts in the German lines, so the fighters would be unable to flee. Their women took position on board the wagons. They watched with tearful eyes, as the men marched forwards. The women called out, not to allow their families to be taken into Roman slavery.

Roman Tactics

Caesar had convinced his soldiers that Roman tactics would prevail.

303 Julius Caesar, *Gallic War*, 1.38–40
If they took the trouble to enquire, they would discover that the Gauls had been worn down by the long duration of this conflict. For many months during the fighting, Ariovistus had been skulking in his camp in the marshes, giving the Gauls no opportunity to attack him. Then finally, when the Gauls had abandoned any prospect of battle and dispersed their army, Ariovistus suddenly launched his assault upon them. He had therefore won more by tactical planning than by conspicuous bravery. Perhaps these tactics were successful when dealing with barbarians who had no military skill. But not even Ariovistus could expect such tactics to overcome the Roman army.

Usipetes and Tencteri

In 55 BC, Julius Caesar approached the main camp of the Usipetes and Tencteri, Germanic tribes that had settled west of the Rhine. The Germans had sent most of their cavalry forces out into the wider countryside and Caesar planned to attack the settlers before their warrior horsemen could return.

304 Julius Caesar, *Gallic War*, 4.11–12
The cavalry officers were not concerned since the Romans had 5,000 cavalry, compared with an enemy force numbering less than 800 horsemen. This was because many Germanic horsemen had crossed the Meuse River on a long-range foraging expedition and had not yet returned to their new territories. Furthermore, the Germanic envoys who had just left Caesar had requested a period of truce.

305 Cassius Dio, *Roman History*, 39.47–48
The Germans were not expecting any hostile move against them, especially as their senior men had recently gone to discuss terms with Caesar. They were living in tents and were taking their noonday rest when the Roman army approached. There were vast numbers of infantry warriors within the German encampment, but they did not have time to pick up their weapons. The Romans advanced and slaughtered them amid their wagons. Their women and children were shamefully scattered about the camp during the attack (this was an encampment formed from family groups, not a regimented military base).

Germanic War Gear

Tacitus provides a composite account of Germanic warfare.

306 Tacitus, *Germania*, 6

Iron is not plentiful among the Germans and this is confirmed by the nature of their weapons. Few Germans use swords or long lances. They mostly carry a spear which they call the *'framea'*. This weapon has a short and narrow spearhead which is very sharp and easy to wield. Each man carries several spears that he can throw for an immense distance. So German infantry can launch dense volleys. Consequently, a warrior can use this weapon to fight effectively at a distance, or in very close range. Each warrior fights naked or lightly clad with a small cloak. Their mounted warriors are equipped with just a shield and a spear. Their military equipment is not designed for display and their shields are adorned with a simple choice of colours. Only a few German warriors wear breastplates and just one or two in a battle line might have a metal or a leather helmet.

German horses are not remarkable for their grace or speed. Their horsemen do not train or practise manoeuvres like the Roman cavalry do. The German horsemen ride straight forwards, but if required they can turn to the right in a compact and inclusive group as an evasive manoeuvre (turning right meant that their shields faced the enemy). I would say that in general, the main battlefield strength of the Germans is their infantry. Many German warriors are well adapted to fight alongside the cavalry due to their swiftness. For this purpose, certain units are selected from the best young warriors and stationed in the front battle lines. The size of these units is fixed at 100 warriors per territory. This designation 'one of the hundred' has therefore become a distinguished title in their society.

The German battle line assembles in a wedge-shaped formation. They often consider it wise to withdraw in a battle and this practice is not considered cowardice if the warriors intend to return to the attack. They will try to carry off the bodies of slain comrades, even in indecisive engagements. German warriors think that the greatest crime is to abandon their shields in battle (drop their weapons to flee the fighting). A man who has suffered this disgrace is not permitted to be present at ceremonies, perform sacred rites, or attend tribal councils. Many who have fled battle and suffered this fate will end their humiliation with suicide by hanging. (…)

The Germans carry certain figures and images removed from their sacred groves into battle with them. Their courage is enhanced by the fact that their squadrons and battalions are not formed by chance or random gatherings. Their warbands are instead composed of kinfolk and clansmen.

Cavalry Tactics

Caesar describes the fighting style of Germanic cavalry as experienced on campaign.

307 Julius Caesar, *Gallic War*, 1.48

The Germans trained in the following form of combat. They deployed 6,000 horsemen supported by an equal number of very swift and brave infantry. These men had been specially selected from the entire force and each horseman was assigned one infantryman for personal protection. They worked together when engaging the enemy. The horseman could withdraw quickly, or converge speedily, if any serious difficulty arose (on the battlefield). They would form up around any fighter who fell severely wounded from his horse. If a longer-range advance was needed, or a more rapid retreat, the infantry was trained to support themselves by the manes of the horses to keep up their pace (they gripped onto the horses to be carried at a gallop).

308 Julius Caesar, *Gallic War*, 4.2

In cavalry attacks the Germans will often leap from their horses and fight on foot. They train their horses to stand still in the very spot where the rider has dismounted. They can therefore retreat to their horses if they are forced back by enemy actions. According to their customs, Germans regard it as inappropriate and unmanly to use excessive horse equipment on their mounts. Consequently, they have the courage to advance against a far larger number of enemy cavalry that is well furnished with riding equipment.

Horse Stabbers

The image of a warrior stabbing at the belly of a horse appears on the funeral monuments of Roman cavalrymen.

309 Julius Caesar, *Gallic War*, 4.11–12

The Germans immediately attacked the Roman cavalry, causing disorder in the forces. When the Romans stood firm, the German horsemen leaped from their mounts and attacked as infantry. They stabbed our horses in the belly, bringing down a great many of our cavalrymen. The Roman forces fled in such alarm that they did not halt the retreat until they reached our main army. In this encounter seventy-four Roman cavalrymen were killed.

The Barritus – War Chant

310 Tacitus, *Germania*, 3
The Germans say that in ancient times the demigod Hercules once visited them. They therefore praise him in the verses that they sing, as first above all other heroes. Some of their songs are known as the '*Barritus*' (deep and resounding Germanic war chants). These battle recitals rouse their courage, and the rising notes predict the outcome of the approaching conflict. All along their battle lines the shouts of the Barritus inspire fear or provoke alarm. In battle, the Barritus is less like an articulate sound and more like a cry of valour. They aim for a harsh note and a confused roar. They also put their mouths close to their shields so that the noise reverberates and swells into a wider, deeper sound.

311 Cassius Dio, *Roman History*, 38.35
Do not fear the magnitude of their large physique, their great violence, or their mighty shouts (the Barritus – war chant). For no voice ever killed a man and their huge bodies have the same hands as ours. With our hands we can impose greater injury because their large, unprotected bodies will be an easy target.

Attacking the Goths

Ammianus describes a Roman attack on a Gothic encampment in AD 377.

312 Ammianus Marcellinus, *Roman History*, 31.6–8
Both armies advanced cautiously then stood immobile. The opposing warriors stared at each other with a savage and penetrating gaze. Then the Romans sounded their war cry in unison – the sound known by the native name Barritus (a Germanic custom adopted by some Roman regiments). It rose from a low murmur to a louder tone, and it roused the soldiers to great strength. But the barbarians countered by reciting the glories of their forefathers in wild shouts (verses recounting ancestral heroics). While this discordant clamour of different languages sounded out, the first skirmishes occurred.

Tacitus describes the noise and tumult of Germanic forces engaged in the Batavian uprising (AD 69).

Women Spectators

313 Tacitus, *Histories*, 4.18
The war song of the men that dominated the battle lines was punctuated by the shrill cries of the women.

Warhorns

The Batavians in the North Rhine region used war horns, perhaps a practice adopted from the neighbouring Celtic peoples.

314 Lucan, *Civil War*, 1.420
The fierce Batavians assemble whose courage is roused by a blare of curved bronze war trumpets.

German Methods of Fighting

The Romans began the invasion and conquest of Germania in 14 BC.

315 Cassius Dio, *Roman History*, 38.35
Even if some of them (the German tribes) should band together to oppose us, they will not prove superior to us in any way. Omitting all other factors, we have greater numbers. Our soldiers are more mature, better experienced and have performed greater deeds. We have armour that fully encompasses our bodies, while our opponents are unprotected. Our military employs reason and organisation, whereas our rivals are unorganised and rush impulsively at everything.

316 Tacitus, *Annals*, 2.21
The Germans matched the Romans in bravery, but they were beaten by style of fighting and the weapons used. They were a vast horde crammed into a confined space where they could not easily thrust, or withdraw, their long spears. In this close engagement the German fighters could not make use of their fast reflexes or more agile bodies (unencumbered by armour and heavier equipment). The Romans fought with their shields pressed right up against their chests as they gripped their sword hilts and repeatedly stabbed. They struck the huge limbs and exposed faces of the barbarians and they cut a passage through the enemy, slaughtering them as they went.

Germanic Warfare and Military Threat 155

317 Tacitus, *Annals*, 2.14
Germanicus explained:

> Roman soldiers fight well on flat plains. But if they use their skills correctly, they can also engage the enemy successfully in woodlands and forest passes. The huge shields and unwieldly spears of the enemy cannot be used effectively amid tree trunks and bushes. Manage the throw of your javelins. Make use of your closefitting armour and short swords (superior protection and capacity to fight at extreme close quarters). Launch your javelins in dense volleys (to maximise injuries). Then strike at the face of your opponents with your sword points. The Germans do not have breastplates or helmets. Their shields are not strengthened with leather or iron (bands binding or reinforcing heavy wooden boards). Instead, their shields are osiers woven together (a lightweight wickerwork frame that could block missile fire). Or they carry a thin painted board.
>
> The front ranks of the enemy are armed with spears, but behind them the rest have only short blades or wooden weapons hardened by fire (wood desiccated by partial charring to produce a more durable material). The German physique is terrifying and formidable, but their strength is quickly spent and they cannot endure wounds. They will ignore their leaders and flee without feeling any shame for their disgrace. The Germans disregard the laws of gods and men when they succeed. But they tremble with fear when they suffer disaster.

Battle Engagement

Caesar describes the Battle of Vosges (58 BC).

318 Julius Caesar, *Gallic War*, 1.52–53
Caesar put the quaestors (state magistrates) in charge of the legions alongside the legates (regular commanders) so that every man would have a witness for his valour (a greater chance of recognition, reward and advancement). He himself took position on the right wing of the Roman force, having noticed that the corresponding division of the enemy was less secure (the left wing of the German force appeared weaker).

When the signal for battle was given, the enemy dashed forwards so suddenly and swiftly that there was no time for the Romans to launch javelins against them. Nevertheless, the Roman troops attacked the enemy with great fierceness. They threw aside their javelins and fought with swords at close quarters. But the Germans, following their custom, speedily formed into solid masses to resist the Roman sword attacks (shield walls). Many of our soldiers were brave enough to leap on the enemy defensive formations. They tore the shields from their hands or dealt them a wound from above.

The left wing of the enemy's army was beaten and put to flight. But their right wing, by sheer weight of numbers, pressed heavily into the Roman battle line. Young Publius Crassus, who was commanding the Roman cavalry, noticed this development. He could respond more quickly than other officers who were occupied in the front lines of battle. He therefore moved his cavalry round to form a third line of attack to support our struggling troops. This restored Roman prospects in the battle, causing all the enemy to turn and run.

The enemy did not cease their flight until they reached the river Rhine about 5 miles from that place. A few of the Germans trusted to their own strength and tried to swim across the river. Others discovered boats that could take them across to safety. Ariovistus found a skiff moored to the bank and escaped across the stream, but our cavalry caught and slew the rest of the enemy.

Shield Wall

Cassius Dio offers further details about this battle, including a German shield wall.

319 Cassius Dio, *Roman History*, 38.48–49

On the next day, the Romans followed their usual practice and drew up their forces in full military array (an invitation for battle). And on this occasion Ariovistus led his full army forwards to attack.

The Romans observed the enemy emerging from their tents and advancing towards them. They responded by rushing forwards so that the Germans could not form a secure battle line. The Germans had special confidence in their ability to hurl spears, but the Romans charged with a battle cry and closed the distance so quickly that their opponents could not effectively launch their javelins. They pushed forwards into such extreme close quarters that the Germans could not even use their tall spears or long swords. The impacted barbarians were pushed, shoved, and forced to fight more with their bodies than with their weapons (punches against blades).

The Germans struggled to overpower the soldiers they engaged (heavily armoured Roman troops) and they could not easily knock down, or topple, those who withstood them (Romans pushing forwards in dense ranks).

Many Germans lost even their short swords in the struggle and fought with their hands and their teeth. They dragged their opponents down, biting, tearing, and ripping at them. They used their greater strength and physique to overpower their Roman adversaries. But this practice did not cause any great loss to the Roman ranks. They continually pushed forwards into their foe. Somehow, Roman armour and skill matched the ferocity of the enemy attack. This struggle continued for a long time, and it was nearly the end of the day before the Romans prevailed.

The Romans had an advantage since they carried daggers that were smaller than Gallic swords and had steel points (short-range stabbing blades). The Roman soldiers were also better accustomed to long-duration combat and had far greater endurance than the barbarians. The Germans could not prolong the strength and fierceness of their attacks. The enemy were therefore defeated, but they did not flee the battle site. Instead, they collapsed into large helpless, exhausted groups. Some of these groups included more than 300 fighters who stood with their shields raised on all sides. These formations were so solid and compact that the Romans could not successfully assault, or dislodge them. Thus, both sides became immobile and were unable to inflict further damage, or suffer additional harm.

The Germans neither advanced against the Romans nor turned to flee. So, the Romans stood immovable on the battlefield as if stationed behind a battlement (a solid wall of shields). They had set aside their spears before the battle had begun, as they thought these weapons would be of no use in combat. The German shield walls were vulnerable since their warriors had no helmets, but the Romans could not use their short swords to strike at the heads of their opponents while they carried their own heavy shields (the Romans had to reach upwards and strike far above the height of their own head). Therefore, the Romans cast down their shields and rushed at the Germans with just their swords. Some charged into the enemy formations from a running start, while others dashed forwards and leapt into the shield wall as though they were scaling a tower. The Romans delivered a fierce array of blows into the huddled German masses.

Many Germans were instantly slain with a single sword thrust (to the face or throat). They were dead before they fell, but they were kept upright in the tightly packed closeness of their defensive formations. Most of the Germans died during this engagement, but some were driven back to their wagons. These men died with their wives and children.

Attack on the Shield Wall

Florus also mentions the German shield wall.

320 Florus, *Roman History*, 1.45

The prospect of fighting this unknown people caused great alarm and concern in the Roman military camps. (…) But (when the fighting began) the giant stature of their German enemies made larger targets for Roman swords and other weapons. The Romans therefore attacked with great resolve and the barbarians retreated into tortoise-like formations formed by solid walls of shields. The Roman soldiers were so determined to finish the fight that they actually leaped on the top of the enemy shields to strike at the throats of the Germans with their swords.

321 Orosius, *History*, 6.7

The fighting was especially fierce, due to the battle formation adopted by the Germans. They formed a dense phalanx-like array of warriors clustered into large groups. The warriors were protected on all sides by interlocking shields and these formations could halt and shatter the advancing Roman battle line. But the most agile and daring Roman soldiers leaped over the front of the enemy 'testudo' shield walls. They tore away their protecting shields like a man might strip scales (of a fish). Other soldiers stabbed at the exposed shoulders (and throats) of the enemy, who were surprised by the sudden assault and had no protection on this part of their bodies. The Germans were horrified by this new danger and their formidable shield walls began to break apart as many warriors started to flee. The Romans pursued them across 50 miles of terrain and inflicted a mass slaughter that seemed to be endless. Afterwards it was impossible to estimate the number of Germans who had fought in that battle, or the vast numbers who were slain.

322 Cassius Dio, *Roman History*, 38.50

Ariovistus fled with some of his horsemen. He abandoned his territory and headed for the Rhine. He was pursued, but not captured, and he escaped on a boat ahead of his followers (Germans escaping the conflict). The Romans overtook and killed many Germans fleeing to the river, but others were swept away in the stream (drowned in their panicked efforts to cross to safety). This was the end of the war.

323 Plutarch, *Julius Caesar*, 19
The German army was routed in this decisive engagement and Caesar pursued the survivors as far as the Rhine. The intervening ground, which stretched across a 50-mile plain, was strewn with dead bodies and the spoils of war. Ariovistus successfully crossed the Rhine with a few of his followers. But the German dead were said to have numbered 80,000.

Germans Attack

At the onset of the imperial era the Romans conducted large-scale campaigns of conquest and subjugation in Germania (15 BC to AD 16).

324 Tacitus, *Annals*, 2.15–19
The Germans were roused by these speeches and demanded immediate battle. Their chiefs led them down into a plain named the Idistavisus, which lies between the Weser and a nearby range of hills. This plain varies in width due to the curvature of the river and the protection of the adjoining hills. Behind the hills was a tall forest with thick branches rising to a great height. However, close to the forest floor the branches were sparse and there were clear spaces between the tree trunks (little undergrowth at ground level due to thick forest canopy).

The barbarian army occupied the plain and the outskirts of the wood. The Cherusci assembled on the high ground where they could rush down on the Romans during the battle (the hillslopes facing the plain). The Roman army advanced in the following order. The auxiliary Gauls and Germans formed the vanguard. Then came the infantry archers, then the four legions and then Caesar Germanicus himself with two praetorian cohorts and some specially selected cavalry. The other legions followed with the light-armed troops, the mounted archers, and the remaining allied cohorts (a total force of perhaps 40,000 soldiers). The soldiers were ready and prepared to form a battle line based on this marching order.

The Cheruscan warbands were impetuous and charged down the slopes to attack the Romans. When Caesar Germanicus saw them move from position, he ordered the Roman cavalry to immediately charge their flank. Meanwhile, Stertinius, who was leading the other squadrons, took a wide detour to attack the enemy from the rear. Germanicus had assured Stertinius that the main army would be fully engaged when this counterattack struck.

At this very moment an augury occurred which gave great encouragement to the Romans. Eight eagles were observed flying towards the woods (matching the number of legions in the campaign army). Germanicus saw the birds and cried out, 'Go! Follow those Roman birds, for they are the true deities of our legions.' At that moment the Roman infantry charged and the cavalry, which had been sent in advance, smashed into the rear and flanks of the enemy army.

Terrain

Ancient accounts indicate the terrain favoured by Germanic forces when fighting Roman armies.

325 Tacitus, *Annals*, 2.19–20

Finally, the enemy chose a battle site flanked by a river and enclosed by forests. This site was a narrow swampy plain and beyond the woods there were further marshlands. On one side of the marshes, the Angrivarii had raised a broad earthwork as a tribal boundary between themselves and the neighbouring Cherusci. The Germans arrayed their infantry along this barrier and concealed their cavalry forces in nearby woods. This deployment would allow the German cavalry to attack the rear of the legions as they entered the intervening forest (en route to the earthwork).

But Caesar Germanicus was fully aware of the enemy's position and their battle plans. He knew both what could be observed and what was concealed. He therefore prepared to use the enemy's stratagems to fulfil their own destruction. He assigned the Roman cavalry to his chief officer Seius Tubero and instructed him to occupy the level ground. Germanicus then arranged the Roman infantry so that only part of this force would advance across the plain to the forest. Meanwhile, a Roman subdivision would assault the enemy earthwork by clambering up the defences and confront the visible section of the German army. This was a complex and difficult military operation (planning, timing and co-ordinating the separate Roman attacks). Germanicus therefore led the Roman charge and left the further arrangements to his senior officers (giving them scope to act and respond as required).

The Roman soldiers who advanced across the level ground made good progress. But the forces who assaulted the earthwork were struck with many heavy blows from above and had to fight as though they were scaling a wall (clambering, climbing, striking upwards, and defending against downward attacks). The commander realised how disadvantaged his soldiers had become and withdrew his legions a short distance from the earthwork.

He then ordered slingers and artillerymen to discharge a dense volley of missiles into the defences to scatter the enemy. Spears were hurled from the engines (long-range field artillery – mobile catapults able to launch harpoon-like javelins). Any defenders who made themselves prominent (in acts of bravado) suffered the greatest wounds, as the Germans were driven back from the earthwork.

The Romans stormed the ramparts while Caesar Germanicus, accompanied by some of the praetorian cohorts, led the charge into the woods. The Romans now engaged the Germans in extreme close-quarter fighting. Both sides fought desperately to maintain their position and avoid retreat. Behind the Germans there was treacherous marshland and behind the Romans the landscape was hemmed in by the river and the hills. Their only hope was valour, and a victory provided the only means for safety and survival.

Teutoburg Forest

The Germanic war leader Arminius inflicted a severe defeat on the Romans at the Battle of the Teutoburg Forest (AD 9). It was a German strategy to attack an enemy in motion (mid-migration). Arminius ambushed the Roman forces when they were crossing dense terrain encumbered by their dependants (women, children and servants).

326 Cassius Dio, *Roman History*, 56.20–22

The mountains of Germania are split by ravines where the trees are densely placed and extend to a great height. From their first campaigns the Romans had struggled to enter and cross the regions contained by these ranges. It was a difficult task to fell trees, construct roads and bridge territories (by building wooden causeways across marshlands). Now they had to perform these tasks while under attack.

Varus had the Roman army travel in a convoy containing many wagons and pack animals as though it were a time of peace. There were women and children accompanying the army along with a large retinue of servants. For this reason, the Roman force was advancing in scattered groups instead of a unified military column. Rain and violent winds further interrupted and separated the advancing force. The surface water made forest roots and logs slippery and treacherous for those who walked the route. Branches torn from the trees kept falling onto the path of the column, causing further delay and confusion.

The Germanic forces were already prepared and waiting. When their leaders arrived, they massacred the Roman detachments posted in their territories. Then they moved forwards to intercept the Roman army led by Varus as they marched through the midst of a vast and almost impenetrable forest (the Teutoburg). As the German warriors approached the Romans, they suddenly revealed themselves to be armed enemies instead of subject allies. Then they wrought great and dreadful havoc on the Romans.

While the Romans were distracted by logistic (supply and terrain) difficulties the barbarians suddenly and simultaneously surrounded them on all sides. They knew the hidden trails and could emerge from the densest thickets of the forest. At first their warriors hurled their spear volleys from a distance. The unprepared Romans put up no defence and a great number were wounded. Seeing this the Germans approached closer to the Roman lines.

The Romans were not advancing through the forest in any regular order and the soldiers were intermixed with wagons and unarmed people (women, children and attendants). The Roman response was therefore chaotic as the soldiers could not form into effective combat units. The Romans were also outnumbered by the Germans at the main points of attack. This meant that they suffered greatly in the fighting and could offer no effective resistance.

Batavian Revolt

In AD 69, a territory on the North Rhine frontier called Batavia revolted from Roman authority. The war leader Civilis prepared a Germanic army to resist Roman retaliation.

327 Tacitus, *Histories*, 5.16–18

After his defeat alongside the Treveri (Gallic rebels), Civilis formed another army recruited from Germanic fighters (tribes east of the Rhine). He took up position at the Old Camp where he had a strategic advantage, and his barbarian troops would gain courage by recalling previous successes at the site. Cerialis followed him to this place with a Roman force that had been doubled in size by the arrival of the Second, Sixth and Fourteenth legions. The auxiliary infantry and cavalry had been summoned earlier, and now hurried to join the legions after their recent victory.

Neither of the commanders favoured delay (German or Roman). But the nature of the terrain, which was widely exposed and waterlogged, prevented them from engaging. Civilis had constructed a dam obliquely across the Rhine, so the river was diverted and overflowed across the adjacent countryside. The flooded landscape was now full of hidden perils such as the varying depth of fords (deep mud pits or flooded trenches). This was unfavourable terrain for Roman soldiers, who wear heavy armour and are afraid to swim. In contrast, the Germans are accustomed to cross to rivers and can fight well in these circumstances, due to their light equipment and greater height.

Civilis did not marshal his army in silence. He called upon the battle lines to witness the coming valour. He told the Germans and Batavians that they were standing on the monuments of their past glory. They were treading on the ashes and bones of defeated legions. He said:

> Wherever the Roman looks he sees confinement, disaster, and everything terrible. Do not be alarmed by the battlefield defeat of the Treveri (Gallic allies). For that Roman victory has benefitted the Germans. Their soldiers have dropped their armaments to pick up plunder. Since then, everything has been favourable to us and adverse for our foe.
>
> Your leader has taken all actions and precautions required. We know these flooded plains and we have made the marshlands fatal to our enemy. The Rhine and the Gods of Germany are watching us. We give battle under their auspices. Remember your wives, your parents, and your homeland. This day, you will surpass all past glories or be remembered with disgrace and shame.

Once the Romans had exhausted their store of missiles, the enemy intensified their attack. Their tall stature and very long spears allowed them to wound the Roman soldiers without receiving counter-strikes. The Roman troops hesitated, and the ranks became weakened and unsteady. Then a column of Bructeri swam across from the place where the dam had diverted the river (the deepest part of the flooded landscape). Their attack caused confusion in the Roman ranks. The front-line auxiliaries were forced back, leaving the legionaries to engage the oncoming enemy. The legionary ranks held against the fury of the foe as the battle became an equal contest.

Battles in the Late Roman Era

Ammianius describes the Battle of Argentoratum when the western Caesar Julian fought an Alemannic army crossing the Rhine frontier (AD 357).

328 Ammianus Marcellinus, *Roman History*, 16.12

Julian now deployed the greater part of his army opposite the forefront of the savages. (…) The trumpeters signalled the call to battle and a ferocious combat began between the armies. First missiles were hurled, then the Germans recklessly charged the Romans, wielding (only) their weapons in their right hands (shock troops who had discarded their cumbersome shields). They dashed into the cavalry squadrons, hideously gnashing their teeth, and raging far beyond their usual manner (berserkers). Their hair was loose (unknotted) and a kind of madness shone from their eyes. This was a terrifying sight. The Roman soldiers resolutely protected their heads with the barrier of their shields (a roof of shields to deflect darts and arrows). Then with sword thrusts (front ranks) and a return volley of darts they killed their opponents and caused great fear among the German masses. During this crisis the cavalry reformed into massed squadrons ready for valiant action. In response the German infantry joined their bucklers together to form a shield wall that could protect their flanks.

329 Ammianus Marcellinus, *Roman History*, 16.12

Meanwhile, the Alemanni, having beaten and scattered the Roman cavalry, surged into the front lines of the infantry. They thought that the Roman courage to resist had failed, and they could finally be driven back. The close-quarter contest continued for a long time on equal terms because the Cornuti and the Bracchiati (Roman units of Gallic origin) had been toughened by long experience in fighting. These veteran troops intimidated the enemy with their fearsome gestures and raised their mighty battle cry.

This shout emerges in the fury of combat and rises from a low murmur that gradually grows louder, like powerful waves pounding against cliffs (a Roman version of the Barritus). Clouds of hissing javelins flew overhead in the exchange of missiles. The dust of the battlefield began rising up on either side of the combatants to obstruct their view (and irritate their eyes). The fighters began striking blindly at each other – weapon against weapon and body against body. The enemy savages were thrown into disorder by their violence and anger. But suddenly they flamed up like a renewing fire and hacked furiously with repeated strokes of their swords against the close array of Roman shields, which were still locked into the tortoise-formation.

330 Ammianus Marcellinus, *Roman History*, 16.12

The Alemanni were still eager for battle, and they increased their efforts to destroy everything in their path. A fit of rage spread through their fighters, but the darts, javelins and iron-tipped arrows continued to fly into their forces (increasing casualties). At close quarters blade clashed on blade and breastplates were cleft with sword strikes. Some of the severely wounded, before their blood was gone, rose up to commit some incredible act of bravery (realising they had received a mortal wound and had only minutes to live).

331 Ammianus Marcellinus, *Roman History*, 16.12
The combatants were evenly matched. The Alemanni were stronger and taller, but the Romans were experienced by long-term practice. The enemy were savage and uncontrollable, but the Romans were disciplined and wary. They depended on courage to overcome the physical might of the Germans. Often the Roman soldiers were pushed out of position by the weight of the enemy combatants. But they rose up again and reclaimed their place (restoring the shield wall). Sometimes the enemy savages would collapse as their legs gave way to fatigue (the extreme exertion of the push). They would drop down to their knees and with great resolve continue the effort (shoving forwards from a crouching position).

332 Ammianus Marcellinus, *Roman History*, 16.12
Suddenly a furious band of enemy nobles surged forwards (Alemanni warrior-elites equipped with the best armour and weapons). Their kings fought within these units (perhaps a hearthguard). Together with the common soldiers the nobles broke through the battle lines of their opponents and cut a path into the Roman army that the other fighters followed.

333 Ammianus Marcellinus, *Roman History*, 16.12
On the Roman side, 243 soldiers and 4 high-ranking officers were killed in the fighting. This included Bainobaudes, tribune of the Cornuti, Laipso and Innocentius, who were commanders of the armoured cavalry, and one unattached tribune whose name is not recorded. There were reckoned to be about 6,000 corpses of the Alemanni on the battlefield. The heaps of dead swept away by the river were impossible to estimate.

Roman Defeat

Two decades after the victory of Argentoratum, the Roman army engaged a Gothic settler force in Thrace (Battle of the Willows, AD 377). The Goths had crossed the Danube frontier as supposed allies of Rome, but due to mistreatment, they rebelled from Roman authority.

334 Ammianus Marcellinus, *Roman History*, 31.6–8

The Roman leaders watched and prepared for any further movement that the Goths might attempt. The enemy frequently transferred their camp to a new location. So when this occurred, the Romans planned to attack from the rear. They anticipated killing many and seizing their plunder. But the Goths guessed their intentions, or were informed by deserters who revealed the Roman plans. They therefore remained for a long time in the same position. The Goths were terrified by the opposing army and the additional Roman soldiers that they expected would arrive. They therefore summoned the predatory bands of Gothic warriors scattered over various nearby places (engaged in looting and scavenging supplies). They returned like fire-darts (incendiary missiles launched in unison to ignite a siege target). These warbands returned at great speed to the Gothic camp known as the 'Wagon City' and this gave their kinsmen an incentive for bold action.

There was incessant activity on both sides with only a brief armistice. Reinforced by their warbands, the Goths crowded within their defensive ring (a palisade of spikes reinforced by a dense wall of rawhide-covered wagons). They uttered terrifying yells (war cries) and roused themselves into a furious temper. They prepared to rush headlong at the enemy despite the extreme dangers. The chiefs of the nation encouraged this response. But it was nearly sundown and nightfall subdued the Goths, though their camp remained restless. (…)

It was barely daylight when the war trumpets on both sides sounded the call to arms. Following their customs, the enemy fighters took an oath together (a battle pledge). Then they advanced towards the high-ground hoping to make an overwhelming charge down the slope when the Romans drew near. Seeing this the Roman soldiers hurried into their regimental ranks. Then they stood firm without moving or rushing forwards (to claim the hill). (…)

The two armies began attacking each other from a distance with javelins and other missiles. Then they advanced with menace for direct hand-tohand combat. The Romans fixed the edges of their shields together to form a 'tortoise-shed' (a box-like shield wall where the soldiers behind the front line raised their shields upwards and level to protect themselves from downward missile fire). The Romans stood in close quarters against the enemy (toe to toe), but the barbarians were always alert and nimble. They fought with huge fire-hardened clubs (a method that strengthened simple but sturdy weapons). Then they drove their swords through the chests of the Romans who showed the most resistance (battering the shield wall and trying to pierce holes in the Testudo formation). Using these tactics, the enemy managed to break through the left wing of the Roman force.

When the left wing gave way, a strong troop of Roman soldiers held in reserve bravely rushed forwards to assist their comrades. They rallied and reinforced them when death was already at their throats (an imminent slaughter averted). The pace of the battle then increased and a great many were slain.

All the most active and eager fighters rushed into the dense combat and were killed by arrows that flew like hail, or by sword strikes. Those who fled on either side were pursued by troops of cavalry. The horsemen used mighty downward strokes to slash at the heads and backs of the fleeing fighters. On both sides the advancing infantry mutilated those who stumbled and fell as they fled in terror.

Finally, the whole battlefield was covered with corpses and the mortally wounded fell among the dead. Some of the casualties maintained a futile hope of survival, if they had been struck from a sling-shot or pierced by an arrow. But others had been hacked and split between the forehead and the top of their skull (caused by a powerful downward sword strike). Their wounds extended deep into their shoulders. This was a horrifying sight (Ammianus had served as a soldier and writes from experience).

But the two armies were still not exhausted by this stubborn conflict. Both sides continued to assail one another without an outcome. Both sides were undiminished while eager courage maintained their strength. Evening ended the murderous contest for supremacy. Both forces withdrew in disorder wherever the opportunity arose, and survivors returned in sorrow to their tents (both military camps).

Battle of Adrianople

The Eastern Roman Field Army launched a larger attack on this Gothic force at the Battle of Adrianople (AD 378). The Romans were led by the Eastern Emperor Valens.

335 Ammianus Marcellinus, *Roman History*, 31.12
The (Eastern) Roman Army marched a long distance over rough ground under the full glare and heat of the sun. At the eighth hour (early afternoon) they saw the wagons of the enemy arranged in a perfect circle as the scouts had reported (the well-defended enemy encampment). The barbarian soldiers followed their usual customs by uttering savage and disturbing

howls. Meanwhile, the Roman commanders drew up their line of battle with the cavalry on the right wing ready to advance and the greater part of the infantry held in reserve. But the Roman horsemen on the left had great difficulty forming up because many of them were still scattered along the roads and still hastening to the battle site. The left wing of the Roman army was therefore being continually extended by late incomers. The barbarians were terrified by the sight and sound. The Roman soldiers clashed their shields and a volley of whirring arrows was released from their army. (…)

Meanwhile, the enemy deliberately delayed the Romans with this apparent truce, so that their cavalry might return in time. They hoped that the Gothic horsemen would suddenly appear while the Roman soldiers were still exhausted and thirsty, waiting in the glaring summer heat. The gleam of fires could be glimpsed in the distance. The enemy had lit wildfires to burn the dry shrub and send further heat and smoke billowing across the arid battlefield. But there was a further detriment to the Roman forces. Both men and animals (horses and pack mules) were tormented by severe hunger (as they waited in formation). (…)

The Roman archers and the targeteers rushed forwards too eagerly to reach the enemy with their missiles. The Goths charged them, and these Roman units were forced into a cowardly retreat. This was an ominous omen for the battle to come.

Massacre at Adrianople

Valens, like Julius Caesar, planned to attack the opposing camp while the enemy cavalry was absent (engaged in long-range foraging). But the Gothic horsemen suddenly returned, reinforced by skilled steppe riders from the Alani nation. The Romans did not have the battle formations or war equipment to successfully resist (see Arrian, *Battle Order Against the Alani*).

336 Ammianus Marcellinus, *Roman History*, 31.12–13
Richomeres acted quickly to save the situation (allowing the missile troops to disengage). But the conflict was also interrupted by the return of the Gothic cavalry led by Alatheus and Saphrax. They had combined with a band of Alani (mounted warriors from the steppe who had also entered Roman territory). The enemy cavalry dashed into the Roman army like a thunderbolt descending from high mountains. They threw the Roman ranks into confusion, overcoming everything in their path and slaying many in their swift onslaught.

Armour and weapons clashed on every side (as the armies engaged). Bellona (the goddess of war) raged with madness to destroy the Romans as the war trumpets sounded (a rallying call). The Roman soldiers who were giving way rallied and exchanged many encouraging shouts. But the battle was spreading like a fire, and they were filled with terror as many of their comrades were struck by whirling spears and arrows.

Then the two battle lines dashed together like the armoured prow of war galleys (Gothic infantry forces crashing against the Roman ranks). The opposing lines pushed each other back and forth with alternate movements like the surging waves at sea.

The left wing of the Roman force was able to push forwards almost to the wagons (encircling the enemy camp). But they did not have cavalry support because the Roman horsemen (on the flank) were hard-pressed by great numbers of the enemy. Suddenly their formation was crushed and overwhelmed like the downfall of a mighty rampart (the Goths broke through the Roman cavalry). The Roman infantry were now unprotected and their companies were so compacted that hardly anyone could thrust out his sword or retract his arm (their method for killing). Great clouds of dust filled the air obscuring their vision (dust kicked up by the cavalry). Frightful cries echoed through the (trapped) and compacted Roman ranks. Then a hail of whirling arrows fell into their midst from every side. These missiles could not be guarded against or seen until they struck their target. The falling arrows always hit something and impacted with lethal effect (because the Romans were so closely crammed together).

The barbarians pushed forwards in huge hordes, trampling horses and men. The extreme press of ranks gave the crowded and crushed Romans no scope for retreat or escape in any direction. But the soldiers still scorned death and as they received death blows, they struck down their assailants. Helmets and breastplates were split by powerful downward strikes (the easiest attack in the crush of combatants).

Among the enemy the Romans would sometimes glance a single barbarian overcome with courage, his face contracted into a hiss (a bestial snarl). He might be hamstrung with his leg tendons sliced, or his right hand severed, or pierced through the side (all debilitating mortal injuries). But on the very verge of death, he would still look around with fierce and threatening glances for a new opponent to engage. The dead and fallen on both sides covered the battlefield. Corpses were strewn over the ground, while the dying cries of those severely injured, amplified the Roman terror.

There was great clamour and confusion amongst the Roman infantry. They were exhausted by their efforts and the extreme danger. Their strength began to fail, along with their mental ability to plan any effective strategy. Most of their spears had been broken in the constant fighting, so equipped only with drawn swords, they plunged into the dense mass of the foe. They were now heedless of their lives, since all prospect of escape seemed lost. The ground was covered with streams of blood that made the surface slippery. The Romans strained with all their remaining might to inflict injury upon the enemy before they succumbed to death. They opposed the onrushing foe with such great resolution that some died from the weapons of their own comrades.

Everything in sight was stained and discoloured by the taint of dark blood. Wherever the Romans looked there were heaps of dead. They trod upon the fallen bodies without regard or mercy. But the sun was still high overhead, scorching the Romans who felt the greater effects of hunger, thirst, and the burden of heavy armour. Finally, the main Roman infantry line was broken by the onrushing mass of barbarians. All those that could escape fled in disorder and scattered into the landscape along rough paths. (…)

The frenzied barbarians pursued the fleeing Romans, who were dumbfounded with fear and horror. Some of the soldiers were struck down without seeing the killing blow (hit from behind while running away). Others were buried beneath the weight of their assailants (dragged down and slain by multiple attackers). Some soldiers were also slain by the sword of a comrade (a mercy killing). The soldiers often rallied and regrouped, but the enemy were relentless and did not spare anyone.

The roads were obstructed by fallen soldiers who lay crying out in torment with mortal wounds. Mounds of slain horses filled the battlefield. These were irreparable losses for the Roman state.

A night without moonlight ended the fighting (and pursuit). It was assumed that the emperor took refuge among the common soldiers as darkness descended. But no one claimed to have seen him. It was therefore thought that he had been mortally wounded by an arrow and died somewhere on the battlefield. His body was never found.

German Seafaring

Pliny the Elder, who served on the Rhine frontier, describes Germanic seafaring.

337 Pliny, *Natural History*, 16.76

The largest cedar tree is reported to have been grown on the island of Cyprus. It was felled by Demetrius (the Macedonian king) to make a mast for a galley with rowers arranged in teams of eleven men. This tree was reported to be 130 feet long and three men standing with their arms outstretched could touch hands around its circumference. Raiders from Germany make their voyages in boats carved out from the trunk of a single tree. Some of these vessels can carry as many as thirty people.

Body Paint

Tacitus described the use of dyes and paints by German warriors to cause fear among their enemies.

338 Tacitus, *Germania*, 43

The Harii are stronger and more savage than other German tribes in this region. They augment their natural ferocity by dying their shields and their bodies black. They choose dark nights for battle and advance like an army of the dead to strike terror into their foes. The enemy cannot easily deal with their strange supernatural appearance, because in all battles, sight is the first sense to be challenged and overcome by fear.

German Attitude to Land

Pliny mentions German practices that resembled Roman ceremonies.

339 Pliny, *Natural History*, 22.4

The Civic Crown (a military trophy) is a glorious and hallowed award achieved by saving the life of a fellow citizen. It is granted for saving even the lowest and most commonplace man. A far greater award is therefore due to the courageous soldier who saves, or preserves, an entire army or civic community. By tradition this greater crown is woven from the green grass pulled up from the site where the oppressed or besieged men are rescued or relieved (an award usually given to commanders who rescued garrisons near the point of annihilation). This tradition came from another older custom. In earlier times it was a solemn token of defeat for a conquered people to present grass to their conquerors. This symbolised that they had withdrawn their ancestral claim over the soil that had nurtured them and would one day be their place of burial. I know that the Germans still preserve this custom down to our own time.

Chapter Fifteen

Service in the Roman Army

Germanic auxiliaries remained loyal to the Pompeian faction during the Roman Civil War, Battle of Ruspina (46 BC).

340 Caesar, *African Wars*, 40
Caesar ordered the retreat to be sounded and withdrew all his cavalry inside his own fortifications. It was then, when the battlefield had been cleared, that his attention was caught by the amazing physiques of the Gauls and Germans (men slain in combat). Some of these men had followed Labienus from Gaul because they respected Caesar's authority (loyalty to Rome). But others had been induced to join his cause (the Pompeian faction) through rewards and promises. Others were taken captive after Curio's defeat and since their lives had been spared, they offered unswerving loyalty in supreme gratitude. The mutilated bodies of these men, remarkable in splendour and stature, now lay scattered across the battlefield.

Batavians in Roman Military Service

Batavian troops were involved in the Roman campaign to recover Greater Germania in AD 15. They were skilled at swimming rivers.

341 Tacitus, *Annals*, 2.11
The next day, the German army took up position on the other side of the Visurgis. Caesar Germanicus decided it was not good generalship to engage the enemy with legions as bridges had not been constructed across the river (allowing rapid retreat or reinforcement). He therefore sent the Roman cavalry across the river using the nearby fords. These cavalry forces were commanded by Stertinius, and Aemilius who was one of the senior centurions. They attacked at widely different points in the German line in order to engage and distract their enemy. Meanwhile, the Batavian chief Chariovalda charged into the river where the stream was strongest (his auxiliaries crossing by swimming where an attack was least expected).

Germanic Unit Engages Rebels in Thrace (AD 26)

Battle Display of Cohort I Claudia Sugambrorum Veterana

342 Tacitus, *Annals*, 4.47
Sabinus (the Roman commander) advanced against the enemy (rebel Thracians). The enemy had withdrawn to some wooded valleys, but some of them now ventured out onto the exposed hills. The Roman commander approached in fighting order and easily dislodged these opponents, but he could not kill many of them because they had only a short distance to flee (back into the woods).

Sabinus soon established a camp in this position. He deployed a strong detachment of troops to guard a narrow and unbroken mountain ridge which extended to the next fortress. This line was garrisoned by a large force of well-armed soldiers, along with some irregulars (auxiliaries). The boldest of the enemy approached this force and performed actions in their national custom. They posed in front of the Roman ramparts, chanting and dancing (athletic challenges, displays of courage and martial intimidations). Sabinus sent some select archers against this foe. They discharged arrows from a great distance and inflicted many wounds without loss to themselves. But as the archers advanced, a sudden (counter-charge) manoeuvre by the enemy caused them to rout. They fled back to the Sugambrian cohort, which the Roman general had positioned close to the engagement as an emergency measure. This cohort proved as terrifying as the foe in the noise of their war songs and the clashing of their weapons.

Roman Civil War (AD 69)

The Roman commander Vitellius seized Rome with a Rhineland army, including many Germans.

343 Tacitus, *Histories*, 2.88
There was panic in Rome as the soldiers crowded in from all directions (the victorious Rhineland army). Most of them headed to the Forum because they were anxious to see the place where Galba had been killed (the former emperor). These soldiers were a terrifying spectacle. They bristled with the skins of wild beasts and were armed with huge spears. They found their surroundings utterly strange (an overcrowded urban environment)

and were disturbed by the mass of people. They slipped and tumbled on the streets (slick cobbles worn smooth by constant traffic) and recoiled at casual encounters (aggressive begging, haggling and soliciting).

Military Displays by the Emperor Hadrian

344 Cassius Dio, *Roman History*, 69.9

Hadrian travelled through the provinces, visiting various regions and cities, inspecting all the garrisons and forts. (…) Foreign nations saw these preparations and therefore favoured peace. In return they suffered no aggression and received money to abstain from conflict (Roman pay-offs). Hadrian's soldiers were excellently trained, and his Batavian cavalry even swam the Ister River (Danube) under military arms (fully equipped). When the barbarians saw this spectacle, they were terrified and accepted Hadrian as an arbitrator to settle their disputes (resolving inter-tribal conflicts).

Inscription of a Batavian Cavalryman (AD 118)

Tombstone of a Batavian named Soranus, who died on the Danube frontier. Perhaps a member of the Emperor Hadrian's personal horseguard.

345 *Corpus Inscriptionum Latinarum*, 3.3676 (AD 118)

I am the man, known to the riverbanks of Pannonia, brave and foremost among a thousand Batavians. With Hadrian as my judge, I swam the wide waters of the deep Danube in full battle kit. From my bow I shot an arrow which, as it hung in the air and fell, I hit and broke it with another shot. No Roman or foreigner ever outdid my exploits. No soldier with the spear, no Parthian with the bow, surpassed me. Here I lie, beneath this eternal stone. I have recounted deeds to remember. Let anyone hereafter, see if he can match my actions. I set my own standard and I was the first to accomplish such feats.

Emperor Maximinus Thrax Marches against a Rebellious Rome (AD 238)

346 Herodian, *Roman History*, 8.1

The emperor also brought along a large number of German auxiliaries. He assigned these forces to the rear (of his marching columns) where they might withstand the initial assaults of the enemy. These men are savage and bold in the opening phases of a battle. Furthermore, if any serious risk is involved, these barbarian Germans are expendable.

Roman Retreat from Persia (AD 364)

347 Ammianus Marcellinus, *Roman History*, 25.6
With mutinous bluster the Roman army demanded that they be allowed to cross the Tigris. The Emperor Justin, along with the generals, opposed these demands. They pointed out how since the Dog Star had already risen the river was swollen with floodwaters (summer flood conditions). The commanders begged the soldiers to trust them and not try to swim across the dangerous currents. They added that the enemy had dispersed to attack their forces in various places along the swollen river (far banks).

But the repeated warnings had no effect, and with loud shouts the excited soldiers threatened a full mutiny. Therefore, Jovian reluctantly consented and arranged for a mixed force of Gauls and North Germans to enter the river first. If these men were swept away by the force of the stream, then the other soldiers would abandon their stubbornness. But if they crossed without harm, then the main army could attempt the task with greater confidence.

The most skilful soldiers were therefore chosen for this attempt. These were men, who from early childhood, in their native lands were taught to cross the greatest of all rivers (the Rhine). Under the silent cover of night when they would not be seen, they started off in unison like contestants in a race. They reached the opposite bank of the river much faster than expected. The Persians posted to guard these places were in a state of deep sleep due to their feeling of great security. The onrushing horsemen trampled the Persians underfoot and killed a great number of the enemy. Then they raised their hands and waved their capes in the air to show their bold attempt had succeeded. When the soldiers on the far bank saw this signal in the distance, they were eager to cross. But they delayed to allow the pontoon builders time to make bridges of bladders from the hides of slain animals.

348 Ammianus Marcellinus, *Roman History*, 25.7
King Shapur (the Persian monarch) had further anxieties (leading him to conclude peace terms). He was aware that a force of 500 soldiers had crossed the swollen river unharmed. They had slain his Persian guards and roused their Roman comrades to similar bold acts.

Late Empire

The Batavian reputation as determined and effective soldiers persisted into the fourth century AD. It is attested at the Battle of Argentoratum when the western Caesar Julian fought the invading Alemanni (AD 357).

349 Ammianus Marcellinus, *Roman History*, 16.12

In response, the Batavians (another Roman unit) advanced quickly to assist their comrades. They were led by their 'kings' (native officers awarded 'royal' status in the imperial system). These Batavians were a formidable unit (and of German extraction). The Roman troops fighting in the front lines were embattled and in dire need when the Batavians came to their rescue. The trumpets sounded a savage note and they fought with all their power and determination.

Final Refuge

When the Emperor Valens was losing at the Battle of Adrianople, he sought support from the Batavian regiment as a final refuge from the triumphant Goths (AD 378).

350 Ammianus Marcellinus, *Roman History*, 31.13

These Roman horsemen had stood firmly in place while vast numbers of the enemy had surged at their position (their battle line had held). When (their commander) Trajanus saw Valens, he cried out that all hope was lost unless the emperor leave his bodyguard (of mounted troops). He must be protected by foreign auxiliaries (fierce infantry fighters). A general called Victor went in search of the Batavi who had been posted nearby as a reserve force (a regiment of skilled Germanic soldiers from Batavia). But he could not locate them on the battlefield and he did not return.

Chapter Sixteen

German Bodyguards of the Roman Emperors: Germani Corporis Custodes

The Julio-Claudian emperors maintained a loyal bodyguard of Germanic troops who were stationed in Rome. The practice began with Julius Caesar, who recruited allied Germanic warriors into his armies.

Germanic Troops in Roman Service (Gaul, 52 BC)

351 Julius Caesar, *Gallic War*, 7.13
Caesar ordered the Roman cavalry to be brought out of camp to engage the enemy horsemen (Gauls). Then, when the Roman troops began to suffer in this combat, he sent 400 Germanic horsemen to reinforce them. It had become his practice to keep these Germans close to himself at the onset of any fighting (a rapid reaction force). The Gauls could not resist the Germanic charge and their cavalry suffered heavy losses as they fled back to their main army.

Fighting Abilities of Germanic Auxiliaries in the Gallic War (52 BC)

352 Cassius Dio, *Roman History*, 40.39
Meanwhile, due to Caesar's recent military failures, Vercingetorix (the Gallic War leader) felt increasing contempt for him. He therefore marched against the Allobroges (a Celtic tribe still loyal to Rome). He managed to intercept the Roman general sent out to assist them while in the territory of the Sequani (another Celtic tribe). This Roman force was entirely surrounded by the enemy, but it endured intact. They survived because there was no safety and retreat was impossible, whereas the enemy acted in an imprudent and careless manner due to their vast numbers.

Vercingetorix suffered a defeat in this engagement largely due to the presence of German warriors who were serving as allies to the Roman force. These Germans possessed mighty physiques and had an unstoppable enthusiasm for the fighting. With strength and daring they broke through the Gallic ranks that encircled the Romans. After this good fortune, Caesar continued the conflict and besieged Alesia (an *oppidum* – Celtic settlement) where many of the enemy had fled for refuge.

Use of German Cavalry against the Gauls

353 Julius Caesar, *Gallic War*, 7.67

The next day the Gauls divided their cavalry into three divisions. Two of these divisions appeared on the Roman flanks, while the third moved in front to obstruct their march. When Caesar realised what was occurring, he ordered the Roman cavalry to form three divisions and charge the enemy simultaneously. Meanwhile, the main Roman force halted and the baggage trains were received within the legionary ranks (for protection).

If the cavalry seemed to be distressed, or hard-pressed in any quarter, Caesar ordered his infantry to advance, and the army would move forwards in that direction. This deterred the enemy from pushing forwards in pursuit and encouraged the Roman cavalry to expect support.

Finally, the Germans (serving Roman auxiliary cavalry) who were fighting on the right wing, gained control over the top of the hill. They dislodged the Gallic cavalry from their position and pursued them as far as the river where Vercingetorix was stationed with his infantry forces. During this pursuit, the Germans managed to kill a significant number of the enemy. When the rest of the Gallic cavalry saw what was occurring (on the right flank), they feared being surrounded so they fled the conflict. The Roman slaughter of the enemy took place in every direction and three of the noblest of the Aedui were taken prisoner and brought before Caesar.

Roman Civil War (36 BC)

When a Germanic bodyguard spent the night on the slopes of Mount Etna (an active volcano in Sicily), they protected their commander Octavian (the future emperor Augustus).

354 Appian, *Civil Wars*, 5.117

Octavian planned to intercept Tisienus (the rival general), but he lost his way travelling around Mount Myconium. His forces therefore spent the night on the hillside without tents or shelter. A heavy rainfall began, which was a common occurrence in autumn. In response, some of his armour-bearers (bodyguard) held their Gallic-style shields over his head throughout the whole night (a shield wall shelter). During the night, Mount Etna emitted harsh grumbles and prolonged roars. Fires spat out of the mountain to illuminate the sleeping Germans who sprang from the ground in terror. Some of them had heard stories about the mountain and were afraid that a torrent of fire might roll down towards them (lava).

Imperial Bodyguard

The German bodyguard (corporis custodes) remained with Octavian when he became emperor and received the name Augustus (27 BC). However, the guard had their duties suspended after the Teutoburg massacre (AD 9, when three legions were slaughtered in a Germanic revolt).

355 Suetonius, *Augustus*, 49
Augustus disbanded a troop of Calagurritani (native Spanish soldiers, possibly Iberian Celts), which had formed a part of his bodyguard until the overthrow of Antony. He also dismissed a bodyguard unit of Germans after the defeat of Varus (a temporary suspension of their duties).

Unit Sizes

Cassius Dio mentioned the German bodyguards when he discussed the size of the Roman military. He calls them 'Batavians' (from allied territory on the North Rhine).

356 Cassius Dio, *Roman History*, 55.24
In the time of Augustus, the Romans maintained either twenty-three or twenty-five legions. They also maintained allied forces of infantry, cavalry and sailors, but I cannot find figures for these troops (detailed historical records). There were also 10,000 praetorians (in Rome) organised in 10 divisions. Then there were about 6,000 'Watchmen' in the city organised in 4 divisions (public order forces). The emperor also maintained a force of specially selected foreign horsemen, known as the Batavians (the German bodyguard). This force was recruited from the (riverine) island of Batavia next to the Rhine, which provides excellent horsemen. But I cannot state the exact number of these troops.

Legendary Bodyguards

Livy was writing during the reign of the First Emperor Augustus. He provides an account of Romulus, the legendary founder of Rome (750 BC).

357 Livy, *History of Rome*, 1.15

Romulus had greater appeal to the populace than to the patricians (the nobility). But most of all he was adored by his soldiers. He kept a (mounted) bodyguard of three hundred men around him for service in peacetimes as well as in war. These men were called the 'Celeres'.

Actions of a Possible Germanic Bodyguard

In 9 BC, the Roman commander Tiberius made a rushed journey north beyond the Rhine to reach his gravely ill brother Drusus. He was accompanied by a guide named 'Namantabagius'.

358 Valerius Maximus, *Memorable Deeds*, 5.5.3

Our paternal emperor Tiberius had a very strong love for his brother Drusus. After defeating our enemies, Tiberius came to Ticinum to embrace his parents. There he learnt that Drusus, who was in Germany (on a campaign of conquest), was seriously ill. He was in a dangerous condition and might not live. Tiberius was distraught and rushed off immediately to make the journey in wild haste. He barely paused for breath, crossing the Alps and the Rhine, riding day and night, and changing his horse repeatedly. He keenly completed a journey of 200 miles through a barbarous region that had only recently been pacified. Namantabagius was his sole guide and companion on this journey.

Northern Europeans Serving the Roman Client King Herod

In about 30 BC, the Roman client king, Herod, was given a Celtic bodyguard by Octavian (Augustus). This suggests the size of Germanic/Celtic units used to guard kings and emperors.

359 Josephus, *Jewish War*, 20.3

Octavian (Augustus) presented King Herod with a personal bodyguard of 400 Celts who had served Queen Cleopatra (the former ruler of Ptolemaic Egypt).

Royal Funeral

Josephus describes the death of King Herod the Great in 4 BC. Celtic bodyguards and Germanic troops were prominent in his funeral procession.

360 Josephus, *Antiquities*, 17.8.3

The king was laid out upon a purple bed on a gold bier decorated with precious stones. A diadem was placed upon his head, a crown of gold above it, and a sceptre was placed in his right hand. Close to him were his sons and his numerous relations. The soldiers next to them were dressed in the clothing of their different countries and cultures. First came the Royal Guards, then Herod's Thracian regiment, then the German unit, then the Celtic soldiers. Each was armed and dressed in full war gear. The whole army marched behind these troops, in the same manner as they used to go to war.

Attempted Assassination

In AD 9, the imperial prince Tiberius was almost assassinated by a Germanic warrior who had been able to infiltrate his military camp.

361 Suetonius, *Tiberius*, 19

At his very moment of victory, Tiberius narrowly escaped assassination by one of the Bructeri (a Germanic warrior posing as a Roman auxiliary or custodes?). This man gained access to Tiberius from among his attendants, but he was detected due to his nervousness. Torture was then used to extract a full confession of his intended crime.

Impact of the German Revolt (AD 9)

Cassius Dio describes the reaction in Rome to the Teutoburg massacre (AD 9).

362 Cassius Dio, *Histories*, 56.22–24

There was a large number of Gauls and Germans in Rome during this period. Some of them were serving in the Praetorian Guard (the military unit assigned to the emperor). Others were staying in the city for various other reasons. But Augustus now feared that these people might become involved in an uprising against the empire. He therefore ordered them to leave the city and sent his personal bodyguard (an elite unit of German warriors) to certain islands (offshore Italian islands removed from political affairs in Rome). All unarmed Celts and Germans were also expelled from the capital.

Mutiny by the Danube Legions (AD 14)

The Germanic custodes soon returned to imperial service and when the Emperor Augustus died in AD 14, they transferred their loyalties to his successor, Tiberius (reigned AD 14–37). Soon after Tiberius assumed power some Roman legions on the Danube frontier began to mutiny over pay and conditions. The imperial prince Drusus, son of Tiberius, was sent to restore order, accompanied by a select force of custodes.

363 Tacitus, *Annales*, 1.24

The Emperor Tiberius was careful to conceal serious disasters (from the Roman public). He therefore sent Drusus (his son and heir) north with some leading men of the state and with two praetorian cohorts. He did not give him definite instructions, only advised him to take suitable measures.

The cohorts were strengthened beyond their usual force with some specially selected troops. A considerable part of the praetorian cavalry was included along with the best of the German soldiers from the emperor's bodyguard. The commander of the praetorians, Aelius Sejanus, (…) also came to advise and direct the young prince on whether the mutinous soldiers should be punished, or have their demands acknowledged.

False Alarm

Custodes or praetorians nearly killed a high-born senator who unwittingly caused the Emperor Tiberius to fall.

364 Tacitus, *Annals*, 1.13

Haterius entered the imperial palace to beg the emperor for forgiveness. As he was walking he threw himself at the knees of Tiberius. But this caused the emperor to fall forwards, accidentally entangled in the grip of this suppliant. Consequently, Haterius was almost killed by the soldiers (imperial bodyguards anticipating this was an attack).

Service under Caligula (AD 37–41)

The custodes were not commanded by Roman military officers, thereby ensuring their direct loyalty to the imperial household. The Emperor Caligula appointed a gymnastics instructor named Helicon as commander of the Germanic Guard. A Jewish envoy named Philo recorded these details in a report he wrote for his religious community in Alexandria.

365 Philo, *Embassy to Gaius* (*Caligula*), 175
Helicon fulfils the role of chamberlain (manager of the Royal Household) and chief bodyguard, an office entrusted only to him. He has all kinds of favourable opportunities for the emperor to listen to him at leisure, distant from outside noise and distractions. Through Helicon, the emperor would be able to quietly hear what we desire.

Northern Expedition

In AD 40, Caligula prepared for an expedition into Germany. He was about 30 years old, the same age as his father, Germanicus, and his grandfather, Nero Claudius Drusus, when they subdued Germania as far as the Elbe.

366 Suetonius, *Caligula*, 43
Caligula had only one experience with military affairs and warfare. He had gone to Mevania to visit the river Clitumnus (a scenic site in central Italy). While there he was suddenly reminded of the need to recruit more men for his bodyguard of Batavians. He therefore decided to leave urgently for an expedition to Germany (a forty-day journey to the Rhine frontier).

Rhine Crossing

Caligula sent a group of custodes across the Rhine, possibly to secure an area in preparation for a hunting expedition.

367 Suetonius, *Caligula*, 45
The emperor could find no one to fight with (on the frontier). So, he had a few of his German bodyguard transported across the river (Rhine) and concealed on the far banks. He arranged to be interrupted during his dining with a panicked report that some great disturbance was occurring across the river and the enemy was approaching. He immediately rushed

out with his friends and led part of the praetorian cavalry to the nearby woods. They thrashed about cutting branches and adorned themselves with these pieces like victory trophies.

The emperor returned by torchlight and taunted those who had not followed him, calling them timid and cowardly men. He presented his companions with victory crowns (military awards) ornamented with figures of the sun, moon, and stars. He called these objects *exploratoriae* (awards connected with military scouting ahead of a main army).

Sometime later, he seized some slaves from a common source (perhaps a dealer in barbarian captives). He secretly released these captives and sent them on ahead. Then suddenly during a banquet he got up with his companions and pursued these slaves as if they were fugitives. They were brought back in chains and the emperor reappeared displaying immoderate glee at his actions. When he returned to his table, someone announced that the army was fully assembled (the Rhine legions). He instructed the soldiers who delivered these messages to take a seat at the banquet while they were still in their armour (a breach of decorum).

Murder of Emperor Caligula (AD 41)

The Emperor Caligula was assassinated in AD 41, provoking the Germanic *custodes*.

368 Suetonius, *Caligula*, 58

On the ninth day before the Kalends of February at the seventh hour, Caligula was still undecided whether or not to leave the theatre for a midday meal. His stomach was still disordered from an excess of food on the previous day, but he was finally persuaded by his friends. On leaving the theatre he had to pass along a covered passageway. In this passageway were some noble-born youths who had been summoned from Asia to appear on stage. They were rehearsing their parts, so he stopped to watch them and offer encouragement. He wanted to return to the theatre and make them perform immediately, but the leader of the group complained that he had a chill.

From this point on there are two versions of the story. Some say that as Caligula was talking with the boy, Chaerea came up behind him with a blade drawn. He shouted, 'Take this!' and struck the emperor on the back of the neck causing a deep wound. Then the other conspirator, the tribune Cornelius Sabinus, who was facing Caligula, stabbed him in the chest.

Others say that Sabinus ordered several centurions involved in the plot to remove spectators from the scene before the attack. He then asked the emperor for the watchword as was the usual practice for the soldiers. When Caligula gave him the word 'Jupiter', Sabinus, cried out, 'So be it!' As Caligula turned, Sabinus, struck him with his sword, slicing his jaw with the blow. Caligula immediately fell to the ground and writhed around with his limbs flailing. He cried out that he was still alive. So, the attackers rushed upon him with their weapons drawn and dispatched him with thirty wounds. Their repeated command was, 'Strike again' and some even thrust their blades through his groin. At the start of the disturbance some of his litter bearers ran to his assistance with their polls, but they could not intervene. Later, his Germanic bodyguard (the custodes) went out hunting for the killers. They slew several of his assassins as well as some innocent unarmed senators.

369 Josephus, *Jewish Antiquities*, 19.1.15
The Germans were the first to perceive that Caligula was slain. These Germans were his personal bodyguard and they bore the name of the country where they were recruited. They composed his (so-called) 'Celtic' regiment. These men are subject to strong emotions, which is a common trait of barbarous nations. Likewise, they do not overthink their actions. They have robust physiques and will immediately retaliate when attacked. For this reason, they can perform great exploits.

The German guards were grief-stricken at the report that Caligula was slain. They did not think rationally about public affairs (politics) since they measured everything according to their own advantage (the group interests of an ethnic unit). The emperor had bestowed wealth upon them, this wealth had purchased their affection, so he was beloved by them (gift-giving to purchase tribal loyalty).

The Germans drew their swords and Sabinus, one of their tribunes, led them out. He had received this office, not because his forefathers had performed virtuous actions, but because he had been a gladiator with a strong physique. They marched through the streets searching for the killers. (A senator named) Asprenas had some blood on his toga from animal sacrifices (flamingos killed earlier that day). When the Germans saw him, they rushed forwards and cut him to pieces (thinking he was one of the assassins). Then they encountered Norbanus, who was foremost among the Roman nobility and had many ancestors who had served as generals in past armies. But these high honours meant nothing to the Germans who attacked him. Norbanus was not willing to die without a struggle and he tore a sword from the grip of the first German who struck at him. But as he fought, he was surrounded by a great number of assailants and died by a multitude of wounds.

A third senator named Anteius died with a few companions, but he did not meet the Germans by chance as the others did. Caligula had banished Anteius' father from Rome and later sent some soldiers to kill him. Anteius therefore hated Caligula and wanted to verify his death with his own eyes. He thought it would be a very pleasant sight and he wanted to rejoice at the death scene. Encountering the Germans, Anteius fled into a residence, causing great upset and chaos. Even though he hid himself, he could not escape the accurate search made by the Germans. They slew those who were guilty and those who were not, with equal barbarism.

Custodes Seize and Detain Influential People in the Theatre

370 Josephus, *Jewish Antiquities*, 19.1.17

A multitude of Germans had now surrounded the theatre with their swords drawn. All the occupants were seized by fear as the troops entered the venue and they expected death. It seemed to all those present that they might be immediately cut to pieces. The crowd became distressed, but no one had the courage to leave the theatre, and no one thought they were safe remaining there.

When the German troops closed in, the cries of the crowd were so great that the entire theatre resounded with their pleading. They cried out that they were entirely ignorant of all conspiracies. They knew nothing of any plot and they begged to be spared. They pleaded not to be punished for the murderous crimes of other people and urged the Germans to search for the guilty people in other places. The crowd appealed to their gods for their torment to end. They cried and covered their faces and made every promise and pledge that might prevent imminent danger and preserve their lives. This diffused the fury of the German troops and they regretted the great harm and cruelty they had threatened on the crowd.

The Germans placed the heads of the slain senators, including Asprenas, on the altar (the ceremonial slab where animal sacrifices had earlier been conducted). This caused great alarm among the spectators due to the high status of the slain people and their horrific treatment. The renewed danger caused further disorder as the crowd expected a similar fate. So, even those who despised Caligula could not take pleasure in his death, since they might perish with him. And now they had no certain hope of survival.

Praetorian Response

Chera was an officer in the Praetorian Guard responsible for the assassination and Minucianus was a co-conspirator.

371 Josephus, *Jewish Antiquities*, 19.1.19
Cherea was very afraid for Minucianus in case the Germans had caught him while they were still in their fury (their rampage through the streets). He therefore went and spoke to every one of the soldiers (the Praetorian Guard), pleading with them to preserve his friend, find out his fate and discover if he had been slain.

372 Josephus, *Jewish Antiquities*, 19.1.18
Euaristus Arruntius was a public crier in the market who had a strong and audible voice. (…) He put on the clothes worn during bereavement (the black toga) and entered the theatre as though he was grieving for one of his dearest friends. He announced to everyone that Gaius (Caligula) was indeed dead. This display was convincing and ended all uncertainty.

Followed by the tribunes, Arruntius walked around about the pillars and called out to the Germans. He cried out that Caligula was dead and together they bid the Germans to lay down their weapons. This proclamation saved everyone who had been gathered in the theatre and all the other people that the Germans might later encounter. For the Germans had an immense affection for the emperor and would have undertaken all forms of brutality while they had hope that he still lived. If they had been able to, they would have prevented the plot against him, and secured his escape from this misfortune, even at the cost of their own lives.

The furious zeal they had to punish his enemies quickly diminished. They fully accepted that Caligula was dead. It was now pointless to show further devotion towards him, as he could no longer reward their commitment. The Germans also became afraid that the Senate might punish them if they did any further harm to anyone. For they were worried that the supreme authority of the Roman state might revert back to the Senate (without an emperor). Thus, the violence that occurred after the killing of Caligula was halted. But this was a difficult achievement, given the rage felt by the Germans.

Aftermath of Assassination in the Palace

373 Josephus, *Jewish Antiquities*, 19.3.1

Meanwhile, a multitude of people in the imperial palace were thrown into confusion and dismay (by reports of the assassination). The madness affected the soldiers, and the imperial guard were gripped by the same fear and disorder that affected the civilians (slaves and attendants). The praetorians, the most militarised part of this force, debated over the correct course of action. They had little regard for the murderer of Caligula as they thought he deserved his fate (he had previously insulted and rebuked the praetorians). But their own status and circumstances were now a priority, especially as the Germans were busy killing the murderers of Caligula. These killings were done to gratify the Germans' own savage temper, rather than promote the public good.

During these disturbances, Claudius had been terrified for his own safety, especially when he saw the heads of Asprenas and his comrades being carried about (by the enraged Germans). He had observed these events from an elevated place (a balcony?) so now he stepped back into a dark alcove to conceal himself. Gratus, one of the palace soldiers, saw the solitary figure, but could not make out his features in the gloom. He assumed it was just another man with a private purpose (a visitor to the palace caught up in the turmoil). But as he came closer the man drew back, and he recognised him as Claudius. He called out to his comrades, 'This is a Germanicus, let us make him our Emperor!' (Claudius was the brother of Germanicus.)

374 Cassius Dio, *Roman History*, 59.30

All the soldiers in the Germanic unit began to quarrel and riot, leading to violence and bloodshed.

Thus Caligula, after reigning for three years, nine months, and twenty-eight days, discovered from actual experience that he was not a god. Those who had habitually shown him utmost reverence, even when he was not present, now spat on his memory. He had become a sacrificial victim at the hands of those who had called him 'god' and 'Jupiter'. His statues and his images were dragged from their pedestals and smashed by a populace who now recalled every distress they had endured. (...)

The Praetorian Guard were provoked and began rushing about inquiring who had slain Gaius. But Valerius Asiaticus, an ex-consul, silenced them in a remarkable manner. He climbed up onto a prominent platform and called out: 'If only I could have killed him!' This alarmed the praetorians, who immediately stopped their outcry (their actions had been a pretence of innocence).

Reign of Nero (AD 54–68)

Nero became emperor aged 16. Assisted by the statesman Seneca, he had to assert his own authority and curb the power of his scheming mother, Agrippina.

375 Tacitus, *Annals*, 13.18
Agrippina received tribunes and centurions at the imperial court (the formal responsibilities of a Roman commander). She also honoured the names and virtues of the remaining Roman aristocrats as though she was forming a new political faction. When Nero became aware of these activities, he gave orders to withdraw the military guard that Agripinna had received as the wife (of Claudius), and retained as his mother. He also removed the Germans who had recently been assigned to her as a bodyguard, for this appointment had been made as a further honour.

Loss of Status

Agrippina was denied her praetorian military escort and Germanic Guards (a demotion of status).

376 Suetonius, *Life of Nero*, 34
Nero deprived Agrippina (his mother) of all her political honours including her guard of Roman and Germanic soldiers. Then he forbade her to live in his company and excluded her from the palace.

Public Display

Nero displayed his Germanic bodyguard as mounted hunters in the Roman arena. He also issued bronze coins with the text *Decursio Equitum* ('military exercise involving cavalry') that might be related to these performances.

377 Cassius Dio, *Roman History*, 61.9
At one spectacle in Rome men on horseback rode alongside bulls to slay them (demonstrating their cavalry skills). Then the armoured riders who served as Nero's bodyguard killed 400 bears and 300 lions with their javelins. On the same occasion thirty members of the Equestrian Order (the lesser nobility) also fought as gladiators. These were the public exhibitions that the emperor staged in Rome.

Fighting Styles and Public Acts of Intimidation

Thraex gladiators were trained to fight with small shields and daggers against murmillones, who were equipped with legionary-style swords and shields – the weapons familiar to senators who had served in the Roman military.

378 Suetonius, *Caligula*, 55
Caligula gave some Thracian gladiators command of his German bodyguard (imparting new training methods?). He also reduced the amount of armour used by the murmillones in the combat games (to demonstrate vulnerability, by an uneven contest).

Suppression of Plots

The German bodyguard rounded up the political enemies of Nero in the vicinity of Rome (response to the Pisonian Conspiracy of AD 65). Nero issued coins with the text *Adlocut(io) Coh(ortium)* ('Address to the Troops') that might acknowledge these actions.

379 Tacitus, *Annales*, 15.58
Nero put Rome 'under custody'. He garrisoned its walls with companies of soldiers and placed units on the coast and riverbanks (to prevent unrest and restrict the movement of possible political opponents). Troops were constantly rushing through the public places, intruding on private residences, crossing country fields and occupying neighbouring villages. These soldiers included horsemen and infantry, intermixed with Germans (the imperial bodyguards) since the emperor trusted these men as foreigners (they had no connection to Roman politics or loyalty to the leading senators involved in the conspiracy). These troops were seen leading long lines of prisoners in chains. The captives were dragged along and lined up in front of Nero's Gardens (a large and secure open area that could be used as a base of operations for a military camp).

Custodes Gravestones

About thirty ancient gravestones found in Rome honour members of the custodes. Many of the deceased were Batavians or Ubii who died young (before their service was completed and they presumably returned to their homelands). They adopted more familiar Greek, Celtic or Roman names while in imperial service. Some of the early custodes might have had the status of slaves (in legal service to the imperial household), but later Guards could describe themselves as 'soldiers of the emperor'.

380 Gravestone Inscription from Rome (see Appendix A)
Indus, bodyguard of Nero Claudius Caesar Augustus, of the Second Decuria, of the Batavian nation, who lived thirty-six years, lies here. [This grave-marker] was put here by his comrade and inheritor, Eumenes, from the *Collegium* of the Germans.

The Custodes Abandon Nero

The support of the custodes may have wavered when the Rhine legions began to back a rival candidate for emperor.

381 Joannes Antiochenus, Commentary on Cassius Dio, 63.27
Members of the Senate held conversations with the praetorians and other troops that guarded the imperial court. They persuaded them to join the senators in seizing control over the Roman regime. When these troops had accepted the senatorial plan, they immediately slew Scipulus, the Prefect of their Camp. Then they deserted their post as guardians of the emperor.

When Nero was deserted by his bodyguards, he did not have the courage to kill himself as honour required. Instead, he decided to flee.

382 Plutarch, *Galba*, 2
I have already stated how the prefects of the praetorians, Nymphidius Sabinus and Tigellinus, made Nero's situation more desperate. When it was clear that the emperor was planning his escape to Egypt (Alexandria), they persuaded the soldiers to proclaim Galba their emperor as though Nero no longer ruled. They promised a largess of 75,000 sesterces for any praetorian soldier who followed Galba (a sum equivalent to six years' pay).

383 Cassius Dio, *Roman History*, 63.27
Nero was about to put these measures into effect (an escape by sea to Alexandria) when the Senate withdrew the guard that surrounded him (the praetorians). The senators entered the praetorian camp (their military base) and declared Nero an enemy of the state. Then they pronounced Galba as the new emperor.

Meanwhile, Nero was sleeping in a nearby garden. He awoke to discover that even his bodyguards had deserted him (the Germanic custodes). He therefore decided to flee.

384 Suetonius, *Nero*, 47
Nero awoke about midnight (in the Imperial Palace) and found that his guard of soldiers had left him. He sprang from his bed and sent for all his friends. No reply came back from anyone. With a few followers, he himself went to their rooms. He found that all their doors were closed, and no one replied to him. So, he returned to his own bedchamber. There he discovered that his personal attendants had also fled, taking everything of value with them, including the bedsheets and a box of poison. At once he summoned the gladiator Spiculus and anyone else who might be adept at killing. He thought that by this means he might find death. But when no one appeared, he cried out – 'So then. Have I neither a friend, nor a foe?'

Emperor Galba disbands the Custodes

Civil War of AD 68 – 'Year of the Four Emperors'

385 Suetonius, *Galba*, 12
Galba's reputation was confirmed and augmented when he arrived in Rome (as emperor). (…)

He disbanded a cohort of Germans, who the previous emperors had employed as a bodyguard. These men had been utterly faithful in many emergencies, but Galba sent them back to their native country without any rewards for their service. He alleged that they were favourably inclined towards Gnaeus Dolabella (a political rival) because their military camp in Rome was close to his private gardens. (This sudden dismissal might have provoked the Batavian Revolt, which occupied the Rhineland legions during the civil wars that followed.)

Loyalty of German Units to the Emperor Galba

Galba occupied Rome with his provincial forces, but a military coup occurred, led by a rival officer named Otho.

386 Suetonius, *Galba*, 20
Galba learnt that Otho had taken possession of the main military camp (in Rome). Several advisers urged him to head immediately into the

camp to try to regain control using his presence and imperial prestige. But Galba decided to remain where he was and strengthen his current position. He summoned a strong guard of legionaries, soldiers who were encamped in many different quarters of the city. Meanwhile, for his own protection, Galba put on a linen cuirass (breastplate), though he openly declared that such light armour would provide little protection against so many swords. Galba was then lured into danger by false reports. These reports were circulated by conspirators, to make the emperor reappear in public.

Advisers rashly assured Galba that the disturbances had ended, and the rebels had been suppressed. They said that a group of soldiers were coming to offer their congratulations and receive their new orders. Galba therefore went out to meet them with great confidence. When one of the soldiers boasted that he had slain Otho, Galba asked him, 'On whose authority?' These soldiers accompanied Galba to the Forum (civic centre of Rome), where an ambush had been set. Cavalry were waiting in the nearby streets with orders to slay the emperor. Suddenly they spurred their horses into action, scattering the civilian crowds as they advanced. When they caught sight of the emperor in the distance, they halted momentarily, then charged. When his followers fled, Galba was abandoned and he was butchered where he stood. Some say when the disturbance began, Galba cried out, 'What is your purpose fellow soldiers? I am yours and you are mine.' He may even have promised them monetary rewards. But the more popular account is that Galba offered no resistance and even presented his exposed neck to his attackers. He urged them to do their duty and strike if that was truly *their* will.

It might seem surprising that no one present came to assist their emperor, but all who were sent the summons treated the command with contempt, except for a company of German troops. This was because, recently, when they were suffering and weakened by illness, Galba had showed them compassion and consideration. They rushed to his assistance, but they were not familiar with the layout of the city and did not take the most direct route. They arrived too late to intervene.

German Forces Loyal to the Emperor Vitellius during a Coup (AD 69)

Within a matter of months, Otho was defeated by Vitellius.

387 Cassius Dio, *Roman History*, 64.17

The consuls, Gaius Quintus Atticus and Gnaeus Caecilius Simplex, acted together with Sabinus, who was a relative of Vespasian. They consulted the foremost men in the state and set out for the palace with a force of soldiers who shared their viewpoint. They planned to either persuade, or compel, Vitellius to abdicate from his position as emperor.

But they encountered his Germanic guards and were forced back in the fighting that ensued. They fled to the Capitol (the summit of the civic centre) and fortified their position (among the state temples). Then they sent requests for military assistance to Vespasian via his son Domitian and his other relatives in Rome.

The next day, their adversaries (Roman troops and German auxiliaries loyal to Vitellius) assaulted the Capitol. The defenders were able to repel the attack, but some areas around the Capitol were set on fire and the soldiers on the summit were forced back by the flames. The troops loyal to Vitellius made their way up through the fires and slaughtered many of the defenders. Then they began to plunder all the votive offerings in the sacred precincts. They burned down the great temple (to Jupiter) along with other sacred buildings. Sabinus and Atticus were arrested and sent to Vitellius. But Domitian and the younger Sabinus managed to escape the Capitol early on and in the confusion hid in some residences and remained undiscovered.

Fate of the Emperor Vitellius (Civil War, AD 69)

As rival forces seized Rome, a single German, perhaps a soldier, tried to help the former emperor.

388 Cassius Dio, *Roman History*, 64.20

The city was being pillaged. The inhabitants were fighting, or fleeing, or plundering and murdering one another. They were either seemingly supporting the attackers, or preserving their own lives. The terrified Vitellius put on a ragged and filthy tunic and concealed himself in a dark room where dogs were kept. He intended to escape that night to Tarracina (south of Rome) and there join his brother (who was still in command of several cohorts). But after being emperor he could not go unrecognised for long. Soldiers were searching for him and although he was covered in filth and blood from dog bites, they seized him. They tore off his tunic, bound his hands behind his back and put a rope about his neck.

Then the soldiers led the former emperor down from the palace that he had once revelled in. They dragged him along the Sacred Way (a main thoroughfare), from which he had often witnessed state processions in his chair of office. And they took this 'emperor' to the Forum, where he had often addressed the Roman populace (obedient subject crowds). Some of the crowd pummelled him with their fists while others plucked at his beard (violent humiliations). But all mocked and insulted him. They teased him for his luxuriant living, evidenced by his protuberant belly. In severe humiliation, Vitellius lowered his head to avoid their stares. But the soldiers pricked him under the chin with their daggers, forcing him to look up.

A German who witnessed this sight could not endure the suffering. He took pity on Vitellius and cried out: 'I will help you in the only way I can.' He suddenly launched himself at Vitellius, inflicting a wound and then swiftly slaying himself. But Vitellius did not immediately die from this injury. He was dragged to a place of confinement as his statues were toppled by crowds shouting cries of contempt and ridicule. Then in his great grief and suffering, Vitellius finally called out, 'But I was once your emperor.' Hearing this, the enraged soldiers dragged him to the Gemonian Stairs and cast him down (steep steps where condemned criminals were publicly displayed, executed and their corpses desecrated). Finally, they cut off his head and carried it about the city (as a trophy).

Death of the Emperor Vitellius (AD 69)

389 Tacitus, *Histories*, 3.84

Vitellius returned alone to the desolate and forsaken palace. Even the lowest slaves had fled the building, or avoided his presence. The solitude and silence scared him. He wandered through the building, opening sealed doors and shuddering in vast empty chambers. Finally, he concealed himself in some wretched hiding place.

Vitellius was dragged from his place of concealment by the tribune Julius Placidus. His hands were bound behind his back, and he was led along in tattered robes. This was a revolting spectacle and the remorseless crowd hurled taunts and insults. His degradation was so great that no one could express any pity. Then, when one of the German soldiers suddenly encountered the group, he launched himself at Vitellius, aiming a deadly strike (at the former emperor). Perhaps this furious action was intended to free Vitellius from his great humiliation (a mercy killing). Or maybe the German was aiming his attack against the tribune (trying to free his former commander). He hacked off the tribune's ear in his sudden attack, but he was almost immediately slain.

Batavian serving in the Praetorian Guard (after AD 193)

390 *Corpus Inscriptionum Latinarum*, 6.2548
Sanctinius Probinus, of the Batavian Nation, soldier of the Fourth Praetorian Cohort Pia Vindex, served in the praetorian camp until the day he was released from this life. His monument was put up by his comrade Sanctinius Genialis.

German Campaign by the Emperor Caracalla (AD 213)

The third-century Emperor Caracalla favoured his Germanic troops.

391 Herodian, *Roman History*, **4.7**
Caracalla became especially fond of the Germans in those regions. After gaining their friendship, he entered into various alliances with them. He also selected for his personal bodyguard the strongest and most impressive of their young warriors. Caracalla frequently took off his Roman cloak and wore a short silver-embroidered cape similar to the cloaks worn by the Germans. He also appeared dressed entirely in Germanic-style clothing. This costume included a blonde wig, with his hair arranged in the German manner.

Adopting German Fashions

Emperor Caracalla (AD 211–217)

392 Cassius Dio, *Roman History*, **79.3**
Caracalla could not endure the weight of his armour in hot weather. He therefore wore sleeved tunics fashioned like a breastplate. This outfit had the appearance of armour, but without its weight. It gained him military admiration and made him seem safe from assassinations (sudden attack

from small, concealed weapons). Therefore, he often wore this dress when he was not on campaign. Over this outfit he wore a purple cloak (imperial colours) with a white band down the centre. Although sometimes the cloak was white and the stripe purple. I have seen these outfits myself (as a senator in Rome). However, in Syria and Mesopotamia, the emperor wore German-style clothing and footwear (preparing for campaign).

Assassination of the Emperor Caracalla

Caracalla prepared Roman armies for a large-scale invasion of the Parthian Empire (AD 213). He approached the eastern frontier with a small company of bodyguards and commanders.

393 Cassius Dio, *Roman History*, 79.5
On the eighth of April the Emperor Antoninus (Caracalla) set out from Edessa for Carrhae (northern Iraq). He paused on this journey to dismount from his horse and urinate. Martialis approached him as though he wanted to say something confidential and then stabbed Caracalla with a small dagger.

Martialis immediately fled and would have escaped detection (confirmation of guilt) if he had only thrown away the weapon (the bloodstained blade). But he was recognised by one of the Scythians who attended the emperor (a foreign bodyguard), who struck him down with a javelin. As for Caracalla, the tribunes, pretending to come to his rescue, actually killed him (perhaps exposing his wounds).

The Scythian mentioned attended Caracalla as an ally and a kind of bodyguard. For the emperor kept Scythians and Germans in attendance, both freedmen and slaves. These men had been removed from their former masters and armed by the emperor. Caracalla placed more confidence in these foreigners than in Roman soldiers. Among the various honours that he gave them was the title 'Centurions' and the name 'Lions'.

Furthermore, Caracalla would often converse with foreign envoys, speaking in the native languages of these troops (the Germanic and Scythian bodyguards). On these occasions only the (Roman) interpreters could hear and understand what was really being discussed. It is rumoured that, if anything happened to him, Caracalla instructed these foreign powers to invade Italy and march upon Rome (due to assassination or civil war). And to keep these plans secret (from his Roman commanders) Caracalla would immediately put to death the imperial interpreters (Roman paranoia regarding foreign alliances).

Murder of the Emperor Severus Alexander (AD 235)

Severus Alexander was killed by mutinous troops while campaigning against the Germans.

394 *Historia Augusta, Severus Alexander,* 61

The emperor was resting in his command tent after his meal when one of the Germans performing guard duties entered his quarters. The imperial attendants were asleep, but the emperor was awake and he said, 'What is it, comrade? Do you bring news of the enemy?'

The soldier was suddenly terrified since he had no excuse for bursting into the emperor's tent. He ran back to his comrades (Roman soldiers) and urged them to kill their overdemanding ruler. Then a large group of soldiers grabbed their weapons and rushed into the imperial tent, killing every unarmed attendant and stabbing the emperor to death with many sword thrusts.

German troops used by Maximinus Thrax (Roman Civil War, AD 238)

The military Emperor Maximinus Thrax returned from the northern frontiers to crush a political uprising in Italy led by the Senate.

395 Herodian, *Roman History,* 8.4

In a great rage Maximinus led his army forwards at an increased pace until 16 miles from Aquileia (north-eastern Italy) they came to a large river. This river was very wide and deep since the warm season had melted all the snow that had frozen that winter (in the Alps). A vast snow-swollen flood was therefore surging along its course. His army could not cross this river because the Aquileians had destroyed the main bridge. This bridge was a huge structure of imposing proportions built by earlier emperors using large, squared stones supported on tapering piers. The army halted in confusion, since there were neither bridges nor boats to make the crossing.

Some of the Germans thought that a crossing was possible. But they were unfamiliar with the swift and violent rivers of Italy. They assumed that these water courses flowed down to the plains as calmly as their own rivers (the Rhine and its tributaries). But the German rivers possess a slow current and that is why they can freeze solid. The Germans entered the (Alpine) river with their horses, which are trained to swim, but they were swept away by the current and drowned.

Death of Maximinus Thrax

Pupienus Maximus and Calvinus Balbinus were appointed joint emperors by the Senate in opposition to Maximinus Thrax. Maximinus Thrax and his son began a march on Rome, but his army was opposed at Aquileia and the emperor was assassinated in northern Italy by his own troops.

396 *Historia Augusta, The Two Maximini*, 24
This was the end of the Maximini, the cruel father and the unworthy son. (…) Pupienus was at Ravenna, preparing for war with the aid of his German auxiliaries. There he learnt that the (opposing) Roman army had offered him and his colleagues their allegiance. So, he dismissed the Germans, who were being readied for war, and sent a laurelled dispatch to Rome (announcing his victory).

Bodyguard of the Joint-Emperors (AD 238)

Other evidence suggests that some of the German allies were brought to Rome as loyal bodyguards for the new emperors.

397 Herodian, *Roman History*, 8.6
Not all the troops were pleased about the assassination of Maximinus Thrax. The Pannonians and the barbarians from Thrace were especially enraged since they had placed the Empire in his possession. (…) Meanwhile, Pupienus Maximus (the rival emperor) was in Ravenna levying military recruits from Italy and Rome. The Germans now delivered numerous auxiliary troops into his command. This was because they preserved a longstanding respect for Pupienus due to his good governorship of their country (a former command in the Rhineland provinces).

398 Herodian, *Roman History*, 8.7
The German auxiliaries accompanied Pupienus to Rome. He put great faith in their loyalty, since, before he became emperor, he had successfully governed the province of Germany. Balbinus came to meet his co-emperor on the outskirts of Rome, together with the younger Caesar Gordian. The Senate and the Roman populace welcomed Pupienus with cheers, as if he were celebrating a triumph.

399 Herodian, *Roman History*, 8.8

The praetorians feared that German troops in Rome with Pupienus Maximus would oppose them if they instigated a revolt. They suspected that the Germans were waiting for this opportunity and if the praetorians were discharged for disloyalty, then the Germans would replace them as the permanent imperial bodyguard. They recalled the example of Septimius Severus, who dismissed and replaced the praetorians responsible for the death of Pertinax (emperor in AD 193).

400 *Historia Augusta, Maximus and Balbinus*, 13

It was understood that Maximinus had been made emperor by the soldiers, while Pupienus and Balbinus received their office from the senators. When the soldiers heard what had occurred in the Senate, they were furious because they believed that the politicians had overruled the soldiers' wishes.

To the joy of the Senate and the Roman populace, Balbinus and Pupienus began governing the city of Rome with great moderation. They showed great respect for the Senate; instituted excellent laws, heard lawsuits with justice, and planned the military policy of the Roman state with great wisdom. It was arranged that Pupienus should lead a military expedition against the Persians, while Balbinus took command against the Germans. While they were absent, the younger Gordian would hold office in Rome (a boy from a powerful senatorial family holding commands in North Africa).

Any soldiers who were still seeking an opportunity to kill Balbinus and Pupienus were at first frustrated by a German bodyguard, who were in permanent attendance around the new emperors. There was also some private dissension between Pupienus and Balbinus that was not publicly expressed. Balbinus scorned Pupienus for his lack of noble heritage and Pupienus despised Balbinus as a weakling (possessing less military experience). This gave the soldiers (the praetorians) their opportunity for action, since they knew that disunited emperors could be easily slain. They waited until the Capitoline Games, when many of the other soldiers and palace attendants were busy. They planned to isolate the two emperors in the Imperial Palace, where they would only have the German Guard for protection.

The soldiers instigated the unrest, but they made it known to Pupienus that he must immediately summon the Germans to calm the disturbance. But the German bodyguard were in another part of the Palace under the authority of Balbinus. Pupienus therefore sent word to Balbinus asking him to send immediate assistance. But Balbinus suspected that Pupienus was asking for the German Guard in order to use them against him. He suspected that Pupienus wanted to rule alone, so he refused and blocked the request.

While they were engaged in this dispute, the soldiers (praetorians) suddenly seized both emperors. They tore off their imperial robes, hurled insults at them, and dragged them out of the palace. With rough force they began to hurry them through the centre of the city towards their military base. But when they learned that the Germans were following them to defend the emperors, the soldiers immediately slew both men and left the corpses lying in the middle of the street.

Meanwhile, the other soldiers had acclaimed the young Caesar Gordian as their new emperor (a 13-year-old boy). They did this because there were no other acceptable candidates within immediate reach. Then, jeering at the Senate and the Roman populace, the soldiers withdrew into their military base (the praetorian barracks). As for the German guard, they thought it was futile to fight for emperors who were now slain. So, they left Rome and returned to their stations beyond the city.

401 Herodian, *Roman History*, 8.8
Their rivalry caused their own downfall. When Pupienus learned that the Praetorian Guard was coming to kill them, he tried to summon enough of the German auxiliaries in Rome to resist the conspirators. But Balbinus thought that the request was a ruse intended to deceive him. He knew that the Germans were devoted to Pupienus and he feared that they were being assembled, not to put down a praetorian uprising, but to secure the Empire for Maximus alone. He therefore refused to approve the order.

While the two men were arguing, the praetorians rushed in with a single purpose. When this happened, the guards at the palace gates immediately deserted the emperors. The praetorians seized the old men and ripped off their plain household robes. They dragged them naked from the palace, inflicting every insult and indignity upon them. They jeered at these emperors who had been elected by the Senate. The men were beaten and tormented. Their beards and hair were mauled, and every kind of physical outrage was inflicted upon them. The praetorians brought the emperors through the middle of the city to their military barracks. They did not want to kill them in the palace or any other site. They wanted to torture them in a place where they might suffer longer.

When the Germans discovered what was happening, they snatched up their weapons and rushed to their rescue. But when the praetorians received word of their approach, they immediately killed and mutilated the emperors. They left the corpses exposed in the street. Then they seized Gordian Caesar and proclaimed him as their new emperor, since he was the only available candidate. (…) Keeping their emperor Gordian with them, the praetorians returned to their barracks, shutting the gates, and remaining quiet. When the Germans learnt that the men they were rushing to rescue had been killed, they returned to their quarters. They were unwilling to continue a futile fight for men who were already dead.

Chapter Seventeen

The Baltic Coasts and Scandinavia

The Romans were aware of the Baltic Sea and the southern coast of Scandinavia (ancient Sweden).

Size of Germany

North Sea Geography

402 Strabo, *Geography*, 7.2.3
The Germans populate the north (of Europe) along the coast of the ocean. They extend from the outlets of the Rhenus (Rhine) to beyond the Albis (Elbe). The most well-known tribes in this territory are the Sugambri and the Cimbri. However, the Germans on the ocean coasts, east of the Elbe, are almost entirely unknown to us (Greek and Roman authorities).

I have consulted earlier accounts, and I cannot find any record of a voyage along this coast to any regions near the Caspian Sea (northern Russia). Even the Romans have still not advanced east of the Albis and no one has made the land journey.

However, it is clear from the parallel distances (latitude), that a person travelling eastwards (from the Elbe) will reach the Borysthenes (Dnieper River region) north of the Pontus (Black Sea). But what is beyond Germany? And what lies beyond the countries east of Germany? Most writers believe that this land is occupied by the Bastarnae, but perhaps there are intermediate people such as the Iazyges, Roxolani, or other wagon-dwellers (populations of steppe-based Scythians or Sarmatians).

The geography of this region is not easy to ascertain. Perhaps the Germans extend along the entire length of this ocean coast (northern Europe). Or maybe large stretches are uninhabitable due to the extreme cold. It is also possible that a different race of people is located between the sea and the eastern Germans (the Sami). A similar lack of knowledge exists regarding the other northern peoples. It is not known how far the Bastarnae or the Sarmarians extend, or who exactly dwells north of the Pontus (Black Sea). I cannot say how far the Atlantic is from the Black Sea, or who dwells in the intervening lands (Pontic Steppe).

Extent of the North Coast

403 Pliny, *Natural History***, 4.28**
Beyond the river Scaldis (the Scheldt, near the Rhine) the entire northern shore of the continent is inhabited by Germanic tribes (the North Sea coast). The exact dimensions of the territories inhabited by these tribes cannot be stated with certainty, because writers who have considered this subject have given very different measurements and estimates. Greek authorities and some of our own countrymen (Romans) have stated that the German coast is 2,500 miles long.

The Roman commander Agrippa included the territories of Rhaetia and Noricum in his account of German territory (the Alpine regions in Switzerland and Austria). He therefore recorded that Germany was 686 miles long and 148 miles broad (perhaps 248 miles?). But the breadth of Rhaetia alone almost exceeds that number of miles. Rhaetia (on the Upper Rhine) was only subjugated by Rome around the time the General died (in 12 BC). The greater part of Germany was not entered and explored until several years later. This explains the discrepancy (Agrippa provides measurements for Rhineland Germany).

I suspect that the north coast of Germany could be as long as the Greek authorities have estimated if all the inlets are included (2,500 miles). But if this distance was measured in a single straight line (west to east) it would be closer to the figure given by Agrippa (686 miles).

Outer Germany and the Baltic Sea

Cimbri and Teutoni

404 Pomponius Mela, *Geography***, 3.31–32**
On the far side of the Elbe River there is a huge bay called the Codanus (the Baltic Sea). The bay is filled with both large and small islands. These islands are not far from the shore and the coasts of the various landmasses are almost equidistant. For this reason, the sea within the bay is sheltered and never really looks like an ocean. Its tides are dispersed and rambling like the separate streams and channels of rivers. The currents flow in every direction and cross each other many times. On this seaboard the sea is confined by coastal islands. Here the sea flows through a narrow strait (the North Sea passing through the Skagerrak Strait), then the current will curve along a broad ridge of land (the east coast of Jutland). The Cimbri

and the Teutoni occupy this bay and far beyond them are the Hermiones, who are the most distant people of Germany.

Greek Knowledge of the North Sea (before Roman campaigns)

In the 320s BC, a Greek mariner named Pytheas explored the landmasses of the North Sea. This was the era when Alexander the Great was conquering the Persian Empire.

405 Strabo, *Geography*, 7.3.1
Pytheas the Massalian made many false statements regarding the country that faces the northern ocean (North Sea and Baltic coast). He used his knowledge of astronomy and mathematics to conceal deliberate falsehoods. His writings should therefore be dismissed. Sophocles, who composed tragic plays, describes the Far North when he writes about Oreithyia (a nymph). He explains that she was snatched into the air by Boreas (the personified north-west wind). She was carried 'over all seas to the ends of the earth, reaching the sources of night where heaven unfolds and the ancient gardens of Phoebus (Bright Apollo) stand'. These stories have no importance to the present work and can be disregarded. They can be dismissed like Socrates rejected accounts of the Boreas in the *Phaedrus* (a dialogue by Plato). Let us confine our narrative to what we can learn from both ancient and recent history.

Roman Knowledge of the Atlantic Coast

406 Pliny, *Natural History*, 2.67
At present, the whole of the west coast (the Atlantic seaboard) is navigated from Cadiz and the Straits of Hercules (Gibraltar) all around Spain and Gaul. The greater part of the northern ocean (the Atlantic coast of Germany) was explored under the orders of the late Emperor Augustus. A military fleet sailed for this purpose around Germany to the promontory of the Cimbri (the Jutland Peninsula). Beyond this shore they observed a vast sea (the Baltic). They gathered reports of this expanse and reached a region in Scythia where the climate was excessively wet. The ocean must extend beyond this territory (further east) since there is a superabundance of moisture in the region (sea mists).

Further east this expanse must extend to the Caspian Sea and join with the Indian Ocean because the same constellations are visible in these regions (similar latitudes). The Hellenic kings Seleucus Nicator and Antiochus Soter sent Macedonian forces to navigate and explore the Caspian Sea (292 BC). They planned to rename the expanse after themselves, calling it the 'Seleucis' or the 'Antiochis' Sea. Many coasts of the Caspian have therefore been fully explored by galleys, including most of its northern shore. The Maeotic Marsh has also been explored to its full extent (the Azov inlet to the north of the Black Sea). There is now overwhelming proof that these expanses are not gulfs of the great northern ocean, as many have previously believed.

The North Coast of Germany

Jutland to Scandinavia

Pliny the Elder suggests the possible population size of ancient Sweden.

407 Pliny, *Natural History*, 4.13
Beyond Balcia (Gotland) the north coast of Europe becomes more accessible. The first nation encountered in this region of Germany is the Inguaeones. There is a large mountain in their territory called the Saevo, which is the same size as the mountains of the Ilipaean range. This mountain extends to an enormous bay joining the Cimbrian Promontory (the Jutland Peninsula). The bay is called the Codanian Gulf, and it is filled with islands (Zealand, Lolland and Funen). The most famous landmass in this sea is Scandinavia (the southern edge of the Scandinavian Peninsula). Its size has not been ascertained and only part of it is known to be inhabited. The natives are known as the Hilleviones and they dwell in 500 villages. They refer to their island as 'another world' (the edge of a vast landmass experiencing a different climate – the Scandinavia Peninsula extending north and east).

Aeningia is thought to be as large as Scandinavia (Estonia to the east). Some authorities report that regions as far as the river Vistula are inhabited by the Sarmatians, Venedi, Sciri and Hirri. There is a gulf called Cylipenus in this place and the island of Latris is positioned at its entrance (perhaps Saaremaa). The gulf next to it is called the Lagnus and it is the frontier of the Cimbri (the coastline of Poland). The Cimbrian promontory projects a great distance into the sea and forms a peninsula called the Tastris (Jutland, Denmark). The Roman military has documented the existence of twenty-three islands in this vicinity. The most significant is Burcana, which was called 'Bean Island' by our forces due to the quantity of wild beans growing there.

Another island visited by our soldiers became known as Glass Island because of amber found on its shores. The barbarians called these places Austeravia and Actania.

The whole of the seacoast as far as the German river Scheldt is (...) inferior to none in grandeur.

The Baltic Sea (East to West)

408 Pliny, *Natural History*, 4.13

I will describe the outer regions of Europe beyond the Black Sea. Beyond the Riphean Mountains (the Volga region) the coastline extends west as far as Cadiz (Atlantic Europe from Scandinavia to southern Spain). Several islands are reported to exist off the northern coast, but many have not yet received names. According to the account of Timaeus, there is an island called Baunonia lying off the coast of Scythia (in the Baltic Sea). This island is one day's voyage from the coast. In springtime, amber is cast up on the shore of Baunonia by the action of the waves. The rest of this shoreline is only known to us through reports of doubtful authority.

An ocean exists to the north of Europe. Hecataeus calls the stretch of ocean next to the Scythian coast the Amalehian Sea (the Baltic). This Amalehian Sea extends to the river Parapanisus and means 'Frozen' in the native language. Philemon claims that the Cimbrian name for this sea is Morimarusa or the 'Sea of Death'. It extends from the Parapanisus and Cape Rusbeae (Gulf of Riga) towards the Cronian Sea (North Sea). Xenophon of Lampsacus reports that about three days' sail from the Scythian coast there is an island of enormous size called Balcia (Gotland or the east coast of the Scandinavian Peninsula). Pytheas names this landmass Basilia.

There are also islands in this sea called the Oeonae where the inhabitants are said to subsist on the eggs of sea birds and a diet of oats.

The Existence of Vast Northern Territories (Norway and Russia)

409 Pliny, *Natural History*, 2.112

Our portion of the earth is situated in an ocean which surrounds the known landmass (Eurasia and North Africa). This landmass is longest from east to west, extending from India to the sacred Pillars of Hercules at Cadiz (the Gibraltar Strait). Artemidorus estimates the east–west extent of the earth's landmass to be 8,568 miles, but Isidore calculates the figure to be 9,818 miles. (...)

In contrast, Isidore estimates that the north–south extent of the earth's landmass is about 5,462 miles, or about half its east–west extent. However, this distance (global latitude) crosses through opposing extremes of great heat and severe cold (from the equator to the Arctic).

I believe the earth is a globe, so that its distance from north to south cannot be smaller than its east–west extent. Perhaps the discrepancy is because there are further uninhabited regions in the extreme north and south that have not yet been explored (the Arctic and Sub-Saharan Africa).

These are the measurements that have been recorded:

The Ethiopic Ocean is located at the extreme south of the known earth (the Romans imagined that Africa ended just south of the Sahara). From the Ethiopic seaboard it is 705 miles north to Meroe, which is well inhabited (a Nilotic kingdom).

From Meroe it is 1,250 miles north to Alexandria (the capital of Egypt, on the Mediterranean coast). From Alexandria it is 584 miles north to the island of Rhodes, 86 miles to Cnidus, 25 miles to Cos, 100 miles to Samos, 94 miles to Chios, 65 miles to Mitylene, and 49 miles to Tenedos (Greek islands and ports in the Eastern Mediterranean).

From there it is 12 miles to Cape Sigeum (on the Anatolian coast), 312 miles to the Bosphorus (entering the Black Sea), 350 miles north to Cape Carambis and 312 miles to the edge of Lake Maeotis (the Azov Sea).

The mouth of the river Don is 266 miles further north (from where it flows into the Azov Sea). The total distance is reduced because the crossings are not exact (on a precise south to north line). The most careful authorities have therefore calculated the full distance from the mouth of the Don to the Canopic mouth of the Nile at 2,110 miles.

Artemidorus knew that the Sarmatians occupied lands around the Don River and the territories further north. But he argued that these regions had not been properly explored (so no trustworthy distances could be added to his calculation). But Isidore added another figure to his calculations and estimated that Thule (Shetland?) might be 1,250 miles further north. This was purely a conjectural estimate (and not based on any actual journeys northwards from the Don). However, if this is accurate, then the Sarmatians must occupy an enormous territory. This area would be large enough to contain many nations, or perhaps it simply contains certain nomadic populations in a continual state of migration (large clan-based groups roving seasonally across vast open steppes). I think that there might be a much larger uninhabitable region to the north of these people. This is because I have been informed that there are vast landmasses beyond Germany (Scandinavia) and these islands were discovered not so long ago.

Eastern Germany and the Black Sea

410 Pomponius Mela, *Geography*, 3.38

The part of the Caspian Sea that extends inland (further northwards) is like a river (the Volga). The passage inland from the Caspian is through a strait that is as wide as it is broad. Beyond this channel (the Volga–Svir rivers) the sea forms three separate bays (perhaps the Gulf of Finland, Lake Ladoga and Lake Onega). The Bay of Hyrcania is positioned where the Caspian flows into the outer ocean (the Svir River). To the west is Scythian Bay and on the east is Caspian Bay. The sea in this region is violent and savage. This coast has no harbours and is exposed everywhere to storms. This part of the ocean is also crowded with sea monsters. For this reason, the bays are not navigable.

411 Pomponius Mela, *Geography*, 3.44

For a long time, it was uncertain what lay beyond the Caspian Bay (Russia beyond the Gulf of Finland). Was there an ocean (White Sea/Barents Sea), or was there just a hostile and cold land extending endlessly northwards without any natural border? Homer, and other philosophers concerned with nature, all claimed that the entire world was surrounded by sea. Cornelius Nepos also makes this claim and he is more reliable since he is a more recent authority. Nepos uses an account of Quintus Metellus Celer to support his argument. When Celer was proconsul of Gaul, certain Indians were presented to him as a gift by the king of the Boii (a Celtic tribe). He asked what route these men had followed to reach Europe. He was informed that they had been caught by a storm in Indian waters and swept along the coast to Germany. Therefore, the sea must be continuous (around the coast of Eurasia). However, due to the unrelenting cold, this coast must be uninhabited.

The North beyond the Black Sea

Hyperborea (Part of Scandinavia?)

412 Pliny, *Natural History,* **4.12**

The Sarmatians and Essedones occupy lands leading to the Azov Sea. The Maeotae inhabit the coast as far as the river Don and they give their name to the sea (the Maeotic Lake). The Arimaspi inhabit territories inland from the Maeotae.

The Riphean Mountains exist to the north of these people in a region called the Pterophorus (the Russian Volga). Featherlike snow continually falls in this part of the world. The region is condemned by nature and has been plunged into dense darkness. It is subject only to frosts and the chilly lurking places of the north wind originating beyond these mountains. But even beyond this, there is said to be a race called the Hyperboreans. The Hyperboreans are a contented people who are said to live to extreme old age and are famous for legendary wonders.

These Hyperboreans occupy the extreme limits of the earth (Scandinavia?). The sky is said to pivot around their territory, so they witness full revolutions of the stars (Polar regions). They receive six months of daylight when the sun is never absent from view. Misinformed people claim that this perpetual sunlight occurs from the spring equinox until autumn. They say the sun rises once a year at midsummer and sets just once at midwinter. Due to this perpetual sunlight, the region is said to possess a pleasant and mild climate that is free from any harmful winds.

Authorities who locate the Hyperboreans in a region with six months of daylight say they sow in the morning, reap at midday, and pluck the fruit from the trees at sunset. Then they retreat into their grottos to endure the long night.

The Hyperboreans live in the woods and groves. They worship several gods in large congregations. Their society does not know discord or sorrow, and death comes to them only when they have obtained an overabundance of life. When this occurs, they hold a banquet, affirm their old age with a celebration, then leap from a certain rock into the sea. The Hyperboreans think that this is the most blissful form of burial.

Some authorities have located the Hyperboreans, not in Europe, but on the northern coast of Asia. This is because there is an Asiatic people who share their customs and occupy a similar location. They are called the Attaci (perhaps the Sami peoples).

Some authorities have located the Hyperboreans midway between the position that the sun disappears at sunset in the Antipodes (the Southern Hemisphere) and reappears at our sunrise (Northern Hemisphere). But this is impossible, because an enormous expanse of sea exists between these positions (north-west to east, crossing the opposite side of the globe).

It is not possible to doubt the existence of the Hyperboreans. Many authorities record that they regularly sent the first fruits of their harvests to the Greek sanctuary at Delos. They presented these offerings to Apollo, whom they revere and worship above other gods. The gifts used to be brought by highly venerated virgins who spent years making the journey and were received and protected by various nations on their route to Greece. But the tradition ended when this good faith was violated. The Hyperboreans therefore began a new custom and deposited their offerings at the nearest frontiers of neighbouring peoples. A succession of different peoples passed these items on to adjoining communities, until the offerings finally reached Delos. But later this practice also passed out of use.

Location of Hyperborea

Mela describes territories beyond Germany that could be Finland or Lapland. These regions were north of Scythia (the Eurasian Steppe).

413 Pomponius Mela, *Geography*, 3.36–37

The Scythian peoples are known collectively as the 'Belcae'. Their frontier joins with Asia and their territory extends into lands where the winter climate is continuous, and the cold is unbearable. On the Asiatic shore their lands stretch towards the Hyperboreans, who are located beyond the coastal north wind (Finland or Scandinavia). The Hyperboreans live beyond the Riphean Mountains in lands directly beneath the pole star (Arctic Zone). Here the sun does not rise every day as it does for us. Instead, it rises for the first time during the vernal equinox and eventually sets at the autumnal equinox. Therefore, this region experiences six months of completely uninterrupted daylight.

The country of the Hyperboreans is narrow (a peninsula). The land is bountiful since it is continually exposed to the sun. Its inhabitants live in equality and have a longer and happier lifespan than any other people. They enjoy themselves in festive leisure and have no experience of wars or disputes. The Hyperboreans devote themselves mainly to the sacred rites of Apollo (the Greek solar god).

According to tradition, the Hyperboreans sent their first seasonal fruits as an offering to Delos (the shrine of Apollo in central Greece). These offerings were delivered by maidens, but later they were handed through a succession of distant peoples to reach their destination. This custom was preserved for a long time until the intervening people committed a sacrilege and profaned the offering. The Hyperboreans inhabit groves and forests. They decide to die when they are fully satisfied by their lives, but this act is not motivated by boredom. They cheerfully wreathe themselves in flowers and throw themselves from a particular cliff into the sea. The Hyperboreans regard this to be the finest death ritual.

The North Atlantic

Britain and Sweden

By the sixth century AD, Roman authorities had a greater knowledge of Scandinavia. The Latin writer Jordanes possessed Gothic (Scandinavian) ancestry.

414 Jordanes, *Getica*, 1
Britain has other islands deep within its own seas. (…) It has an island named Mevania (the Isle of Man) and thirty-three Orcades (the Orkneys), some of which are uninhabited. On its furthest sea is another island named Thule. Thule is mentioned by the Mantuan poet Virgil when he writes, 'Emperor, furthest Thule will obey your commands.'

This mighty sea also has an Arctic region in the north and a great island named Scandza (Scandinavia – Sweden). With the Grace of God, my account of the Goths will begin in this place. For the Gothic nation emerged from this island and spread across Europe like a swarm of bees. By the Will of the Lord God, I will now explain how this occurred.

Claudius Ptolemy described Scandza when he produced his excellent account of the earth (a work of global cartography). He wrote:

> There is a great island situated in the surge of the northern ocean named Scandza. Its coast has the shape a downward-facing juniper leaf (a conifer branch with scaly leaves). The coast of Scandza is formed from long narrow extensions that bulge outwards and end in a tapering point (the rocky fjords and headlands of Norway and Sweden).

Pomponius Mela also mentions Scandza in his *Geography*. He says that it is situated in the Codan Gulf and that the ocean laps its shores.

Scandza is positioned opposite the Vistula River (eastern Europe). The Vistula rises in the Sarmatian mountains (southern Poland and Ukraine). It flows north and enters the ocean within sight of Scandza. Along its course, the Vistula separates Germania from Scythia (the Ukrainian Steppe).

The eastern part of Scandza has a vast lake filled from deep underground sources (perhaps the Vanern in Sweden). The Vagus River flows from this lake and surges into the ocean. The western coast of Scandza is surrounded by an immense sea (western Norway). The northern part of Scandza extends into a vast ocean that cannot be navigated. Scandza therefore resembles a projecting arm which ends near the German Sea (the Scandinavian Peninsula projecting down to the North Sea and enclosing the Baltic).

There are said to be many small islands scattered around Scandza. The climate is so cold that the sea will freeze, and wolves can cross over to these islands. But even these animals can be blinded by the extreme cold. Thus, the country is both inhospitable to men and cruel to savage beasts.

Chapter Eighteen

Baltic Amber

Pliny reviewed the false accounts of amber promoted by the Greeks.

415 Pliny, *Natural History*, 37.11

Amber is an extremely precious item, but it is different from other gemstones as it is a fashion enjoyed only by women. Amber therefore has the same prestige as other precious stones but has fewer uses. Expensive vessels carved from rock crystal are used to serve cold drinks and myrrhine wares (multi-coloured crystals from Iran) can be filled with hot liquids, but the market has not discovered an equivalent use for amber.

A discussion of amber will reveal falsehoods promoted by the Greeks. It is important to know this and understand that not everything the Greeks have said deserves to be admired. The Greeks tell the story of how Phaethon was struck by a thunderbolt and his grief-stricken sisters were transformed into poplar trees. By the banks of the Eridanus, which we call the Po River, the sisters annually shed tears of amber, known to the Greeks as 'electrum'. This is because the sun is called 'Elector' or 'The Shining One'. This narrative is told by numerous poets, beginning with Aeschylus, then Philoxenus, Euripides, Nicander and Satyrus (fifth century BC). The mention of Italy as the origin of amber provides clear evidence that this Greek narrative is false.

Chares states that Phaethon died in Ethiopia on an island the Greeks call the Isle of Arnmon. There is said to be a shrine and oracle on this island that are the true source of amber. Philemon declares that amber is a mineral which is dug up in two regions of Scythia (the Ukrainian Steppe). One of these substances has a glossy white colour and is called 'electrum' (the alloy of gold and silver). But the other mineral is a tawny-coloured product known as '*snaliternicum*' (another alloy?).

More credible Greek writers suggest the existence of islands in the Adriatic Sea named the Electrides. They say that amber is swept along by the Po River and washes ashore on these islands. But certainly, no islands have existed near northern Italy bearing the name Electrides. In fact, there are no islands located nearby to receive anything carried downstream by the Po River.

Aeschylus claims that the river Eridanus is in Spain and is also called the Rhône (the river running down through Gaul to the Mediterranean). By contrast, Euripides and Apollonius assert that the Rhône and the Po meet on the coast of the Adriatic Sea. This account demonstrates an immense ignorance of geography, so their poor knowledge of amber is therefore excusable.

Flawed Greek writers have also described how amber is produced by special trees that grow on inaccessible rocks near the head of the Adriatic Sea. Every summer, at the rising of the Dog Star (Sirius), these trees shed their gum into the water. By contrast, Theophrastus states that amber is dug up in Liguria (north-western Italy).

Demonstratus calls amber '*lyncurium*' or 'lynx urine'. He alleges that amber is formed from the urine of wild cats known as lynxes. This explains why it possesses a tawny translucent colour. The urine of the female cats produces a fainter and lighter-coloured amber. According to Demonstratus, amber is also known as '*langurium*'. He states that the wild animals which produce the substance live in Italy and are called 'languri'. Zenothemis calls these wild cats 'langes' and suggests that they inhabit lands on either bank of the river Po. Sudines and Metrodorus believed that the trees in Liguria which produced amber were called 'lynxes'.

Sotacus, however, believes that amber flows from ravines in Britain called the Electrides. Pytheas describes an estuary of the ocean named Metuonis that extends across 750 miles. Its shores are inhabited by a German tribe, called the Guiones (an early Greek description of the Frisian coast and Scandinavian Goths). From this coast it is a day's sail to the Isle of Abalus. Pytheas reports that amber is swept onto this island by ocean currents that occur in spring. He suggested that amber could be some form of ocean emission formed from solidified brine.

Pytheas also reports that the inhabitants use amber as a fuel instead of wood and also sell it to the neighbouring Teutones. Timaeus provides similar information, but he calls the amber-producing island 'Basilia'. Philemon refuses to believe that amber can produce a flame.

Nicias explains amber as a moisture congealed from the sun's rays. He reasons that as the sun sets in the west, its rays fall more strongly upon the earth at that place. It creates a dense amber fluid which congeals and is later cast ashore in Germany by the tides of the ocean.

Nicias maintains that amber is also formed in Egypt, where it is called '*sacal*'. It also appears in India, where the inhabitants value it more than frankincense (a fragrant gum resin). In Syria, women make whorls (spindles for spinning) of amber and call it '*harpax*', or 'the snatcher' (electrostatic properties). This is because it attracts and picks up leaves and husks from the threads of garments.

Theochrestus maintains that amber is washed up on the capes of the Pyrenees by the turbulent ocean (western Atlantic trade?) Xenocrates shares this view. He is the most recent Greek writer on this subject, and he is still living.

Asarubas records that Lake Cephisis near the Atlantic coast produces amber (north-west Morocco on trade routes supplying orange-coloured carnelian gemstones). The Moors call this lake 'Electrum' because when the lake is heated by the sun, amber is produced in the mud and floats to the surface. Mnaseas describes another district in Africa called Sicyon and a river Crathis which flows from a lake into the ocean. On the shore live the birds known as Meleager's Daughters or Penelope Birds (guinea fowl). This lake is also said to produce amber from its mud.

Theomenes tells us that close to the Greater Syrtes is the Garden of the Hesperides and a pool called Electrum (on the Gulf of Sidra, on the Mediterranean coast of North Africa). Poplar trees grow around this pool and the amber that drips from their branches into the water is collected by the daughters of Hesperus (the nymphs who embody the golden light of evening).

Ctesias states that in India there is a river known as Hypobarus which is known as the 'bringer of all blessings'. It flows from the north into the eastern ocean past a thickly wooded mountain. The trees of this forest are called '*psitthacorae*', a word which means 'luscious sweetness'. They produce the amber which falls into the river stream. Mithridates records that off the coast of Carmania (southern Iran) there is an island called Serita covered with a kind of cedar. This tree exudes sap which also flows down to the rocks as amber.

Xenocrates asserts that amber is known in Italy as '*sucinum*' and '*thium*'. But in Scythia it is called '*sacrium*' and so he believes that it is found in this country. But he is also aware that other authorities claim that amber is produced in the mud lands of Numidia (carnelian trade routes in North Africa).

The accounts of these writers regarding amber are only surpassed by the tragic playwright Sophocles (sixth century BC). This surprises me since his tragedies are so serious and his personal reputation is very great. Sophocles was born of noble Athenian lineage, and he obtained high public achievements and served as a general.

Sophocles describes how amber is formed in the lands beyond India. It is the tears shed for the Greek hero Meleager by the birds known as

'Meleager's Daughters' (guinea fowl). It is amazing that Sophocles held this belief and even hoped to persuade others to accept it. But only a childish and naïve mind would believe that birds could weep large amber tears. If Meleager died in Greece, then why did these birds migrate to India to mourn for him? The works of the poets are full of equally fabulous stories.

Actual Origins of Amber: Expedition by Nero

Using more recent Roman evidence, Pliny the Elder was able to provide a more accurate account of amber and its origins.

416 Pliny, *Natural History*, 37.11

There is no need to invent stories regarding the origins of amber, for this material is a commonplace product in our society. It is imported in great amounts and fills the markets so much that the person who repeats false narratives must be confounded by the reality. Surely the false stories regarding amber are a severe insult to our intelligence.

It is well established that amber is a product from islands in the northern ocean (Baltic Sea). The Germans call amber '*glaesum*' and refer to the main amber-producing island as 'Austeravia'. Roman soldiers reached this island when Caesar Germanicus was conducting military operations on this coast which involved naval squadrons. The troops nicknamed the main island 'Glaesaria' or 'Amber Island'.

Amber is formed from a fluid which seeps out from the interior of a certain type of pine tree. It resembles the sap produced by a cherry tree, or the gum resin which sometimes bursts out of pine wood. The sap is hardened by sharp frosts interposed with periods of moderate heat. Or perhaps it is the effects of the frozen ocean that hardens the sap when pieces are swept across the sea. Amber is swept along so easily that it seems to be suspended in the water without settling on the seabed. It is then washed up on the shore by the actions of the sea.

Our Roman ancestors understood that amber was a sap or '*sucus*' from a tree and that is why they called the product '*sucinum*'. There is confirmation that amber is sap extracted from pine wood because the substance smells like a pine when it is rubbed. Kindled flakes of amber will burn with a strong and distinctly scented smoke that resembles a burning pine torch.

The Germans mostly convey amber into the province of Pannonia (Roman territory south of the Danube frontier). This trade first became prominent through the activities of the Veneti, who are known to the Greeks as the Enetoi (Celtic settlers in north-eastern Italy). The Veneti occupied lands near the Pannonians and inhabited territories next to the Adriatic Sea. This must be the reason why Greek authorities associate amber with the river Po (in northern Italy). Even today, the rural women in Cisalpine Gaul wear necklaces fashioned from pieces of amber. Amber is worn mainly as an adornment, but it is also believed to have medical properties. Amber is supposed to be a preventative against tonsillitis and other harmful conditions that affect the larynx. This is important because some water sources near the Alps have properties that harm the human throat.

It was only recently confirmed that the distance from Carnuntum in Pannonia to the amber-producing coasts of Germany is about 600 miles. A Roman *equites* (nobleman) is still alive who was commissioned to procure amber by Julianus, the man in charge of a gladiatorial display given by the Emperor Nero.

This *equites* travelled the entire trade route and traversed the northern coasts. He brought back such a large supply that the nets used for keeping the beasts away from the parapet of the amphitheatre were adorned with pieces of amber. The weaponry, trolley carts and all the equipment used on that one day of the display were also decorated with amber fittings. The heaviest piece that the *equites* brought back to Rome weighed 13 pounds.

It is certain that amber is also found in India. Archelaus, who was the king of Cappadocia (eastern Anatolia), reports that amber comes from India in a rough state with pine bark adhering to it. The substance is processed by being boiled in the fat of a suckling pig.

There is further confirmation that amber originates as a liquid outflow. Certain things can be found in amber including ants, gnats and lizards. They are visible inside the substance and must have stuck to the fresh sap. There they remained trapped inside the resin as it hardened.

Amber as a Substance

Tacitus examined amber and deduced that it was formed from hardened tree sap.

417 Tacitus, *Germania*, 45
The tribes of the Aestii occupy the eastern shore of the Suebic Sea (Baltic coast). (…) The Aestii also search the seas and are the only people who gather amber on these coasts. They call the substance '*glesum*'. This substance lay amid the other refuse from the sea until Roman consumerism made it a valuable product. Amber is an utterly useless product to the Aestii.

They gather it in a raw state and marvel at the price they receive for these shapeless lumps. These foreigners have never investigated or discovered what natural cause, or process, produces amber. Amber is formed from the sap of trees. Sometimes winged insects and even small lizards can be seen in the substance. These creatures were caught and submerged in the glistening sap before the liquid hardened around them and they were completely enclosed.

From evidence based on these creatures, I think there must be fertile forests in the west (extreme north). These forests must resemble the furthest regions of the east (Sumatra, where lizards and large insects inhabit tropical rainforests), or the fertile woods where frankincense and balsam resins are produced (the monsoon-swept coastal highlands of Yemen). Perhaps amber is created by the rays of the setting sun acting on the tree sap. The sap then falls into the nearby sea and, because of severe storms, it is swept ashore on the opposite coast. Amber will burn like pinewood if you test its composition by applying fire. When burning it will produce a powerful and sweet-smelling flame, but it soon melts into something resembling pitch or resin.

'Glass Island'

418 Pliny, *Natural History*, 4.13
Another island visited by our soldiers became known as Glass Island because of amber found on its shores. The barbarians called these places Austeravia and Actania.

The Island of Glaesaria

Writing in the third century AD, Solinus mentions the amber-producing island known as Glaesaria.

419 Solinus, *Polyhistor*, 20.9
Glaesaria is a crystal and a type of amber. The Germans call amber '*glaesum*' in their language. Past peoples believed that this substance came from the 'Padanian Woods' (Po Valley), but further investigation was necessary, for the characteristics of this material were only vaguely known before Germanicus Caesar explored the (northern) shore of Germania.

Amber is produced by a type of pine tree that exudes this resin from its trunk in autumn. We can confirm that amber is indeed a sap by burning it, which releases the smell of pine. The barbarians brought this splendid substance (south) into Illyria, from where it passed through Pannonia via Transpadani trade (trade routes leading to Cisalpine Gaul). This is where the Romans first saw amber, so they assumed it was produced there (in Cisalpine Gaul). Through a gift, Nero was able to adorn many furnishings with amber (in the arena). This was easily accomplished because a king of Germania sent him a gift that included 13,000 pounds of amber.

420 Solinus, *Polyhistor*, 20.12
Raw amber is rough and covered with a rind. It is boiled in the fat of a suckling pig then polished to produce the gloss seen in the finished product. Amber has other names which originate from its appearance. It is called '*melleum*' ('honey-like') and '*Falernum*' (a famous Italian wine) from its similarity to honey and to wine. It is well known amber snatches up dry leaves and attracts chaff to itself. Doctors assert that it cures many ailments affecting the vital organs. India also has amber, but Germania has the most amber and the best varieties. This is why I have written about amber when discussing the island of Glaesaria.

Amber in Roman Fashions

Pliny describes the uses and consumer value of amber in Roman society.

421 Pliny, *Natural History*, 37.12
There are several kinds of amber. The pale kind has the finest scent, but it is like the waxy type and has no great value. The tawny form of amber is more valuable, but the transparent type is the most highly prized. But the colour must not be a fiery glare, as we admire amber that has just the slightest tint of a fiery tone. The most sought-after ambers are called '*Palernian*' because they have the tinted translucency of wines (from Palermo). They are transparent but seem to gently radiate in the light. This amber has the mellow tint of honey that has been concentrated by boiling. It should be generally known that amber can be tinted using suet and alkanet root (an orange-red colourant). But nowadays it is even stained with purple dyes (to create replica Indian amethysts).

When amber is rubbed vigorously between the fingers it produces a 'hot exhalation' (an electrostatic force). This attracts straw, dry leaves and fragments of linden bark (sawdust from wood carvings). The process resembles the way a magnet will attract iron. When amber chippings are steeped in oil they will burn brighter and longer than the pith of the flax plant (traditional kindling).

Even among other luxuries, amber has a tremendous value (elite competitive consumer spending). A small figurine carved from amber is more costly than several slaves. An object merely representing human life has therefore greater value than actual people who are alive and in good health. No comment would be sufficient to rebuke this situation.

In the case of Corinthian bronze tableware, people are attracted by the fine appearance of the alloyed metal, which has the sheen of gold and silver. Embossed metalwork is admired for the skill and inventiveness of the artisan. Vessels fashioned from coloured fluorspar and translucent rock crystal have extraordinary beauty. Pearls can be worn in tiaras and gemstones can be used to decorate the valuable rings worn on fingers. Every precious product sought by our society pleases some aspect of display or practical use. But amber is the exception. This product gives us only the private satisfaction of knowing that we possess a luxury.

Among the ominous events of his reign, the Emperor Nero praised the hair colour of his wife Poppaea. In one of his popular poems, he eulogised her hair for being '*sucint*' or 'amber-coloured'. And so, a peculiarity was represented as an asset. From that time onwards, respectable Roman women began to aspire to this as another possible hair colour.

Amber has been found to have some use in medical matters and that is why it is favoured by women. Amber will benefit babies when it is attached to them as an amulet. Callistratus says that amber is beneficial to people of any age as it alleviates panic attacks and reduces strangury (bladder blockage or irritation causing an urge to urinate). For this purpose, it can be worn as an amulet or powdered amber can be ingested in a liquid.

I am adding a further category of amber to the accounts of other writers. There is another form of amber that I will name '*chrys-electrum*', or 'gold amber'. This substance is golden coloured and has an even more spectacular appearance. In early morning sunshine, it easily catches the light and it flares up as though it contains flames itself. According to Callistratus, this type of amber can be worn as an amulet on a necklace to cure diseases that cause fever. It can be powdered and mixed with honey and rose oil to treat conditions involving the inner ear. Powdered amber is also blended with honey from Athens to alleviate eye conditions. Stomach problems can be treated by ingesting just the powder, or by swallowing amber residue in water or a mix of mastic gum (tree resin). I have already mentioned how amber can be used to make replica gemstones. It can be dyed any colour, but the preferred colour is purple to make artificial amethysts.

Amber in Ancient Egypt

Clement of Alexandria suggests that Egyptian temples were once richly adorned with amber (writing in AD 198).

422 Clement of Alexandria, *Paedagogus*, 3.2

The porticos and vestibules of Egyptian temples are ornately constructed. They allow passage to groves and sacred gardens (in precinct grounds). The temple halls are surrounded by many pillars and the walls gleam with the reflection of precious stones. There is an abundance of painted images and ornaments made from gold and silver. The decorations include amber and the glitter of coloured gems from India and Ethiopia. The shrines are also veiled with gold-embroidered hangings.

Amber on Roman Goblets

Writing in the second century AD, Juvenal describes how expensive cups used at the banquets of rich patrons were adorned with gemstones and amber pieces.

423 Juvenal, *Satires*, 5.30

The patron Virro drinks from large goblets decorated with amber and encrusted with beryl. But you will not be permitted the use of gold drinking vessels (as a low-status client). If you are given such cups, there will be a servant observing you. He will be watching your sharp fingernails and counting the gems (since low-status dinner guests might feel tempted to steal from wealthy patrons).

The Appeal of Amber

Martial confirms that part of the appeal of amber was its extraordinary radiance.

424 Martial, *Epigrams*, 8.51

Whose workmanship is displayed in this bronze cup? Was it fashioned by the skilful Mys or by Myron (the sculptor of the *Discus Thrower*)? Is this craftmanship of Mentor or Polycletus? There is no tarnish to blemish the reflective brightness of this cup. Its perfect coloration requires no assayer (tester of metals). Even purest amber radiates light that is less yellow than this glorious metal.

Electrostatic Properties

Writing in about AD 200, Clement of Alexandria compares the spread of Christian teaching to a natural force like the electrostatic attraction of amber.

425 Clement, *Stromata*, 2.6
It is like that famous ore that attracts iron through some special affinity (crude magnets). It is like the amber teardrop that can pull threads towards itself, or the amber ball that can set the chaff in motion. Substances obey because they are attracted by a subtle unseen force. They themselves are not the cause of the movement. They are responding to an impulse compelling them to move.

Use of Amber by Roman Women

Wealthy Roman women carried small amber globes that they rubbed for warmth or aroma.

426 Juvenal, *Satires*, 6.570
Beware that type of wife that you see clutching a well-worn calendar in her hands as if it were a lump of warming amber. She doesn't consult soothsayers anymore, for she is the one who is now consulted. If her husband is leaving for a military posting, or returning home from foreign lands, she will not meet him unless the calendar calculations of Thrasyllus agree. (The 'signs' must be auspicious for that day. Thrasyllus was the favourite astrologer of the Emperor Tiberius.)

427 Martial, *Epigrams*, 3.65
This perfume is like the scent produced when a young woman bites into an apple. It is like the light breeze that passes over saffron fields in Corycia. It is the smell of the first white blossoms appearing on the vine, or new grass cropped by the grazing sheep. It is flower of myrtle, the scent of Arabian incense gatherers and the aroma of amber rubbed with the hand.

428 Martial, *Epigrams*, 11.8
(Kisses like) the fragrance of balsam extracted from incense trees; the heavy odour yielded by teeming saffron flowers; the scent of fruits mellowing in their winter stores. It is the flowering spring meadows, or the silken robes the empress takes from her Palatine wardrobes (a vast collection of exotic

dresses). It is the amber warmed by the hand of a maiden, or a jar of dark Falernian wine scented from a distance. (...)

None of these scents is sufficient for my description. But mix them all together and you will have a perfume that resembles of the morning kisses of my favourite.

A Man who Receives Amber

Juvenal mentions an attractive Roman youth who received gifts from male admirers including items usually given to women.

429 Juvenal, *Satires*, 9.50
So, the pretty youth might have presents sent to him of green sunshades, or big amber globes on his birthday, or on the first showery day of spring. He will lounge on a long couch admiring the secret gifts that he received upon the Matron's Day! (The first day of March.)

Imperial Excess

The teenage Emperor Elagabalus (who reigned in AD 218–222) was despised for his feminine character and wasteful excess.

430 *Historia Augusta, Elagabalus*, 31
The Emperor Elagabalus had gold dust and silver particles scattered onto the floors of the palace porticos. And when he walked to his horse or carriage, gold dust was often sprinkled in his path. This practice is now performed with golden-coloured sand (the ritual continued without the expense). And it is said that Elagabalus lamented that he could not add amber dust to his scatterings of precious gold.

Creatures in Amber

Some pieces of amber were admired for the prehistoric creatures caught in the substance. Martial wrote the following verses to accompany amber gifts.

431 Martial, *Epigrams*, 4.32
This bee is enclosed in amber and shines, perfectly preserved, in a tear produced by the sisters of Phaethon. It looks like it is encased in its own precious nectar (clear golden honey). This bee has therefore obtained a

worthy reward for its great toils. And perhaps it would have desired such a laudable death.

432 Martial, *Epigrams***, 4.59**
A viper was winding along the weeping branches of the Heliades – the (transformed) 'Daughters of the Sun'. Suddenly, an amber drop flowed along the serpent. It wondered at being stuck by this gummy extrusion. Rapidly the substance grew stiff, and the congealing mass confined the creature. Queen Cleopatra – do not pride yourself on your royal sepulchre. For this viper reposes in a more splendid tomb.

433 Martial, *Epigrams***, 6.15**
An ant was wandering under the shade of a Phaethon tree when a drop of amber sap suddenly enveloped the tiny insect. Thus, a life that was held in no regard was made precious by death.

Epilogue

The early Anglo-Saxons were a North Germanic population who preserved stories from their ancestral homelands.

Beowulf

Old English Verse

434 *Beowulf*, 1. 'Scyld Scefing'
Harken!
We, the Spear-Danes, in past days,
We had Clan-Kings who proclaimed their glory.
We had Nobles who performed courageous deeds.

Scyld Scefing often scourged enemy hordes,
He seized the mead-benches from many peoples,
He scarified the Eorlas (Heruli – North Germans).

But at first, Scyld had been a babe-abandoned.
He endured distress and destitution,
But survived, and grew strong from obscurity.

He thrived to gain high respect,
Until each nearby nation over the Whale-Road,
Submitted to him, and yielded him Tribute.

That was one good king!

Final Battle and Death

Duties of the Hearthguard

435 *Beowulf*, **36**
Wiglaf was his name, son of Weohstan, a noble shield-warrior of the Scylfings (…) Wiglaf spoke many true words. He said to his comrades:

> I am disheartened. I recall the times we drank mead,
> When we pledged to our Household Lord in the Beer-Hall.
> He who gave us arm-rings (awards of wealth and status),
> So that we would have the guild-stock (war gear).
> We wished to repay him for this. And now foreseen hardship has come,
> (A battle need) for helmets and hard swords (hearthguard equipment).
> He selected us from his army for this adventure (chosen warriors).
> He deemed us worthy of renown.
> He gave us these precious objects, because we are Spear-Warriors,
> That he considered excellent, bold, Helm-Bearers (helmeted hearthguard).
>
> Our Lord intended us alone to perform this valiant work.
> 'The Keeper of the Folk' ('Clan Protector' – a war chief title),
> Placed forward the foremost men,
> Those with glories already achieved, and audacious deeds (expected).
> Now the day has come that our Liege-Lord needs the strength of good warriors.
> Let us go to aid our Battle-Chief while the heat lasts, that grim fire-terror.
>
> God knows that, to me, it is far more desirable,
> That my body be engulfed in fire along with my Gold-Giver
> (to die with the chief rather than flee in fear and shame).
> I do not think it proper that we who bear shields,
> Should go back to our own land,
> Unless we can first fell this foe and defend the life of the Chief of the Wederas (the Geats).
> I know well of his past (heroic) deeds.
> He does not deserve to (stand and fight) alone without a retinue of Geats (his hearthguard of kinsmen).
> He should not suffer sorrow or sink in strife (alone).
> For we must (stand together), sword and helm,
> Mail-coat and clan-tabard and all share (the same fate).

> We must advance through the smoke of slaughter,
> With helmet full-on (face-plates lowered) to support our lord.

These few words he spoke (to Beowulf):

> Beloved Beowulf. You must conduct yourself well, as you did in youth,
> Long ago when you said, that you would not allow,
> Glory to become doom, while you still lived.
> You must act now with bold deeds
> And a noble steadfast mind
> And with all your strength, defend your life.
> And I shall support you.

Honouring a Fallen Chief

After the Battle of the Catalaunian Plains, the body of the Visigothic King Theodorid was found among the dead (AD 451). The Visigoths possessed Scandinavian ancestry, but their nation had migrated through eastern Europe. Similar sentiments are expressed in the Anglo-Saxon work *Beowulf*.

436 Jordanes, *Getica*, 44

During this delay, the Visigoths sought their king Theodorid among the dead. The king's sons were perplexed by his absence when victory had been obtained. So, they searched among the corpses and after a long time they found his body where the dead lay thickest on the battlefield. He lay fallen among many brave men.

The Visigoths honoured him with valiant songs and bore him away with the enemy as their witness. While the battle had raged the enemy had seen bands of Goths shouting with dissonant cries and paying death honours to the fallen king. But now his demise was confirmed. The Visigoths shed tears for the death of a brave leader and the Huns witnessed a glorious passing that must have diminished their pride. The body of Theodorid was carried in procession with due honours. The Goths sounded the muster and assembled under arms to follow the royal funeral train. The valiant Thorismund acted as befitted the son of a beloved king. He honoured the glorious spirit of his dear father and followed his remains.

Chronological Index of Ancient Authors

Julius Caesar (assassinated 44 BC)
Julius Caesar was a Roman general, politician and dictator. Caesar wrote an account of his military campaigns in Gaul leading to the conquest of the territory (58–52 BC). *The Gallic Wars* describes Roman conflict against the Germans, who were intruding across the Rhine. These commentaries are written in the third person. Julius Caesar was about to launch a campaign of further conquests, which included new plans for Germania, when he was killed by a group of senators. They believed he wanted to end the republican system of government by retaining supreme power.

Vellius Patercullus (born about 19 BC – died after AD 30)
Vellius Patercullus was a Roman soldier, political figure and Latin historian. Vellius served as a military tribune in Thrace, Macedonia, Greece and the Eastern Mediterranean. He was a cavalry prefect and legate in Germany and Pannonia under the future Emperor Tiberius (AD 4). He held office as quaestor in AD 7 and praetor in AD 15. Velleius wrote a compendium of Roman history up to AD 29. He witnessed and participated in many of the events he describes about Roman conflicts in Germany.

Strabo (died after AD 21)
Strabo was a Greek historian and geographer writing during the reign of the first Emperor Augustus (27 BC to AD 14). Strabo lived in Alexandria, the Greek capital of Egypt, before moving to Rome. His *History* has not survived into the modern era, but his multi-volume *Geography* has been preserved. The *Geography* describes all the countries and populations known to the Greeks and Romans of his era, incorporating many historical details. Strabo wrote in Greek, the second language of the Roman Empire.

Pomponius Mela (writing in about AD 43)
Mela was a Latin writer who composed a *Geography* in about AD 43. Little is known of his life, but he was cited as a source by Pliny the Elder in his *Natural History*. Mela's *Geography* contains a Roman perspective on Germania, the

campaigns fought to control this territory, and imperial knowledge of the northern ocean.

Pliny the Elder (AD 23–79)
Pliny was the author of the *Natural History*, a vast encyclopaedic work considering mankind and the natural environment. Aged 23, Pliny began a military career in Germany, reaching the rank of cavalry commander. He returned to Rome to study and practise Law. He served as procurator (governor) of Spain and other provinces. Pliny devoted much of his time to writing, including a *History of Rome* and a multi-volume work describing Roman campaigns in Germany. In Rome, Pliny served in the advisory council of the Emperor Vespasian (AD 69–79). He was commander of the Roman fleet in the Bay of Naples when Mount Vesuvius erupted (AD 79). Pliny succumbed to volcanic fumes while leading a rescue attempt.

Flavius Josephus (AD 37–100)
Josephus was a Jewish priest, scholar and historian from an aristocratic family. He was a commander in the Jewish Revolt against Rome (AD 66) and became a captive of the Roman general Vespasian. Josephus was freed when Vespasian became emperor and served as an advisor to his son Titus. After the conflict, Josephus was granted Roman citizenship and moved to Rome with the imperial family as his patron. Josephus wrote an account in Greek of the Jewish Revolt (AD 66–70) and a multivolume history of the Jews known as the *Antiquities*. These works provide interesting insights into the activities of the Roman Empire, along with ancient perceptions of Germanic peoples.

Tacitus (died about AD 120)
Tacitus was a Roman orator, legal advocate, public official and Latin historian. He held the following career roles: military tribune attached to a legion, quaestorship with a possible provincial posting, praetorship with legal jurisdiction, and member of a Priestly College in Rome. He may also have served as a legionary commander for four years. Tacitus wrote the *Annals*, dealing with the Empire from AD 14 to AD 68, and the *Histories*, describing the era between AD 69 and AD 96. He also wrote a short biography of his father-in-law, Gnaeus Julius Agricola, who was governor of Britain from AD 77 to AD 84, during the Roman conquest of Caledonia. In AD 98, Tacitus wrote an ethnography of the Germans, known as the *Germania*, which was possibly based on a multi-volume history by Pliny the Elder that has not survived.

Suetonius (died after AD 122)
Suetonius was a Roman author who wrote a collection of short biographies concerning Julius Caesar and the first eleven Roman emperors (*The Twelve Caesars*). Suetonius was from the *equites*, the lesser nobility that held a rank below the ruling senatorial class. He began a legal career in Rome with the friendship and support of Pliny the Younger, the nephew of Pliny the Elder. Suetonius entered imperial service during the reign of the Emperor Hadrian (AD 117). He served as controller of the libraries, keeper of the archives, and adviser to the emperor on cultural matters. In about AD 121, he was briefly promoted to Secretary of the Imperial Correspondence. His work *The Twelve Caesars* describes the activities, behaviours and characteristics of the early Roman rulers up to the death of Emperor Domitian in AD 96. It contains many anecdotes that reveal their morals, capacity and intent. It offers an important insight into the inner politics of Rome.

Martial (born about AD 38 – died about 103).
Martial was a Roman poet and friend of the Latin satirist Juvenal. Early in his career, Martial wrote verses in praise of the dictatorial Emperor Domitian (reigned AD 81–96). But most of his epigrams concern the life and social conduct of people in Rome. Martial also wrote witty verses to accompany gifts exchanged between friends, clients and patrons during popular Roman festivals. These offer an important insight into the consumer culture of Rome and its attitudes towards Germanic society.

Juvenal (born about AD 60 – died about 127)
Juvenal was a Roman satirist and friend of the Latin poet Martial. Juvenal served as a military officer in preparation for a career in the administrative service of the Emperor Domitian. But he failed to obtain promotion and was banished for criticising the court favourites who influenced the allocation and award of state offices. After the assassination of Domitian in AD 96, Juvenal returned to Rome, where he published his *Satires*, offering a pessimistic and scathing view of contemporary Roman society.

Plutarch (first to second century AD)
Plutarch was a Greek author and biographer who wrote the *Parallel Lives*. The work describes the character and careers of leading Roman generals and statesmen, paired with accounts of comparable Greek figures. Plutarch obtained the Chief Magistracy of Chaeronea, a leading Greek city in Boeotia, central Greece. He directed a philosophical school in the city and visited Rome as part

of his official duties. He also held a lifelong priesthood position at Delphi, the most prominent religious centre in Greece.

Claudius Ptolemy (writing AD 150)

Claudius Ptolemy was a Greek mathematician, astronomer and geographer who lived in the Egyptian capital Alexandria during the Roman imperial era. His *Geography* proposed new methods for constructing maps of the ancient world using data assembled by an earlier Greek geographer named Marinus of Tyre (active in about AD 100). Ptolemy's data includes a sequence of territories stretching from Ireland across Europe and Asia to China. Germany appears in book ten and is represented in Map 4 of Europe (preserved in medieval manuscripts). The map can either be plotted from the original co-ordinates listed by Ptolemy, or redrawn from the medieval renderings.

Appian (second century AD)

Appian was a Greek historian who wrote a history of Roman conquests. He held public office in Alexandria and after receiving Roman citizenship went to Rome to practise Law. He became a procurator (government financial agent) under the Emperor Antoninus Pius (reigned AD 138–161). His *Roman History* is written in Greek.

Cassius Dio (born about AD 150 – died 235)

Cassius Dio was a Roman administrator and historian who wrote a multi-volume *Roman History* in Greek. Dio was a member of the Roman Senate. He served as the administrator of Pergamum and Smyrna, leading Greek cities in Anatolia. Returning to Rome, he was made consul (senior magistrate in the Capitol). Afterwards, he obtained the proconsulship (office of governor) in the Roman province of 'Africa' (Tunisia). Later, he served as a legate in Dalmatia, then Pannonia (Danube frontier) before being granted a second consulship in the reign of the Emperor Severus Alexander (AD 229). His *Roman History* contains the insights of a soldier and senior statesman. Large extracts of his work survive as summaries by later authors.

Ammianus Marcellinus (born about AD 330 – died 395)

Ammianus was a Latin historian who wrote an account of the later Roman Empire. He served as a soldier in Gaul and fought against the Persians on the eastern frontiers. In AD 359, he served in the army commanded by the Emperor Julian during a failed invasion of Babylonia. Ammianus later resigned from the army and settled in Rome, where he composed his multivolume *Roman History* in Latin. His account began in AD 96 with the reign of the Emperor Nerva, which was the year that Tacitus ended his account. Ammianus finished his study in AD 378 with the Gothic invasion of the Roman Empire (Goths – Eastern Germans from the Far North).

Orosius (writing in AD 414–417).
Orosius was a prominent Christian author and theologian from Roman Spain. He wrote a world history from the Christian perspective, which provides important information for events after AD 378.

Jordanes (writing in AD 551)
Jordanes was a historian of Gothic ancestry who wrote an account of his people in Latin called the *Getica*. Jordanes probably lived in the Danube region after the fall of the Western Roman Empire (AD 476). The *Getica* was completed in AD 551.

Chronology

Germanic Migrations into Gaul and Italy (115–100 BC)
- 115–113 BC Cimbri and Teutones migrate into Gaul. They are joined by a Celtic tribe called the Ambrones.
- 113 BC Cimbri and Teutones defeat a Roman army at Noreia.
- 105 BC Germanic tribes invade Gallia Narbonensis, defeating the Romans at Arausio.
- 102 BC Rome defeats the Teutones at the Battle of Aquae Sextiae.
- 101 BC Rome defeats the Cimbri at the Battle of Vercellae.

Rhine Crossings (62–31 BC)
- 62 BC War between the Celtic Sequani and Aedui tribes in central Gaul. Sequani recruit Suebi (Germanic) warriors and allow them to cross the Rhine.
- 60 BC Sequani defeat the Aedui. The Suebi settle in Gaul.
- 59 BC Germanic king Ariovistus acknowledged as an ally of Rome.
- 58 BC Julius Caesar begins the Roman conquest of Greater Gaul.
- 58 BC Battle of Vosges, Caesar defeats the Germans settled west of the Rhine.
- 56 BC Caesar crosses the Rhine and conducts an inconclusive campaign in Germania.
- 50 BC Caesar completes the conquest and subjugation of Greater Gaul.
- 44 BC Julius Caesar assassinated.
- 30s BC Germanic Ubii allowed to relocate across the Rhine to Oppidum 'Ubiorum' (modern Cologne).

Augustan Conquests (31 BC–AD 9)
- 31 BC Octavian wins the final civil war of the Roman Republic. Under the name 'Augustus' he becomes the first Roman Emperor (27 BC).
- 17 BC Three Germanic tribes declare war on Rome. Marcus Lollius defeated by an alliance of Tencteri, Sugambri and Usipetes. Led by a warlord named Maelo, the Germans invade Belgica and seize the eagle standard of Legio V Alaudae.
- 14 BC Imperial prince, Drusus, legate (commander) of Tres Galliae, prepares the Roman invasion of Germania. Batavi brought into alliance and Roman military camps established along the Rhine.

Chronology 235

- 12–9 BC Drusus campaigns in Germania Magna (Greater Germany).
- 9 BC–AD 9 West Germania as far as the Elbe is under Roman control.

Germanic Revolt and Resistance (AD 9–17)
- AD 9 Revolt: Battle in the Teutoburg Forest. Arminius and the Germans destroy three entire Roman legions. Rome withdraws from Germania Magna (Greater Germany) to the Rhine frontier.
- AD 10–13 The imperial princes Tiberius and Germanicus campaign in Germania.
- AD 14 Death of Emperor Augustus, succession of Tiberius.
- AD 14–15 Germanicus, son of Drusus, leads further retaliatory campaigns against the Germans.
- AD 17 Tiberius abandons plans to fix the Roman frontier on the Elbe. Rhine–Danube frontier now the northern limits of the Roman Empire.

Stalemate with Free Germany (AD 17–100)
- AD 37–41 Reign of Caligula (son of Germanicus).
- AD 40 Caligula prepares to invade Germany. Campaign halted.
- AD 41–54 Reign of Claudius (son of Drusus, brother of Germanicus).
- AD 43 Claudius conquers southern part of Britannia.
- AD 47 Gnaeus Domitius Corbulo suppresses the Frisii.
- AD 54–68 Reign of Nero (grandson of Germanicus).
- AD 68–69 Roman Civil War: 'Year of the Four Emperors'.
- AD 69–70 Batavian Revolt.
- AD 81–96 Reign of Domitian.
- AD 83 Domitian invades Germania to engage the Chatti.
- AD 88 Romans defeated by Quadi and Marcomanni on the Danube frontier.
- AD 98 Tacitus writes the *Germania*.

Second and Third Centuries AD
- AD 161–180 Reign of Marcus Aurelius.
- AD 165–180 Antonine Pandemic, an ancestral form of smallpox, devastates the Roman population and its essential military forces. Casualties in affected communities are as high as one-third (deaths and debilitating medical conditions that prevent further military service).
- AD 166–180 Marcomannic Wars. Marcomanni and Quadi threaten the Danube frontier. Sarmatians (steppe horsemen) attack the Lower Danube. Prolonged series of savage military campaigns conducted by the stoic Emperor Marcus Aurelius.

- AD 235–284 Third Century Crisis: upheaval and repeated civil wars in the Roman Empire.
- AD 284–305 Reign of Diocletian. Order restored in the Roman Empire. Diocletian reorganises Roman administration. The Empire is divided into East and West.

Age of Migrations (AD 370–476)
- AD 370–374 Huns defeat the Alani and Goths (East Germans) on the Pontic Steppe. The defeated populations flee westwards.
- AD 375 Visigoths ask Emperor Valens for sanctuary within imperial territories. The Tervingi are settled south of the Danube frontiers, but are abused by Roman officials.
- AD 376 Gothic Revolt. Battle of Marcianople: Goths defeat a Roman army in Thrace and seize imperial armouries.
- AD 378 Battle of Adrianople: Eastern Field Army destroyed by the Goths. Roman Emperor Valens killed in battle.
- AD 406 Mass of Germanic tribes and steppe forces cross the Rhine frontier invading Gaul (Asding Vandals, Suebi, Marcomanni, Quadi and Alani).
- AD 410 Visigoth King Alaric sacks Rome.
- AD 428 The Asding Vandals cross from southern Spain into North Africa.
- AD 446 Final appeal of Roman provincials in Britain for imperial assistance against Pictish, Scots-Irish and Saxon invaders.
- AD 451 Battle of Catalaunian Fields: Attila invades Gaul with a vast army of Huns and vassal Germans. Invaders defeated by a coalition force of Romans, Visigoths, Burgundians and Salian Franks. Attila withdraws his army from the Western Empire.
- AD 450s The Anglo-Saxons begin the conquest of Britain.
- AD 453 The Vandals sack Rome.
- AD 476 Romulus Augustulus is deposed, the last emperor of Rome. Germanic soldier named Odoacer is declared king of Italy with the support of barbarian troops.
- AD 476 Fall of the Western Roman Empire.

Appendix A

Germanic Bodyguard of the Roman Emperors: Inscriptions from Rome

Gravestones and altar inscriptions in Rome honour Germans who served in the imperial bodyguard (the Germani corporis custodes). Many were Batavians, but Rhineland Ubii and Frisians, from the north coast, also appear on the memorials (30 inscriptions, 12 Batavians, 9 'Germans', 5 Ibians, 2 Frisians, 1 Suebian and 1 'Baetesian').

Imperial Princes (27 BC–AD 19)

Corpus Inscriptionum Latinarum, 6.4437
Sinnio, bodyguard of Caesar Drusus.
Sinnio Caesar(is) / corpore custos / Drusianus.

Corpus Inscriptionum Latinarum, 6.4337 (inscription on the Via Appia thoroughfare in Rome)
Bassus, German (bodyguard) of Germanicus Drusus Caesar, of the Ubian Nation, lived 30 years.

Bassus / Germanus / Germanician(us) / Drusi Caesaris nat(ione) / Ubius; u(ixit) a(nnos) XXX.

Emperor Tiberius (AD 14–37)

Corpus Inscriptionum Latinarum, 6.20216
Honored: Posides freedman of Marcus Julius Augustus [---], Neber freedman of Marcus Julius Augusta [---], Actius freedman of Tiberius Claudius Augustus, of the German Guard, Aratus Bithi slave and comrade [---], Bathyllus freedman of Gaius Julius Augustus [---], Marcus Livius Bithus [---].

Hono[rati]: / M(arcus) Iulius Aug(ustae) l(ibertus) Posides, [---], / M(arcus) Iulius Aug(ustae) l(ibertus) Neber, [---], / Ti(berius) Claud(ius) Aug(usti) l(ibertus) Actius cur(ator) Ge[rmanorum], / Aratus Bithi (seruus) frat[er ---], / C(aius) Iulius Aug(usti) l(ibertus) Bathyllus, [---], / M(arcus) Livius Bithus [---].

Corpus Inscriptionum Latinarum, 6.4338
Bassus, German (bodyguard) of Tiberius Germanicus.

Bassus Tiberius / Germanicus Germanus.

Corpus Inscriptionum Latinarum, 6.4339
Macro, German (bodyguard of) Germanicus Tiberius Caesar, of the Ubian nation.

Macro / Germaniciano / Ti(beri) Caesaris / Germano / natione Ubius.

Corpus Inscriptionum Latinarum, 6.4340
Macer, German bodyguard of Tiberius Germanicus; lived 30 years.

Macer / Ti(beri) Germanici / Germanus / corpore custos; / u(ixit) a(nnos) XXX.

Corpus Inscriptionum Latinarum, 6.4341
Valens the German, (bodyguard of) Tiberius Caesar Augustus Germanicus, of the Batavian nation; lived 35 years.

Valens Germanus / Germanicianus / Ti(beri) Caesaris Augusti / nation(e) Batauus; u(ixit) a(nnos) XXXV.

Corpus Inscriptionum Latinarum, 6.4345
Proculus, *Collegium* of the Germans. Tiberius Germanicus.

Proculus / decurio / Germanorum / Ti(beri) Germanici.

Corpus Inscriptionum Latinarum, 6.4716 (inscription inside a *columbarium* – structure containing funeral urns).
Fuscus, bodyguard of Tiberius Caesar Germanicus.

Fuscus T »[i(beri) Caesaris?] / German[icianus? uel -us] / corpor(e) c[ustos]: T[i.] / German[ici].

Corpus Inscriptionum Latinarum, 6.8807
Paetinus, bodyguard of Tiberius Claudius Caesar Augusti, of the Pacati Decuria of the Batavian nation; who lived 20 years, lies here. [This grave marker] was put here by Virus of the Pacati Decuria, his inheritor from the *Collegium* of the Germans.

Paetinus / Ti(beri) Claud(i) / Caisar(is) Aug(usti) / corp(oris) cust(os) / dec(uria) Pacati / nat(ione) Bata(u)us; / uix(it) ann(os) XX; / h(ic) s(itus) e(st); / pos(uit) Virus dec(uria) Pacati / h(eres) eius ex col(legio) Germa[norum].

Corpus Inscriptionum Latinarum, 6.8809
Postumus, bodyguard of Tiberius Claudius Caesar Augustus, of the Synerotis Decuria, of the Ubian nation; lived 25 years, lies here. [This grave marker] was put here by Capito of the Synerotis Decuria, his inheritor, from the *Collegium* of the Germans.

Postumus / Ti(beri) Claudi / Caisar(is) Aug(usti) / corpor(is) cust(os) / dec(uria) Synerotis / nat(ione) Vbius; / uix(it) an(nos) XXV; / h(ic) s(itus) e(st); / pos(uit) Capito dec(uria) / Synerotis her(es) eius / ex col(legio) Germ(anorum).

Corpus Inscriptionum Latinarum, 6.37754a
Sabinus (bodyguard) of Tiberius Claudius Caesar Augustus Germanicus [---].

[S]abin[us] / [T]i(beri) Clau[di] / Caisari[s Aug(usti)] / Germa[nici] / [---].

L'Année épigraphique (1968) 32 (inscription slab from a walled-up entrance to the burial ground of Callisto, between the Via del Casale and the Via Aurelia Antica)
Saturninus, bodyguard of Tiberius Claudius Caesar Augustus Germanicus, of the Laeti Decuria, of the Batavian nation; lived (---) years, lies here. [This grave marker] was put here by Laetus, Curator from the *Collegium* of the Germans.

Saturni[nus] / Ti(beri) Clau(di) / Caesaris [Aug(usti)] / German[ici] / corporis [custos] / dec(uria) La[eti] / natione Ba[tauus?]; / uixit ann[os ---]; / h(ic) s(itus) [e(st)]; / posuit La[etus] / curator ex [coll(egio)] / Germanor[um].

Corpus Inscriptionum Latinarum, 6.8811 (possible funeral altar on the Via Portuense)
Ducto, freedman of Tiberius Claudius Augustus, Decurio of the Germans, who lived 30 years. [This grave marker] was put here by himself and his spouse Luria Paezusa.

Ti(berio) Claudio / Aug(usti) lib(erto) Ducto / dec(urio) / Germanorum; / uix(it) an(nos) XXX; posuit Luria / Paezusa coniugi suo et sibi.

Corpus Inscriptionum Latinarum, 6.8810 (slab inscription possibly from a *columbarium* – structure containing funeral urns).

Severus, bodyguard of Tiberius Caesar Germanicus of the Suibian nation; lived 20 years (---) Germanicus Augustus.

Seuerus / corpore custos / Ti(beri) Caesaris / Germanician[us ?] / natione Sui[bus ?]; / u(ixit) a(nnos) [---]: Germanici Au[g(usti)].

Emperor Caligula (AD 37–41)

Caligula was the son of Germanicus. As an infant he was partly raised in Roman military camps (Suetonius, *Caligula*, 9).

Corpus Inscriptionum Latinarum, 6.4344
Nereus of the German Nation, (bodyguard of) 'Little' Germanicus Nero Caesar; lived 27 years.

Nereus nat(ione) German(us) / Peucennus Germanici/anus Neronis Caesaris; / uixit annis XXVII.

Emperor Claudius (AD 41–54)

Corpus Inscriptionum Latinarum, 6.8802 (Necropolis of Villa Doria Pamphili on the Via Aurelia Thoroughfare)
Alcimachus, bodyguard of Claudius Nero Caesar Augustus Germanicus, Decuria of Albani, of the Batavian Nation; who lived 35 years, lies here. [This grave marker] was put here by the Bavarian 'Mountain' Decuria, his inheritors in the *Collegium* of the Germans.

Alcimachus / Neronis Claud(i) / Caisar(is) Aug(usti) Ger(manici) / corpor(is) cust(os) / dec(uria) Albani / nat(ione) Bata(u)us; / uix(it) ann(os) XXXV; / h(ic) s(itus) e(st); posuit / Batauus dec(uria) Montani / her(es) eius ex coll(egio) Ger(manorum).

L'Année épigraphique (1952) 145 (slab inscription, Baths of Diocletian, 'Garden of the Five Hundred')
Fannius, bodyguard of Claudius Nero Caesar Augustus, of the Cotini Decuria, of the Ubian nation; lived 29 years; lies here. [This grave marker] was put here by Corinthus from the same Decuria, from the *Collegium* of the Germans.

Fannius / Neron(is) Claudi / Caesaris Aug(usti) / corpori(s) custos / dec(uria) Cotini / nation(e) Vbius; / uixit ann(os) XIIX; h(ic) s(itus) e(st); / posuit Corinthus / dec(uria) eadem heres eius / ex colleg(io) German(orum).

L'Année épigraphique (1952) 146 (slab inscription, Baths of Diocletian, 'Garden of the Five Hundred')

Tertius, bodyguard of Claudius Caesar Nero Augustus, of the Prudentis Decuria, of the Batavian nation; lived 37 years, lies here. [This grave marker] was put here, a solum act, by his inheritors in the 'Royal' Prudentis Decuria, from the *Collegium* of the Germans.

Ter[tius?] / Ner(onis) Claud(i) Ca(esaris) / Aug(usti) corp(oris) cust(os) / dec(uria) Prudentis / nat(ione) Batau(u)s; / uix(it) ann(os) XXXVII; / h(ic) s(itus) e(st); posuerunt / Sollemnis optio / et Reginus dec(uria) Prudentis / heredes eius ex collegio / Germanorum.

Emperor Nero (AD 54–68)

Corpus Inscriptionum Latinarum, 6.4342

Bassus, bodyguard of Nero Caesar, of the Frisian nation; lived 40 years.

Bassus Neronis / Caesaris corpore / custos natione Frisius; / uix(it) a(nnos) XL.

Corpus Inscriptionum Latinarum, 6.4343

Hilarus, bodyguard of Nero Caesar, of the Frisian Nation; lived 33 years.

Hilarus Neronis / Caesaris corpore / custos natione Frisiaeo; / uix(it) a(nnos) XXXIII.

Corpus Inscriptionum Latinarum, 6.8803

Tiberius Claudius Chloreus bodyguard of Nero Claudius Caesar, of the Decuria of *Spiculi* ('Spear-tip'), of the Batavian nation; lived 40 years, lies here. [This grave marker] was put here by Tiberius Claudius Diadumenus and the Censor (office-bearer in charge of membership) of the Decuia of Spiculi, who were his inheritors in the *Collegium* of the Germans.

Ti(berius) Claudius / Chloreus / Neronis Claudi / Caesaris Aug(usti) / corporis custos / dec(uria) Spiculi, / natione Bata(u)us; / uix(it) ann(os) XL; h(ic) s(itus) e(st); posuerunt / Ti(berius) Claudius Diadumenus et / Censor dec(uria) Spiculi / heredes eius ex / collegio Germanorum.

Corpus Inscriptionum Latinarum, 6.8804
   Linus, bodyguard of Nero Claudius Caesar Augustus, of the Decuria of Epagati, of the Batavian nation; lived 20 years, lies here [---] [This grave marker] was put here by his inheritor, Macer from the *Collegium* of the Germans.

   Linus / Ti(beri) Claudi / Caesaris Aug(usti) / corporis custos / dec(uria) Epagati / natione Batauus; / uix(it) ann(os) XX[---]; h(ic) s(itus) e(st); / posuit / Macer heres / eius ex collegio / Germanorum.

Corpus Inscriptionum Latinarum, 6.8806
   Nobilis, soldier of the Emperor Nero Augustus, bodyguard, (member) of the Rabuti Decuria, of the Batavian nation. He served for 2 years; he lived 20 years, he lies here. [This grave marker] was put here by Baebius, his inheritor in the Decuria of Rabuti.

   Nobilis / miles Impera(toris) / Neronis Aug(usti) / corp(oris) cust(os) / dec(uria) Rabuti / nat(ione) Bata(u)us; / milit(auit) an(nos) II; / uix(it) an(nos) XX; h(ic) s(itus) e(st); / posuit Baebius / d(ecuria) Rabuti heres.

Corpus Inscriptionum Latinarum, 6.8808 (Necropolis of Villa Doria Pamphili)
   Phoebus, bodyguard of Nero Claudius Caesar Augustus, of the Rabuti Decuria, of the Baetesian nation, served for 8 years; he lived 25 years, here he lies. [This grave marker] was put here by Gnostus from the same Decuria, his inheritor, from the *Collegium* of the Germans.

   Phoebus / Neronis Claud(i) / Caesaris Aug(usti) / corp(oris) cust(os) / dec(uria) Rabuti / nat(ione) Baetesius; / mil(itauit) an(nos) VIII; uix(it) an(nos) XXV; / h(ic) s(it) e(st); posuit Gnostus / dec(uria) eadem heres eius / ex colleg(io) German(orum).

Corpus Inscriptionum Latinarum, 6.37754
   Silua, bodyguard of Nero Claudius Caesar Augustus [---].

   Silua / Neron(is) Claudi / Caesaris Aug(usti) / [corpor(is) cu]stos / [---].

L'Année épigraphique (1952) 147 (slab inscription, Baths of Diocletian, 'Garden of the Five Hundred')
   Gamo, bodyguard of Nero Claudius Caesar Augustus, of the Pacati Decuria, of the Batavian nation, lived 25 years; lies here. [This grave marker] was placed by Hospes ('Guest'), his comrade and inheritor from the *Collegium* of the Germans.

Gamo / Ner(onis) Claud(i) Caes(aris) / Aug(usti) corp(oris) cust(os) / dec(uria) Pacati / nat(ione) Batau(u)s; / uix(it) ann(os) XXV; / h(ic) s(itus) e(st); posuit / Hospes dec(uria) Pacati / frater et heres eius / ex collegio / Germanorum.

L'Année épigraphique (1952) 148 (slab inscription, Baths of Diocletian, 'Garden of the Five Hundred')
Indus, bodyguard of Nero Claudius Caesar Augustus, of the Second Decuria, of the Batavian nation; who lived 36 years, lies here. [This grave marker] was put here by his comrade and inheritor, Eumenes, from the *Collegium* of the Germans.

Indus / Neronis Claudi / Caesaris Aug(usti) / corpor(is) custos / dec(uria) Secundi / natione Batauus; / uix(it) ann(os) XXXVI; h(ic) s(itus) e(st); / posuit / Eumenes frater / et heres eius ex collegio / Germanorum.

L'Année épigraphique (1952) 149 (slab inscription, Baths of Diocletian, 'Garden of the Five Hundred')
[---]inus, bodyguard of Nero Claudius Caesar, of the Benigni Decuria, of the Batavian nation; lived 25 years, lies here. [This grave marker] was put here by Calyx from the Benigni Decuria, his inheritor from the *Collegium* of the Germans.

[---]inus / [Ne]ronis Claud(i) / [C]aes(aris) corp(oris) cust(os) / dec(uria) Benigni / nat(ione) Batau(u)s; / uix(it) ann(os) XXV; h(ic) s(itus) e(st); / posuit Calyx dec(uria) Benigni / her(es) eius ex col(legio) Germ(anorum).

L'Année épigraphique (1983) 58 (slab inscription)
Vetus, bodyguard of Nero Claudius Caesar Augustus, of the Batavian Nation (---) bodyguard of the (---) nation, Polverini.

Vetus / Neronis Claud(i) / Caesar(is) Aug(usti) / corp(oris) cust(os) n[at(ione)] / Ba[tauus ---]. r. 4 cus(tos) n[atione], Polverini.

Corpus Inscriptionum Latinarum, 6.8812
[---]ore[---] bodyguard of Nero Caesar lies here; (---) his wife placed (this memorial) (---) Caesar.

[---]ore[---] / [Neroni]s Caesa[ris] / [corpore?] custos hic sit[us est]; / [---]ma coniux p[osuit] [---]s Caesa[ris], CIL.

Served an Unnamed Emperor

Corpus Inscriptionum Latinarum, 6.8805
[------] Decuria [---] of the Ubian nation; lived 25 years, lies here. [This grave marker] was put here by the Decuria of Cotini, his inheritors from the *Collegium* of the Germans.

[------] / dec(uria) [---] U[bius]; / uixit ann(os) XXV; h(ic) s(itus) e(st); / posuit Marsus / dec(uria) Cotini / heres ex / collegio Germanorum.

L'Année épigraphique (1923) 73 (slab inscription from the Baths of Diocletian, Room 8)
Julian, 'Roman Citizen', bodyguard of Caesar, (and) Fausta Julia, dedicated this.

Romano Iuliano / corpore custos / Caesaris / Fausta Iulia / fecet.

German Beast Fighter

Corpus Inscriptionum Latinarum, 6.3220 (a Batavian beast fighter in the Roman arena at Parma, northern Italy)
To the Spirit of 'Vitalis Invicti', of the Batavian Nation. Here (he lies). He fought well against the adversary, he was good with his fist; H[---] long-time companion.

Dis Manibus Vitalis invicti retiari, natione Batavus; hic sua virtute, partier cum adversario depugnavit; alacer fuit pugnis; Hi[---] convictor eius.

Appendix B

Details of Germania: Claudius Ptolemy's Map Data

Claudius Ptolemy, *Geography*, 10 (second century AD)
The Rhine River is the western boundary of Germany. Its northern boundary is the Germanic Ocean. The following is a description of that shore (west to east):
- river mouths of the Rhine
- river mouths of the Vidrus
- the port of Marnamanis
- river mouths of the Amisia
- river mouths of the Visurgis
- river mouths of the Albis.

Next is the Cimbrian Peninsula (Jutland). This is formed from:
- the cape after the Albis River
- the next cape
- the northernmost cape
- the first cape after the bend
- the easternmost part of the peninsula
- a cape beyond this
- a shore extending eastwards again.

(Northern frontier beyond Jutland):
- the river mouths of the Chalusus
- the river mouths of the Suevus
- the river mouths of the Viadua
- the mouths of the Vistula
- the head of the Vistula
- the source of the Vistula which is to the west in the direction of Albis.

(Southern edge of Germany – Danube frontier running west to east):
- the southern limits of Germany are formed by the western stretch of the Danube River
- the head of the Danube River

- the first river that flows into the Danube from Germany
- a river called the Aenus flows into the Danube from the south side
- a second river flows from the Forest of Gabreta into Danube the from the northern side
- a river traversing the Luna Forest rushes into the Danube from the north
- on the next bend the Danube turns southwards
- a river called the Arabo flows into the Danube from the north
- a bend in the Danube near Curta
- another bend in the Danube near Carpis, which is the northernmost extension of the river.

(Eastern limits of Germany)
The eastern side of Germany stretches from the last bend of the Danube to the Sarmatian mountains. It consists of:
- the southern limits
- the northern limits
- the interval between these mountains and the head of the Vistulae River, which extends to the sea.

(German Mountains):
The most famous German mountains are properly called the 'Sarmatian mountains'. These are the 'Alps', located beyond the head of the Danube River:
- the Abnoba Mountains
- the Melibocus mountain, which rises from the Semanus Forest
- Mount Asciburgius
- the Sudeti Mountains, which rise from the Gabreta Forest. The Orcynian Valley lies between the Sudeti and the Sarmatian mountains.

(Rhineland German populations):
German tribes on the eastern side of the Rhine River. From north to south:
- the Bructeri minors and the Sygambri
- beyond them are the the Suebi Langobardi
- then the Tencteri and the Incriones, who occupy territories between the Rhine and the Abnoba mountains
- then the Intuergi and the Vangiones and the Caritni
- beyond them are the Vispi and the Deserted Lands of the Helvetii, which stretch to the Alps.

(North coast German populations):
The shore of the ocean is inhabited beyond the Bructeri up to the Amisia River. From west to east:
- to the north are the Cimbri
- the Saxons
- the Farodini occupy lands from the Chalusus to the Suebian River
- the Sidini extend to the Viadua River
- the Rugiclei occupy lands leading to the Vistula River.

(Interior populations – western Germany)
The most important populations living in the interior of Germany are:
- the Suebi Angili who live east of the Langobardi. Their territory extends northwards to the central part of the Albis River
- the Suebi Semnones, whose territories extend from the Albis River to the Suevus River
- the Burguntae, who inhabit lands from the Suevus River to the Vistula
- the Silingae are located south of the Semnones
- the Lugi Omani are south of the Burguntae
- the Lugi Diduni are south of the Lugi Omani and extend to Mount Asciburgius
- the Calucones and the Camavi are south of the Silingae tribe and Mount Melibocus. Their territories extend eastwards to the Albis River and Mount Asciburgius
- the Corconti and the Lugi Buri extend to the head of the Vistula River
- to their south is the Sidones
- to their south is the Cotini
- south is the Visburgii, who live beyond the Orcynius Valley.

(Interior populations – eastern Germany)
Eastwards from the Abnoba Mountains:
- the Casuariy live south of the Suebi
- the Nertereanesy
- then the Dandutiy
- south are the Turoni and the Marvingi
- the Chattae and the Tubantiy are south of the Camavi
- the Teuriochaemaey live north of the Sudeti Mountains
- the Varisti live south of the mountains
- then there is the Gabreta Forest
- south of the Marvingi are the Curiones
- then the Chaetuoriy

- then the Parmaecampi, who extend as far as the Danube
- south of the Gabreta Forest are the Marcomanni
- south of the forest are the Sudiniy, who extend to the Danube River
- then the Drabaecampi
- the Quadi are south of the Orcynium Forest
- there are iron mines to the south in the Luna Forest
- south of this a large population called the Baemi extend as far as the Danube
- the Racatriae are on the Danube bordering the Baemi
- the Racatae live near the main bend of the river.

The following 'towns' (major settlements) are found in the northern regions of Germany:
- Phleum
- Siatutanda
- Tecelia
- Fabiranum
- Treva
- Leufana
- Lirimiris
- Marionis
- another Marionis
- Coenoënum
- Cistuia
- Alisus
- Laciburgium
- Bunitium
- Virunum
- Viritium
- Rugium
- Scurgum
- Ascaucalis

The southern regions of Germany contain the following 'towns' (major settlements and notable sites):
- Asciburgium
- Navalia
- Mediolanium
- Teuderium
- Bogadium

Details of Germania: Claudius Ptolemy's Map Data

- Stereontium
- Amisia
- Munitium
- Tulifurdum
- Ascalingium
- Tulisurgium
- Pheugarum
- Canduum
- The Trophy of Drusus (a Roman campaign monument)
- Luppia
- Mersovium
- Aregelia
- Galaegia
- Lupfurdum
- Susudata
- Colancorum
- Lugidunum
- Stragona
- the grove of Limis
- Budorigum
- Leucaristus
- Arsonium
- Calisia
- Setidava

Further south, Germany contains the following 'towns' (notable population centres and significant sites):

- Alisum
- Budoris
- Mattiacum
- Arctaunum
- Novaesium
- Melocabus
- Gravionarium
- Locoritum
- Segodunum
- Devona
- Bergium
- Menosgada
- Bicurgium

- Marobudum
- Redintuinum
- Nomisterium
- Meliodunum
- Casurgis
- Strevinta
- Hegetmatia
- Budorgis
- Eburum
- Arsicua
- Parienna
- Setovia
- Carrodunum
- Asanca

The part of Germany near the Danube River has the following 'towns' (population centres and monuments):
- Tarodunum
- The Flavian Altars (Roman campaign monument)
- Riusiava
- Alcimoënnis
- Cantioebis
- Bibacum
- Brodentia
- Setuacotum
- Usbium
- Abilunum
- Furgisatis
- Coridorgis
- Mediolanium
- Felicia
- Eburodunum
- Anduaetium
- Celamantia
- Singone
- Anavum (Adiabum?)

(German Islands – Scandinavia)
- There are three islands located to the north of Germany near the mouths of the Albis River. These islands are known as the Saxon Isles.

- North of the Cimbrian Peninsula (Jutland) there are three other islands. These are called the Alociae Islands.
- East of the Cimbrian Peninsula there are four islands called the Scandian Islands. Three of the islands are far smaller than the central isle, which is very large (the southern tip of Norway/Sweden). This landmass, known as Scandia, extends eastwards beyond the mouth of the Vistula River.
- The western part of Scandia is inhabited by the Chaedini. The eastern region is occupied by the Favonae and the Firaesi. The northern region contains the Finni. Its southern region is home to the Gutae (Gautae) and the Dauciones. The central part of Scandia is occupied by the Levoni.

Appendix C

German Tribes in Tacitus and Ptolemy

List of German Tribes in Tacitus' *Germania* (first century AD – 26 tribes)

1. Aelvaeones
2. Ampsivarii
3. Angles
4. Chamavi
5. Dulgubnii
6. Frisii
7. Gambrivii
8. Harii
9. Helveconae
10. Herminones
11. Ingaevones
12. Istvaeones
13. Manimi
14. Nahanarvali
15. Narisci
16. Nervii
17. Peucini
18. Quadi
19. Scordisci
20. Semnones
21. Sitones
22. Suebi
23. Treveri
24. Tubantes
25. Tungri
26. Varini

German Tribes documented in Claudius Ptolemy's *Geography* (second century AD – 49 tribes)

1. Bructeri – Northern German
2. Cimbri – Northern German
3. Farodini – Northern German
4. Rugiclei – Northern German
5. Saxons – Northern German
6. Sidini – Northern German

1. Burguntae – Western German
2. Calucones – Western German
3. Camavi – Western German
4. Corconti – Western German
5. Cotini – Western German
6. Langobardi – Western German
7. Lugi Buri – Western German
8. Lugi Diduni – Western German

9. Lugi Omani – Western German
10. Semnones – Western German
11. Sidones – Western German
12. Silingae – Western German
13. Suebi Angili – Western German
14. Suebi Semnones – Western German
15. Visburgii – Western German

1. Baemi – Eastern German
2. Camavi – Eastern German
3. Casuariy – Eastern German
4. Chaetuoriy – Eastern German
5. Chattae – Eastern German
6. Curiones – Eastern German
7. Dandutiy – Eastern German
8. Drabaecampi – Eastern German
9. Marcomanni – Eastern German
10. Marvingi – Eastern German
11. Nertereanesy – Eastern German
12. Parmaecampi – Eastern German
13. Quadi – Eastern German
14. Racatae – Eastern German
15. Racatriae – Eastern German
16. Sudiniy – Eastern German
17. Suebi – Eastern German
18. Teuriochaemaey – Eastern German
19. Tubantiy – Eastern German
20. Turoni – Eastern German
21. Varisti – Eastern German

1. Chaedini – Scandia
2. Dauciones – Scandia
3. Favonae – Scandia
4. Finni – Scandia
5. Firaesi – Scandia
6. Gutae (Gautae) – Scandia
7. Levoni – Scandia

German tribes appearing in both Tacitus and Ptolemy
(indicating possible instability in German tribal politics):
- Angles (Angili Suebi) – Western German
- Semnones – Western German
- Suebi – Eastern German
- Quadi – Eastern German

Dear Reader,

We hope you have enjoyed this book, but why not share your views on social media? You can also follow our pages to see more about our other products: facebook.com/penandswordbooks or follow us on X @penswordbooks

You can also view our products at www.pen-and-sword.co.uk (UK and ROW) or www.penandswordbooks.com (North America).

To keep up to date with our latest releases and online catalogues, please sign up to our newsletter at: www.pen-and-sword.co.uk/newsletter

If you would like a printed catalogue with our latest books, then please email: enquiries@pen-and-sword.co.uk or telephone: 01226 734555 (UK and ROW) or email: uspen-and-sword@casematepublishers.com or telephone: (610) 853-9131 (North America).

We respect your privacy and we will only use personal information to send you information about our products.

Thank you!